The Global
Philosophers

Issues in World Politics Series

James N. Rosenau and William C. Potter, consulting editors

The Global Philosophers

World Politics in Western Thought

Mark V. Kauppi
Paul R. Viotti

Lexington Books
An Imprint of Macmillan, Inc.
New York

Maxwell Macmillan Canada
Toronto

Maxwell Macmillan International
New York   Oxford   Singapore   Sydney

To Joe —
The best of colleagues, best of friends.
Mark Kauppi
6.11.93

This book is published as part of Issues in World Politics Series,
James N. Rosenau and William C. Potter, consulting editors

Map illustrations by Christine Veblin Bishop.
Copyright © 1992 by Christine Veblin Bishop, Spirit Lake, Idaho

Library of Congress Cataloging-in-Publication Data

Kauppi, Mark V.
 The global philosophers : world politics in western thought /
Mark V. Kauppi, Paul R. Viotti.
  p.   cm.
 Includes bibliographical references and index.
 ISBN 0-669-18033-5
 1. International relations—Philosophy. 2. International
relations—History. I. Viotti, Paul R. II. Title.
JX1245.K37 1992
327'.01—dc20   92-7874
                                                      CIP

Lexington Books
An Imprint of Macmillan, Inc.
866 Third Avenue, New York, N. Y. 10022

Maxwell Macmillan Canada, Inc.
1200 Eglinton Avenue East
Suite 200
Don Mills, Ontario M3C 3N1

Macmillan, Inc. is part of the Maxwell Communication Group of Companies.

Printed in the United States of America

printing number
1 2 3 4 5 6 7 8 9 10

To our children
NATALIE
and
MICHELLE, DAVID, and PAUL
as they look toward the future.

Contents

Foreword

James N. Rosenau

This innovative volume develops several themes that can all too easily be lost in the rush of climactic events. In our time of restless, pervasive change it is useful to be reminded that not all is new, that historical context matters, that the creative mind can sort out the important from the trivial, and that those who do the sorting—the global philosophers—leave a trail of ideas that guide subsequent generations.

These reminders are not self-evident. Each is embedded in a complex set of tensions. All is not new, but much is changing. Historical context matters, yes, but history is also marked by breakpoints that transform the old context. The creative mind focuses on crucial issues, yes, but it can also exaggerate them. Theorists leave an ideational trail, yes, but they are also bound by both cultural and temporal concerns, each of which can divert travelers into unnecessary detours and dead ends.

It is precisely because of the endless and contradictory tensions between change and continuity, specific contexts and broad universals, theory and practice, that the study of international relations is pervaded with controversial issues. No problem has a clear-cut solution. No pattern is free of exceptions. No situation derives from a single cause. No actor is consistently moral. No system is fully integrated. Rather, everything is discrepant, nuanced, perplexing, thereby compelling us as students to evolve ways and perspectives that tolerate ambiguity and value complexity.

Kauppi and Viotti are keenly aware of the many tensions and contradictions that have long pervaded global politics and long challenged those who dare to comprehend its patterns and judge its practices. They do not shrink from complexity, nor do they offer a skeletal view of the world and its observers. They do not hesitate to use modern social science concepts—such as meta-theoretical images or the systems approach—as a basis for comparing philosophical premises articulated at very different times in history. And they are no more averse to teasing out the factors that differentiate historical eras as they are to delineating the commonalities.

The foundations of their analysis should be reassuring for the reader. It is all too easy to avoid, and thus to dismiss, the complexity that attaches to

probes of the historical record. By high-mindedly asserting that it is important to be familiar with the writings of history's philosophical giants, one
builds confidence that clarity lies ahead, that current challenges can be met
by drawing on the wisdom of the ages. On the face of it, after all, the notion
of falling back on the ideas of Thucydides or Plato in order to comprehend
the present seems to make a lot of sense, or at least one can hardly quarrel
with the thought that understanding is enriched through an awareness of
intellectual roots. Such reasoning is deceptive, however. It encourages confidence in one's broad, cultural perspective, but there is no magic in the
works of our intellectual forebearers, no blueprint for discerning the suit-
ability of their formulations to the present scene. To discern their applicability takes imaginative insight and an explicit set of criteria for sorting out
those of their ideas that have enduring relevance from those that do not.
Thucydides observed acts of war and diplomacy that occurred in an ancient
context—more than four centuries before Christ—some of which parallel
current conflicts and some of which do not, thus posing the danger of excessive reliance on the simple premise that Thucydides's observations, or
those of any other earlier writer, are necessarily worthwhile. Kauppi and
Viotti are fully cognizant of this danger. Their chapters are sensitive to both
the uses and abuses of history and, consequently, their claims of present-
day relevance are modest and cautious. Readers need not fear that a deep
engagement with this book will prove misleading or foster simplistic asser-
tions about the relevancy of the past and its observers.

On the contrary, a deep engagement can only be enlarging. In the pages
that follow one will find a sensitive and subtle appreciation of how a succession of observers, from the ancient philosophers to those who confronted
the 19th Century, were affected by the very relationships, institutions, and
crises they sought to understand. Here one encounters great minds trying to
puzzle through the nature of war and conflict, the underpinnings of peace
and the dilemmas of collective action, the limits of power and justice, and
a host of other substantive issues that arise again and again from decade to
decade and from century to century. Here one can trace both the recurring
preoccupations of different generations and the specific circumstances that
each had to face. Here one gets an incisive introduction to the dynamics of
interaction that link thinkers to actors, theorists to their milieu, observers
to their methods. Here one has to puzzle about the eternal verities in relation to the momentary event. Here one must acknowledge that alternative
images of the world can give discrepant meanings to the same developments. And here one can derive comfort from knowing that neither our
problems nor our proposed solutions to them are entirely unique and that
our predecessors somehow managed to muddle through and pass along
their accumulated wisdom.

Furthermore, even as the ensuing chapters sweep across millenia of international experience and thereby suggest the large extent to which indi-

viduals and societies are prey to powerful forces beyond their control, so do they collectively highlight the diverse ways in which the course of world events is shaped by the ideas and urgings of those who reflect on world affairs. Let those among us who wonder whether their research findings and theoretical formulations matter take heart. One may not be a Hobbes or a Rousseau, but one does contribute to an intellectual milieu out of which an era's philosophical giants emerge and to which its political leaders respond. Kauppi and Viotti do not probe this causal process at any length, but it is clear that diverse and circuitous channels of communication continuously circulate the interpretations of those who teach and write about international affairs and thereby create a milieu which shapes the thinking of leaders and publics. The milieu defines the actors, attaches meaning to the past, reinterprets the present, posits desired futures, accords legitimacy to some actions and withholds it from others, or otherwise serves as a backdrop for the conduct of public affairs. Teachers and writers are not the only contributors to the prevailing milieu, but their work does matter, as can be readily discerned in the various chapters that follow.

And throughout it is also clear that the processes of influence work both ways, that the reflections of intellectuals are shaped by the historical context in which they labor even as their formulations shape the milieu. A distinguished historian succinctly sums up this interactive process:

> I am not sure that I should envy any historian who could honestly claim to have lived through the earth-shaking events of the past fifty years without some radical modifications of his outlook. . . . It is not merely the events that are in flux. The historian himself is in flux.[1]

If both history and the historian are simultaneously in flux, how does one uncover the continuities of world politics and differentiate them from the changes? This book provides no easy solution, but the analysis does offer ample empirical materials out of which readers can fashion their own answers. So there are good reasons for them not to be in awe of what they are about to undertake. The key is to relax and enjoy the task, to ponder and probe the analysis, and then to experience the enlargement and satisfactions that are bound to follow.

---

[1]E.H. Carr, *What Is History?* (Harmondsworth, England: Penguin Books, 1964), p. 42.

The Global
Philosophers

1
Introduction

This book has been written for a wide range of readers with interest in the field of international relations. Our primary purpose, quite simply, is to identify the intellectual and historical roots of the ideas that underlie much of the present-day literature on international relations, particularly that which is conceptually and theoretically oriented. In surveying selected works from ancient Greece through the nineteenth and early twentieth centuries, we cull insights from a number of authors. Some might argue that if one wished to understand the basics of thought about world politics, an in-depth study of Thucydides, Machiavelli, Hobbes, Rousseau, Kant, and perhaps Grotius is sufficient. This would be a mistake. Authors usually not associated with the discipline also have had some interesting things to say about world politics and are deserving of comment. Furthermore, many of these writers directly influenced some of the more illustrious names in the field. Machiavelli, for example, owed an intellectual debt to such ancient writers as Polybius, Livy, and Plutarch. Indeed, in comparison to much of the current literature on international relations, the extent to which the authors surveyed here were familiar with the arguments of their predecessors is striking.

Aside from examining the intellectual roots of much of the contemporary literature on international relations, a second important purpose of this volume is to discuss the historical context within which the writers we cite made their observations. These authors were obviously influenced not only by the arguments and insights of their predecessors, but also by the times within which they lived. It must be emphasized that our goal is not to provide an overview of the history of ancient Greece, the Middle Ages, the Roman Empire, or the rise of the modern state system. Rather, it is to illustrate how the nature of the international system at a particular point in time influenced the works of the writers under consideration and how writers living in similar historical circumstances could nevertheless conceive of international politics in different ways.

Of equal importance, the discussion of historical contexts is also intended to show how different types of international systems have existed over time. By studying earlier regional and international political systems, we can discern how they differ from present-day forms of international politics. Such contrasts allow us to gain insights into how change has occurred and reminds us that the contemporary state system, which we take for granted as a permanent fixture, has not always been the norm. This issue of change is particularly important at a time when many observers believe that fundamental shifts in the pattern of world politics are underway. In sum, an understanding of present-day efforts in the field of international relations is enhanced when one sees such works in their intellectual–historical context.

This understanding leads one to ask how much of the current work on international relations really offers new insights. We believe it is fair to say that much less is completely new in present-day international relations theory than one might first suppose—a comment that no doubt applies equally well to political theory in general. There is a certain hubris caused by lack of attention to intellectual antecedents; political scientists sometimes cloak their ideas in present-day theories with a "newness," originality, or uniqueness that may not be warranted. In point of fact, international relations as a field of inquiry tends to suffer from the problem of fads. Research programs come and go and sometimes return under new titles. By studying classic and even somewhat obscure works, as any historian will tell you, one becomes more skeptical toward fashions and can gain an appreciation for the continuity of thinking about international politics.[1]

A third purpose of this work is to illustrate how various writers have contributed to the development of three images of international relations that we have argued elsewhere currently dominate the field of international relations—realism, pluralism, and globalism.[2] All too often realism monopolizes the discussion. In this book realism dominates, but we attempt to give, if not equal time, at least greater attention to writers who have influenced the pluralist and globalist modes of thought.

Finally, central and enduring questions relevant to the theoretical enterprise are our concern. For example, we ask to what extent international phenomena such as the actions of states are best accounted for by the structure of the international system, the nature of the international system's political units, or human nature. Do the writers examined believe individuals have the capacity to affect events (more specifically, whether their theories allow for such voluntarism) or do they see individuals primarily in a reactive mode, responding to circumstances largely imposed on them (thus producing theories with a heavy dose of determinism)? How one answers such questions will influence resultant expectations of peaceful change and the transformation of the international system.

Scope

Anyone who engages in a project such as this is faced with two basic problems involving selectivity and interpretation. We used three criteria for deciding which authors to discuss. First, there are those writers who most would agree are central to the study of international relations: Thucydides, Machiavelli, Hobbes, Grotius, Rousseau, and Kant. Secondly, we were interested in discussing authors and ideas that did not rely almost exclusively on the modern state as the key unit of analysis—the Greek and Roman Stoics and their emphasis on the individual and a community that transcended parochial allegiances; Livy and Plutarch and their analyses of the Roman empire; Augustine and Aquinas and their view of the role of the church and religion in the international system of the Middle Ages; Dante's call for a secular world empire; nineteenth-century liberals and their claim for the pacifying effects of republicanism and international commerce; and Marx's and Lenin's conceptualization of politics and economics in transnational class terms. Finally, we have included authors who had little interest in international relations as such, but whose interest in domestic and comparative politics or methodology directly or indirectly influenced later scholars more expressly concerned with international politics. This group includes Plato, Aristotle, Polybius, More, Bodin, Montesquieu, Hegel, Smith, and Weber. Indeed, we would go so far as to observe that the reason it is questionable even to conceive of international relations as a "discipline" is the fact that even such luminaries as Machiavelli, Hobbes, and Rousseau were primarily interested in domestic politics. Their views of the violent world of international politics were, to a great extent, a contrast to their preferred form of domestic polity that would supposedly ensure a civil peace.

While most scholars will have no problem with the writers we have chosen to discuss, there will certainly be grounds for disagreement as to which ones have been left out of our account or which have been mentioned only in passing. We would expect even more disagreement concerning our interpretation of certain aspects of these classic works. Even those who devote their professional lives to studying these works—whether political theorists or historians—disagree on trivial as well as important matters; consensus is very hard to achieve in most academic areas of inquiry. This is the nature of scholarship. Nor is consensus necessarily a very good thing. What makes these works important is the fact that they are subject to different interpretations, with different insights being culled from them by scholars with different interests and orientations. We hope, however, that the reader does not find our interpretations of these works to be unduly idiosyncratic. Our goal is to provide a synthesis not only of our own views, but also of those interpretations of the wider community of international relations scholars.

We must admit, however, to what some readers may claim to be cultural and geographic parochialism. The authors and ideas we discuss developed out of the experience of Western civilization. This does not necessarily mean we wholeheartedly embrace Western notions of progress or the supposed benefits of modernity.[3] Our major purpose, however, of identifying the intellectual and historical roots of the contemporary literature on international relations justifies this Western focus. Contributors to this literature have been observers of what began as a Western experience but has since become global. Arab scholars, for example, are to be credited with saving many classic Greek texts that all too easily could have been lost to history. These scholars obviously believed that the insights of Plato, Aristotle, and Thucydides transcended any particular time and place.[4]

Furthermore, the state and world capitalist systems as we know them today had their roots in Western thought and were spread from Europe to the rest of the world in the period of discovery and colonialism. Either as intended or unintended consequence, colonialism and imperialism would be the vehicles for the spread of these Western ideas. Even though peoples in the Americas, Asia, and Africa in time separated formally from their colonial masters, they did so on European terms by adopting (or adapting) political and economic ideas drawn from the European experience and becoming sovereign states according to the European model. We do not, therefore, address Confucian, Hindu, and other ancient Asian traditions because these ideas, though enormously important in their regions of origin, did not spread to the world as a whole. For example, the writings of the Hindu scholar Kautilya are very much in the realist tradition. His work, however, was only rediscovered in the twentieth century and even during his lifetime had little impact outside India.[5]

We readily acknowledge, of course, that international relations as a field of inquiry is increasingly becoming truly international as reflected, for example, in the diversity of membership in professional organizations. Nevertheless, in our discussions with non-Western academics, we have been impressed by the extent to which the writings of a writer like Thucydides, Hobbes, or Marx have shaped the conceptual and philosophical orientation of international relations scholars from all over the world. In a similar fashion, what we call the realist, pluralist, and globalist images of international relations dominate the field not only in Washington and London, but also in Johannesburg, Tokyo, New Delhi, and Mexico City.

Methods

As it has become fashionable—and, we believe, useful—in recent years for authors to declare their biases up front, several comments concerning our methodological orientation are in order. An examination of the table of contents might lead one to assume that we are associated with the so-called traditionalist camp of international relations, given our interest in scholarship over the past 2,500 years and the historical context within which these works were written. In fact, in training and temperament we fall more into the behavioralist school of thought, although we recognize that the promise of the behavioral revolution in terms of the accumulation of knowledge has not been achieved to anyone's satisfaction. Be that as it may, we have always felt uncomfortable with this methodological bifurcation of the field, which is what the old traditionalist–behavioralist debate was all about.[6] We find such a juxtaposition counterproductive in terms of the accumulation of knowledge about international relations. In fact, the traditionalist emphasis on "insight" can be seen as a spur to the development of testable hypotheses, using history as the laboratory. Indeed, in recent years an increasing number of scholars of international relations have followed such a path.[7] Furthermore, it is not as if the behavioral orientation to the study of politics merely dates from the post-World War II era, or even the Renaissance and Enlightenment. As K.J. Holsti has noted:

> We do not read Thucydides, Aristotle, or Rousseau as historical curiosities. We may and do add to them, and often criticize them, but we do not replace them. Long before the behavioral revolution, Aristotle claimed that generalizations about political life can be derived from the empirical data of common sense and historical experience, and that these generalizations can be treated in terms of cause and effect. Thucydides' hypothesis on the causes of pre-emptive war is as germane today as it was in 431 B.C. Rousseau's insights about the sources of war and the difficulties of cooperation in a condition of anarchy command our attention as much today as they did when first published.[8]

In another earlier collaborative effort, our behavioralist tendencies were quite evident.[9] In this volume we show greater appreciation for scholarship in the traditionalist vein. We feel what makes this work unusual, however, is the fact that we consciously attempt to link much of the recent conceptual and empirical research on international relations to its intellectual and historical roots.

As a final comment, we sympathize with our academic colleagues who have found that a twelve-to-fifteen week semester is simply insufficient time to cover adequately World Politics or Introduction to International Relations Theory. The premium is understandably upon current events and trends or current theoretical writings. There is simply not enough time in such courses to delve deeply into the original works to find the intellectual origins of the discipline or to address the issue of how earlier writers have directly or indirectly influenced thinking about contemporary problems. It is for the time-constrained reader who nevertheless wishes a brief overview of the historical and intellectual development of the international relations field up to the early twentieth century that this book has been written. The book may also be viewed as a starting point for a more in-depth inquiry.

Notes

1. As Lawrence Freedman has stated about the literature on nuclear strategy, "Much of what is offered today as a profound and new insight was said yesterday; and usually in a more concise and literate manner." *The Evolution of Nuclear Strategy* (London: The Macmillan Press, 1981), xv.

2. Paul R. Viotti and Mark V. Kauppi, eds., *International Relations Theory: Realism, Pluralism, Globalism* (New York: Macmillan, 1987, 1992).

3. What is progressive naturally depends on one's perspective. As A.J.P. Taylor noted, in terms of talk about the decline of Western civilization, all this "means only that university professors used to have domestic servants and now do their own washing-up." For former domestic servants, professors doing their own washing-up is a sign of progress. Similarly, while the loss of African colonies may symbolize decline from the perspective of the British and the French, for Africans it epitomized the idea of progress. As cited by E.H. Carr, *What Is History?* (Harmondsworth, Eng.: Penguin Books, 1964), 112–13.

4. The Muslim philosopher Alfarabi (circa 870–950), for example, attempted to reconcile classical political philosophy with Islam. Muhsin Madhi, "Alfarabi," in *History of Political Philosophy,* ed. Leo Strauss and Joseph Cropsey (Chicago: Rand McNally, 1963), 160.

5. Narasingha P. Sil, *Kautilya's Arthasastra: A Comparative Study* (New York: P. Lang, 1989).

6. Hedley Bull, "International Theory: The Case for a Classical Approach," *World Politics,* 18, no. 3 (April 1966): 361–77; and J. David Singer, "The Incompleat Theorist: Insight Without Evidence," in *Contending Approaches to International Politics,* ed. James N. Rosenau and Klaus Knorr (Princeton: Princeton University Press, 1969), 63–86.

7. Just as some historians have seen the utility in historians learning from the political scientist's approach to knowledge. John Lewis Gaddis, "Expanding the Data Base: Historians, Political Scientists, and the Enrichment of Security Studies," *International Security,* 12, no. 1 (Summer 1987): 3–21.

8. K.J. Holsti, "Mirror, Mirror on the Wall, Which Are the Fairest Theories of All?" *International Studies Quarterly,* 33, no. 3 (Sept. 1989): 257–58.

9. Viotti and Kauppi, *International Relations Theory.*

2
Questions, Images, and Historical Systems

To lend order to our analysis of thinking about international relations from before the time of Thucydides to the early twentieth century, in this chapter we will list the basic questions to be addressed in the body of the work, discuss the three images that have tended to guide much of the contemporary research on international relations, and outline four types of historical international systems.

Questions

Those individuals who over the centuries have given a great deal of thought to political issues have raised again and again a series of basic questions. Political philosophers, for example, have dwelt on such questions as: What is the best type of political community? What should be the nature of the relationship between the rulers and the ruled? The emphasis tends to be on what could be termed the state or societal unit of analysis.

Writers and observers of international relations are, not surprisingly, primarily concerned with understanding patterns of conflict and cooperation among various types of political units, whether they be fourth-century B.C. Greek city-states, Roman and Carthaginian empires, or modern nation-states. In the course of research, thinking, and writing, a voluminous literature has been produced and a diverse series of questions and topics have been discussed. One of these questions has been of primary interest to a number of scholars of international relations: Why do wars occur? Although a different emphasis, many writers ask what factors account for the maintenance of peace. War and peace are often viewed as opposite sides of the same coin; the absence of factors that help maintain peace may lead to war in the international system.[1]

Explaining the origins of war and the maintenance of peace is a daunting task that has been undertaken by some of the best minds over the past 2,500 years. The preoccupation with war is understandable. At the risk of stating the obvious, we would simply note that war has been the most destructive activity of mankind. It has been estimated, for example, that approximately 2 million people lost their lives on the battlefields during the Thirty Years' War (1618–1648), 2.5 million during the French revolutionary and Napoleonic wars (1792–1815), 7.7 million in World War I (1914–1918), and 13 million in World War II (1939–1945).[2] And these estimates do not include all of the death and destruction suffered by civilian populations. No wonder so much intellectual labor has gone into the study of war in all of its manifestations!

Although an interest in, if not personal commitment to, understanding war and peace underlies much of the literature on international relations, in the course of their work writers also have often focused on more specific questions relating to the dynamics of world politics. It would be a daunting task to catalog all of these questions. For the purpose of this book, however, we offer six of the most interesting and most important questions about international relations. These questions have been either directly or indirectly addressed through the ages by the scholars under consideration in this work, although not every question was addressed by each author.

1. In understanding international phenomena, what is the relative importance of the overall nature of the international system, the nature of the international system's political units, and human nature? (That is, the levels of analysis.)[3]

2. What is the relation between the international economy and the international political system?

3. Why is it so difficult to predict the course of international events?

4. How much control do statesmen have over international events and outcomes? (That is, determinism versus voluntarism or free will.)

5. What is the relation between justice and power in international affairs, particularly concerning the conduct of war?

6. How should one approach the study of international relations?

The first two questions essentially deal with the problem of explanation, the third with the problem of prediction, the fourth with the problem of policy implementation, the fifth with normative-policy considerations, and the sixth with epistemological and methodological matters concerning the study of international relations. It should also be noted that these questions reflect a desire to make generalizations about international relations that transcend time and place. The questions are not restricted in their importance or relevance to the golden age of Greece, the Middle Ages, the time of absolute kings in Europe, or the twentieth century. Those writers who wish to generalize, for example, about the basic and recurrent causes of war and peace and related questions can be loosely termed theorists. This is not to suggest that a single case study does not have theoretical importance. Thus, if a scholar examines a particular war in detail, but the effort is undertaken in order to draw larger lessons about war that can be applied to other cases, the work is of a theoretical nature.

The term "theory," or "theorist," of course, elicits skepticism from many people. The old adage of "In theory that may be true, but in reality . . ." captures the common assumption that theory and reality have very little to do with each other. We must confess that if one examines contemporary journals, some of the articles seem to lend credence to this sentiment. It should be noted, however, that in attempting to make broad generalizations about such a phenomenon as war, it is to be expected that the level of abstraction would be higher than if one wanted to restrict one's attention to outlining the causes of a specific war. We are in agreement with Thomas Aquinas, who argued that "the slenderest knowledge that may be obtained of the highest things is more desirable than the most certain knowledge obtained of lesser things."[4] Hence, although the preceding questions seem to be rather broad and sweeping and, as we will see, the answers to them are sometimes of a similar nature, this does not mean that a theorist is necessarily someone who lives in an ivory tower and devotes his or her life to the contemplation of abstract ideas that have little relation to reality. Attempting to develop what could be termed "generic knowledge" about something so important, for example, as the causes of war is a formidable and certainly worthwhile task, one which by definition forces the researcher to grapple with the "real world."[5]

Of course, over the past two millennia thousands of observers and practitioners of international politics have made generalizations about war and peace and many other issues. Do they all deserve to be discussed? Hardly. We are not interested in every generalization about international relations, but rather those that later generations have deemed to be insightful or important and worthy of praise, debate, modification, or refutation. In a way, those enduring insights on world politics have lasted simply because they are the end product of what amounts to a process of intellectual natural selection. The resultant tapestry of often conflicting, yet insightful generalizations has given definition to international relations or world politics as a field of inquiry. Perhaps the greatest compliment that can be paid to these earlier scholars is the fact that today many of their observations and assumptions concerning international politics continue to provide guidance and inspiration to contemporary scholarship. This is particularly true in the case of basic underlying assumptions that tend to guide a scholar's research. It is to the matter of underlying assumptions we now turn.

Images

It is now widely accepted in the international relations discipline that scholars approach the study of world politics from what has been variously termed different perspectives, paradigms, metatheoretical constructs, or images.[6] However defined, they involve basic and often competing underlying assumptions about the nature of world politics and hence influence which types of questions are addressed and how one answers them. In other words, images influence not only what is studied but by which methods the chosen international phenomena are studied. In this work we examine the contributions various authors have made over the years to the development of three basic contemporary images of world politics that we label realism, pluralism, and globalism.

We wish to emphasize that these images refer to what Max Weber termed ideal or pure types. An "ideal" in this sense is not an evaluation or a normative preference. An ideal type is an analytic construction consisting of certain aspects of reality that are logically interrelated. As exemplified by the terms "feudalism" and "kingship," ideal types represent a heightened standard against which a particular era or ruler's reign can be measured.[7] Not any particular era designated as feudal nor every king would necessarily perfectly match this standard. An ideal type thus allows one to see the proverbial forest for the trees—before one can determine what is unique about a particular phenomenon, one needs to judge what it has in common with other similar phenomena. In the case of the three images, therefore, the following observations are in order.

First, and most important, our primary concern is to emphasize how the authors under discussion contributed to the development of one or more images, not to delineate the images and then assign a particular author to a particular category. Individual scholars may be prone to see the world through one or another of these images or blend them in various ways depending, in part, upon the subject, problems, or issues under study. Although the work of some scholars may conform closely to one of these images, leading to their categorization with others of like mind, this will not always be the case. Secondly, to state that any particular author was a realist, pluralist, or globalist is not to suggest that his work reflects all of the image's assumptions. The three contemporary images, being ideal types, are cast broadly enough to capture different strands of realist, pluralist, and globalist thought as they have developed over the years.

Realism

We start with realism, perhaps the oldest of these images. The basic elements of the realist image purport to reflect the world more as it is, less how it should be. Hence, for the realist the world is filled with conflict and struggles for power. Peace and harmony may indeed be preferable, but the sad reality is that too often this is not the case. More than any other image of international politics, realism most closely approximates the perspective of statesmen down through the ages. This is one reason it seems intuitively plausible to so many people.

What are the basic realist assumptions? First, the state is far and away the most important actor in international politics, whether one is talking about the city-state system of ancient Greece or the modern state system as it has developed since the seventeenth century. Although certainly aware of the historical existence of geographically expansive empires, realists are primarily interested in the relations and dynamics among states. The distribution of power among states will vary, with some states more powerful than others. All states, however, claim to be sovereign, meaning they do not recognize any authority above them, certainly none with a right to tell them what to do. Competition among states with different degrees of power is, therefore, for the realist, the hallmark of international politics. This competition has continued over the centuries; hence, realists tend to emphasize the timeless quality or repetitive nature of world politics.

It should be noted, however, that different realists place different emphases on how one explains the pervasive existence of international competition and conflict among states. Some see humanity as innately aggressive and believe that this predisposition explains wars. Other realists concede that, while the notion of innate aggressiveness might be overstated, certain types of states or societies nevertheless tend to bring out the worst in people. What all agree on, however, is that the mere existence of states claiming sovereignty in a world without a central authority creates a dynamic that encourages competition and violence. In other words, international politics takes place in a condition of international anarchy, or, as the seventeenth-century writer Thomas Hobbes termed it, one of "no common power." Anarchy can be viewed as a permissive cause of war because in a world without a central authority no effective obstacles (other than other states or coalitions of states) prevent states wishing to go to war from doing so.[8] It is essentially a self-help system resulting in what is known as the security dilemma. The dilemma is that, while a state may arm for sincerely defensive reasons, it may set off a chain of events that ironically end up making the state feel less secure as other states respond in kind.[9] But no matter which explanation or level of analysis (the nature of individuals or groups, the nature of the state and society, or the nature of the international system) a realist may include, the examination of the state and its behavior is a primary focus of attention.

Secondly, realists view the state as essentially a unitary actor. To a certain extent this concept is simply a matter of descriptive convenience; it is common, for example, for newspapers as well as scholars to refer to "American policy," "Britain's decision," or "German actions," knowing full well that in most cases the action is the culmination of a decision-making process involving participation and input from a number of individuals and organizations. Nevertheless, realists would argue that, despite internal debates, the state ultimately speaks with one voice when dealing with the outside world. One particular policy is followed at any given time. Exceptions certainly occur, but they highlight the general rule that the state acts as a single, integrated entity when dealing with other states.

Third, the state decision-making process is essentially rational or purposive—aimed at achieving objectives understood to be in the national interest. Particular foreign policy goals are decided upon and then what are understood to be the most effective means to achieve these goals are selected. Do realists assume that optimal choices are always made? No, of course not. Statesmen will never know if they have all the relevant information necessary to make a well-informed decision, and they will have to deal with a certain amount of ambiguity about the international environment. Furthermore, realists are aware that even if a rational decision-making process occurs, the implementation of the policy could be poor, or the complex nature of real-world circumstances could result in unfavorable and unintended consequences. Nevertheless, realists believe that decision makers struggle to engage in rational decision making and seek to choose what seems the best course to them, even if the results of the decision may be less than satisfactory. Furthermore, realists argue that accepting the rationality assumption also provides an analytic payoff in terms of predicting state behavior. Few people are privy to the deliberations of government leaders. By assuming decision making is essentially rational, however, one can place oneself in the shoes of the statesman and ask, "Given these goals, capabilities, and threats, what would I do in such circumstances?" Realists argue that this is how governments attempt to discern the possible actions of either friend or foe.

Finally, realists believe national security concerns top the agenda of relevant issues in international affairs. The major concern of decision makers is protecting the security of the state through the maintenance and expansion of state power. Power, which could perhaps be an end in itself, is usually viewed as a means by which a state attempts to maintain its independence, freedom of maneuver, and, most basically, its existence. However important such issues as human rights or the environment might be, the concern for maintaining the political autonomy and territorial integrity of the state is supreme. Each state wishes to avoid being the subject of another. Independence and freedom of action typically are the goals, with alliances being formed essentially to protect as much freedom of maneuver as possible. The key question decision makers ask themselves is whether or not a given policy is in the national and, in particular, the national security interests of the state, which first and foremost concern state survival.

Pluralism

The pluralist image consists of a different set of starting assumptions. First, nonstate actors are important players on the international stage. Investment and lending decisions by multinational corporations and international banks, for example, may directly affect the economic well-being of a country by determining where money should be invested and when it should be transferred from one country to another. Terrorist groups that operate internationally seem to have a disproportionate impact on world politics, despite their small memberships. International organizations such as the United Nations or the European Economic Community (EEC) are quite often independent actors in their own right, more than simply an arena in which states compete for influence. While states may still be the critical international actors, pluralists argue that nonstate actors play an increasingly important role.

Second, the pluralist image emphasizes that the state is not a unitary actor. The realist assumption, both descriptively and analytically, is misguided because it is an abstraction that masks the way politics are actually played out within a state. Rather than viewing the state as a unified entity acting with single-minded determination, pluralists see the state as composed of various bureaucracies, interest groups, and individuals that attempt to influence foreign policy. The state, in other words, is disaggregated—broken down into its components parts. Competition, cooperation, and coalition-building is the essence of politics. Even if, as realists argue, the state ultimately speaks with one voice to the outside world, pluralists are interested in tracing how individual bureaucracies may intentionally or unintentionally circumvent that policy in the process of its implementation.

For pluralists, there are two international implications or corollaries of this assumption of disaggregation. First, not only must one take into account the multitude of interactions *within* the state, but also one must include the transnational dimension of state and nonstate actors that operate across national borders. Foreign ministries of different countries, for example, may have more in common with each other in terms of policy preference than they do with the defense ministries of their own countries. As a result, an informal coalition may develop concerning a particular issue. Similarly, an international bank or organization may influence the bureaucratic struggle within a state over a particular foreign policy decision. Second, and somewhat paradoxically, although pluralists offer a complex image of the world through their focus on nonstate actors and the disaggregation of the state into smaller players, the transnational dimension of the pluralist image also holds out the possibility of greater international cooperation. As a generalization, while realists often emphasize how the division of the world into competing states makes cooperation very difficult to achieve, pluralists (with some exceptions) tend to emphasize the existence of common values and concerns that transcend state borders and have the potential to bind people together. Cooperation, not just conflict, is a hallmark of international politics, and political leaders and bureaucratic elites of different countries can learn to cooperate to their mutual benefit. There is, therefore, a long tradition of international thought that addresses the problem of how to get leaders and peoples of the world to emphasize what they have in common as opposed to what divides them.

Third, pluralists challenge the realist assumption of the state as a rational or purposive actor seeking to achieve objectives consistent with the national interest. According to the pluralist image, in a disaggregated state in which foreign policy is very often the result of individuals, interest groups, and bureaucracies attempting to see their policy preferences accepted so as to enhance their own prestige, power, or other micro interests and objectives, the resultant decision may not be best for the country as a whole. If the parochial interests of the few very often supersede the interests of the many, how can this be viewed as rational decision making? Furthermore, authors influenced by the pluralist image also examine the problem of misperception and bias on the part of key decision makers operating at the pinnacle of state power. Even if bureaucracies and interest groups could be tamed and the initial stages of the decision-making process made more rational, problems of incomplete information, bias, uncertainty, and stress would still undercut the idea of a rational decision-making process on the part of elites.

Finally, pluralists argue that the agenda of international politics is extensive. While often agreeing with the realists that traditional security issues are important, many pluralists with a transnational focus may broaden their definition of national security to include such matters as global warming, pollution, population growth, and refugees. While the realist usually views economic issues in terms of how they can augment or threaten to reduce a state's power and ability to act independently, pluralists are more interested in attempting to identify how international cooperation can be maintained and expanded in such areas as international trade and monetary policy. Once again, the realist focuses on impediments to international cooperation; conversely, the pluralist concentrates on the identification of common interests, learning, and means to achieve those interests.

Globalism

The globalist image of world politics, as we use the term, is fundamentally different from the realist and pluralist images. First, those we identify as globalists, both Marxists and non-Marxists, argue that one must comprehend the global context within which states and other entities interact. Understanding the overall economic or class structure of the international system means one must examine more than the distribution of power among states (realists) or chart the movements of transnational actors and the internal political processes of states (pluralists). While important, such actors, processes, and relations are part of a world shaped by global social and economic forces whose impact is not always readily apparent in the day-to-day world of domestic and international political competition. These forces not only condition and predispose actors (state as well as nonstate) to act in certain ways, they account for the generation of these actors in the first place. In other words, while realists tend to view state actors and their interests as givens, globalists are interested in explaining how they came into existence.

Second, and following from the above, globalists argue that it is absolutely necessary to view international relations from an historical perspective. Realists and pluralists would agree. But while realists tend to emphasize the timeless and repetitive nature of world politics back to ancient times, globalists use as a benchmark the historical emergence of capitalism. Globalists argue that the emergence of capitalism in sixteenth-century Western Europe was a fundamental breaking point in the structure and dynamics of world politics. Capitalism continued to spread to the point where today we can speak of a world capitalist system. Similarly, while pluralists tend to emphasize the increasing transnationalization of world politics and foresee the possibility of a fundamental change in the nature of international politics, globalists instead emphasize how the continual, incremental evolution of capitalism goes a long way toward accounting for recent changes in world politics. While individual countries over the years may claim to have based their domestic economic systems on something other than capitalism (such as socialism), globalists argue they nevertheless must operate internationally as part of a global or world capitalist system that conditions and constrains the behavior of all states and societies.

Third, while recognizing the importance of states as actors (as to realists) and nonstate actors such as international organizations, multinational corporations, and banks (as do pluralists), globalists frequently view these entities in light of how they act as mechanisms of domination. Specifically, globalists examine how some capitalist states, elites, or transnational classes manage to extract benefits from the world capitalist system at the expense of others. The exploited occupy what has been termed the Third World or lesser-developed countries (LDCs), which are characterized by large, poverty-stricken sections of their population. Some globalists argue that these countries and populations are kept dependent not because they have failed to develop capitalist economic systems or because they are poorly integrated into the world capitalist system. It is quite the opposite: these countries play an important role in the world capitalist system as a source of cheap labor and raw materials. Far from being outside the world capitalist system, they are therefore an integral part of it; their exploitation helps to account for the continued economic dominance of the northern capitalist states in North America, Western Europe, and Japan. LDCs are unable to choose their own path toward economic development because they are ensnared in the net of the world capitalist system and often are poorly served by their own elites or "comprador class," who derive personal benefits from the dependency relationship.

Finally, even more so than the realists and pluralists, globalists empha-size the critical importance of economic factors in understanding interna-tional relations. For globalists, economic considerations are the key starting point for understanding international relations and the creation and devel-opment of the current international system.

In sum, the realist, pluralist, and globalist images represent conceptual lenses through which individuals view world politics. They influence how one defines terms, what data are examined, how information is interpreted, which questions are asked, and how they are answered. These images are not theories of international relations, but rather are general perspectives out of which particular theories may develop. By way of example, take the term "international relations." When realists use the term, they are essen-tially referring to relations among states, a rather restrictive use of the con-cept. Pluralists, as we have seen, are interested in much more than relations among states—nonstate actors such as multinational corporations, terrorist groups, and international organizations are also important. Globalists ex-amine class relations or other global structures that transcend state bound-aries. Hence, "international relations" means different things to different people.

Similarly, a close reading of the realist, pluralist, and globalist images as outlined previously would provide an indication of how an author influ-enced by one of them might answer the basic questions addressed in this book. For example, a realist and globalist would tend to emphasize the overall structure of the international system in accounting for international phenomena and behavior. The realist would point to anarchy and the dis-tribution of power among states; the globalist would note the slow histor-ical development of international capitalism and structures of domination. Similarly, one of the reasons realists have been given this title is because of their pessimistic belief that statesmen do not have a great deal of power to control the outcome of international events. Hence, realists counsel pru-dence. Some globalists, while hoping for the spiritual, political, and eco-nomic liberation of the downtrodden, are nevertheless pessimistic about the ability of people to overturn historically entrenched structures of domina-tion on a world-wide basis. Thus, there tends to be a determinist cast to much of the writing in the realist and globalist vein. Pluralists, however, are more optimistic about the possibilities of transforming the international sys-tem because of their assumption that individuals can exert a degree of con-trol over their fate and life circumstances. This viewpoint reflects a volun-tarist orientation to political and economic change. Finally, by way of example, realists tend to subordinate economic factors to those of a political–military nature, or to see economic power as simply one aspect of overall power designed to enhance the autonomy of a state. Pluralists gen-erally keep an open mind on the relative importance of economic and political–military factors, arguing that it depends on the issue at hand. Globalists tend to emphasize the explanatory power of economic factors.

Historical Systems

Writers on international relations are not only influenced by the ideas and perspectives of those who came before them, but also by the world or international system in which they live. The concept of "system" as applied to international politics has a long history. Perhaps the first formal definition of an international system was provided in 1675 by Samuel Pufendorf, an important contributor to the development of international law: "several states that are so connected as to seem to constitute one body whose members retain sovereignty."[10] Unfortunately, Pufendorf's definition views states as the only components of the system and also emphasizes a perspective of sovereignty that is closely tied to the emergence of the state in the late Middle Ages. The concept of system used in this book is defined as "an aggregation of diverse entities united by regular interaction that sets them apart from other systems."[11] The idea of diverse entities is useful in that it allows not only for different types of state actors—such as city-states, empires, and nation-states—but also for international organizations and such nonstate actors as corporations and terrorist groups. "Regular interaction" varies depending on the nature and intensity of the interactions. For example, the interaction could be war, of greater or lesser intensity. Or the interaction could involve trade, ranging from minimal to intense. Finally, the nature of the system's units and their interactions set the system apart from other systems. This distinction allows one to speak of a system having "boundaries." In this regard, the present-day international or world system can be said to cover the entire globe and to lack the boundaries between separate international systems of earlier historical periods.

It should be remembered, of course, that a system is simply an analytic device that allows the observer to isolate and deal with an aspect of international relations that is of interest. It is not meant to be a precise description of reality. For example, one could focus on a "Peloponnesian system" limited, for the most part, to the interactions of the Greek city-states. This was the approach essentially used by Thucydides for the first part of his work. Conversely, one could enlarge the system being analyzed to include the Persian Empire, which played an intermittent (yet at times crucial) role.[12] Whether one views the Peloponnesian city-state and Persian Empire as separate systems with distinct boundaries or as subsystems within a single system is up to the analyst.

In this book, we examine four very different types of international systems.[13] First, the fourth- and fifth-century B.C. Greek city-state system, which was composed of the Greek polis as principal unit. The polis blurred the modern distinction between state and society and tended to encompass the two in an organic whole.[14] To a certain extent it is also fair to say that this organic conception of state–society relations in ancient Greece was as much a function of the normative preferences of such theorists as Plato and Aristotle as it was a reflection of reality.[15] Nevertheless, particularly among the democratic city-states such as Athens during the time of Pericles, the state was not viewed as an entity antagonistic to, or apart from, the general populace.

Second, the Roman Empire is an example of what could be called a suzerain system. This type of system, as with the Greek city-state system, involves separate societal units associated by regular interaction, but in this case one among them asserts supremacy and the others formally or tacitly accept this claim.[16] While in the Greek polis there was a close relation between state and society, an empire or suzerain system is the opposite; because of the geographic expanse of the empire, the state claiming supremacy is content to devolve power to local authorities and only indirectly have dealings with the diverse societies that comprise the population of the empire. The Romans, of course, were heavily influenced by Hellenistic thinking, but the intimacy of the early Roman Republic—similar to the state–society relations in such Greek city-states as Periclean Athens—began to fade as the powers of imperial Rome grew.

Third, the Western European medieval era from roughly the fifth to the fourteenth century is perhaps the most interesting time period we will examine. Particular emphasis is placed upon the feudal system from the ninth to the fourteenth century. What makes the medieval system so unusual is the diversity of the entities that composed it and the manner in which the relations among these units was structured. Power was claimed by a diverse group of governmental units, only some of which evolved into modern states. Other actors included trading associations, the great houses of merchant bankers, and local feudal barons. Claiming universal jurisdiction in the secular realm was the Holy Roman Empire, which came to be based in the Germanic area of northern Europe. While the papacy in Rome claimed universal jurisdiction in the spiritual realm, it also claimed temporal authority and exhibited great political power through its international bureaucracy. The church was also important in that it argued for a single, undivided *societas christiana*. Rather than emphasizing separateness, the church emphasized unity among the disparate political entities of medieval Europe.[17]

Finally, we will examine the rise of the modern state (or nation-state) system in Europe. While the key actors are, by definition, modern states, writers from the seventeenth through nineteenth centuries also emphasized the importance of taking into account transnational actors, international norms, and social and economic forces that transcended territorial boundaries. Due to European colonialism and imperialism, other cultures were forced to come to terms with the formidable power of the modern state, as well as Western ideas and values.

We now turn to our primary task: the identification of the intellectual and historical roots of many of the ideas that underlie present-day images and much of the literature on international relations.

Notes

1. And the outbreak of peace is very often the result of the end of a destructive war. As one scholar has noted, "For every thousand pages published on the causes of war there is less than one page directly on the causes of peace." Geoffrey Blainey, *The Causes of War* (New York: Free Press, 1973), 3.

2. Jack Levy, "Theories of General War," *World Politics,* 37, no. 3 (April 1985): 373.

3. Are international phenomena best explained at the level of the international system, the level of the state or society, or the level of the individual? Kenneth Waltz, in examining the causes of war, utilizes all three levels in *Man, the State and War* (New York: Columbia University Press, 1959). In an influential article, J. David Singer distinguished between the international system and the national subsystems levels of analysis: "The Level-of-Analysis Problem in International Relations," in *International Politics and Foreign Policy,* ed. James N. Rosenau (New York: Free Press, 1969), 20–29.

4. As cited by John Mueller, *Retreat from Doomsday: The Obsolescence of Major War* (New York: Basic Books, 1989), xx.

5. The term "generic knowledge" is from Alexander George, "Is Research on Crisis Management Needed?" in *Avoiding War: Problems of Crisis Management,* ed. Alexander L. George (Boulder, Col.: Westview Press, 1991), 5.

6. See, for example, Michael Haas, "Metaphysics of Paradigms in Political Science," *The Review of Politics,* 48, no. 4 (1986): 521–48; Michael Haas, "The Comparative Study of Foreign Policy: The Need for Theory and Policy Relevance," *International Studies Notes,* 13, no. 3 (Fall 1987): 69–74; K.J. Holsti, *The Dividing Discipline* (Winchester, Mass.: Allen and Unwin, 1985); Michael Banks, "Where We Are Now," *Review of International Studies,* 11 (1985): 215–33; Michael Banks, "The Interparadigm Debate," in *International Relations: A Handbook of Current Theory,* ed. Margot Light and A.J.R. Groom (London: Pinter Publishers, 1985); Hayward Alker and Thomas Biersteker, "The Dialectics of World Order: Notes for a Future Archeologist of International Savoir Faire," *International Studies Quarterly,* 28, no. 2 (1984): 121–42; R.D. McKinlay and Richard Little, *Global Problems and World Order* (Bristol, Eng.: Frances Pinter, 1986); James N. Rosenau, "Order and Disorder in the Study of World Politics," in *Globalism Versus Realism: International Relations' Third Debate,* ed. Ray Maghroori and Bennett Ramberg (Boulder, Col.: Westview Press, 1982), 1–7; Yosef Lapid, "The Third Debate: On the Prospects of International Theory in a Post-Positivist Era," *International Studies Quarterly,* 33, no. 3 (Sept. 1989): 235–54; and Paul R. Viotti and Mark V. Kauppi, *International Relations Theory: Realism, Pluralism, and Globalism* (New York: Macmillan, 1987, 1992).

7. H.H. Gerth and C. Wright Mills, trans. and eds., *From Max Weber: Essays in Sociology* (New York: Oxford University Press, 1946), 59–60.

8. By contrast, more specific causes for a given war are referred to by one analyst, following Kant, as "efficient" causes. Kenneth N. Waltz, *Man, The State and War* (New York: Columbia University Press, 1954, 1959), 233–34. One of the best statements of the implications of anarchy is by Robert Jervis, "Cooperation Under the Security Dilemma," *World Politics*, 30, no. 2 (Jan. 1978): 167–214. On confusion over the term anarchy, see Helen Milner, "The Assumption of Anarchy in International Relations Theory: A Critique," *Review of International Studies*, 17, no. 1 (Jan. 1991): 67–85.

9. John Herz is credited with the term "security dilemma." See his "Idealist Internationalism and the Security Dilemma," *World Politics*, 2, no. 2 (Jan. 1950): 157–80.

10. As cited by Martin Wight, *Systems of States* (Leicester, Eng.: Leicester University Press, 1977), 21.

11. This definition is modified from that provided by Robert A. Mundell and Alexander K. Swoboda, eds. *Monetary Problems of the International Economy* (Chicago: University of Chicago Press, 1969), 343, as cited by Robert Gilpin, *War and Change in World Politics* (Cambridge: Cambridge University Press, 1981), 26. The original definition is: "A system is an aggregation of diverse entities united by regular interaction according to a form of control."

12. In the second Peloponnesian War, for example, both Athens and Sparta tried to curry favor with the Persians. Following the destruction of the Sicilian expedition, the Persians contributed to the Spartan defense budget and after the revolt of Miletus from Athens, Persia and Sparta agreed to an alliance. It was a rocky relationship, but eventually it was critical to the outcome of the war. In 407 B.C. an Athenian diplomatic mission met a Spartan delegation returning from a meeting with the Persian king, who had agreed to increase support for Sparta. Furthermore, the money provided by Cyrus to Lysander helped to expand and refurbish the Spartan allied fleet, which then gained the decisive Spartan naval victory at Aegospotami that marked the beginning of the end of the war. Donald Kagan, *The Fall of the Athenian Empire* (Ithaca, N.Y.: Cornell University Press, 1987), 380–81.

13. S.N. Eisenstadt distinguishes among the following types of political systems: (1) primitive political systems, (2) patrimonial empires (for example, Carolingian and Parthian), (3) nomad or conquest empires (for example, Mongols and the Arab kingdoms under the first caliphs), (4) city-states (ancient Athens, republican Rome), (5) feudal systems (Europe, Japan, Middle East), (6) centralized historical bureaucratic empires (Rome, Macedonia), (7) modern societies (democratic, autocratic, totalitarian). Our focus is on numbers 4 through 7. *The Political Systems of Empires* (New York: The Free Press, 1963), 10.

14. For a discussion, see H.D.F. Kitto, *The Greeks* (Harmondsworth, Eng.: Penguin Books, 1957), ch. 5.

15. For qualifications to the "classical image" of city-states, see Peter Burke, "City-States," in *States in History*, ed. John A. Hall (Oxford and New York: Basil Blackwell, 1986).

16. Wight, *Systems of States*, 23.

17. Ibid., 26–28.

3
Before Thucydides: Homer and Herodotus

I n studying a number of the ancient Greek and Roman writers who will be discussed in this and the following three chapters, one finds the roots of realist thought in their obvious concern for the security of the state. This concern is particularly true in the case of Herodotus, Thucydides, Livy, and Plutarch. The impact of these writers on the scholars who followed them cannot be overstated. Machiavelli's reading of the ancients, for example, led him to draw conclusions that he applied to sixteenth-century domestic and international politics. There was little new in Machiavelli's rendering. By his own admission, Machiavelli's ideas were drawn not just from observation of events in his own time, but also from the parallels he drew from extensive reading of ancient writers such as Polybius, Livy, and Tacitus. What Machiavelli provided was a synthesis that would become a foundation or point of departure for the realists who followed him.

The roots of pluralist and globalist thought are also present in ancient writings, although usually less developed. In reading Plato and Aristotle, who wrote their works shortly after the time of Thucydides, one can find class analysis, prescriptions for maintaining societal harmony and thus avoiding class conflict, a labor theory of value, and a defense of slavery—what Marx later referred to as an ancient mode of production. Pluralist and liberal (or democratic) modes of thought also received considerable attention from Greek writers, but the application of these ideas typically was contained within the bounds of a given city-state. Applying these ideas—even in principle—beyond the citizens of that unit did not seem to enter their minds. It was the late Greek and Roman writers, known as the Stoics, who developed notions of a community of mankind that transcended the boundaries of individual units and thus provided a conceptual basis for applying principles developed within a city-state to the larger world.

Our study of the ancients necessarily is limited to the written records and artifacts left behind by these civilizations. Greece and Rome figure so prominently in our view of the ancients in part because we know more about them than we do of such civilizations as the Sumerians or Hittites. We cannot know of great philosophical insights or other accomplishments

21

Invasion, Conquest, and Empire:
Security as a Central Problem in Ancient Western History

Date (B.C.)	Historical Developments
3500	The Bronze Age: Sumerian civilization in Mesopotamia (Iraq); Egyptians settle Nile valley
2800	Minoans settle Mediterranean island of Crete
2300	Akkadians dominate Mesopotamia
2000	Amorites and Elamites invade Mesopotamia: Sumerian rule ends and Babylonian Empire established; Hittites settle Anatolia (Turkey)
1900	Greece settled by Achaens (Mycenians)
1800	Legal Code of Hammurabi established in Babylon (Iraq); Hyksos invade Egypt
1300	Phoenician (Canaanite) trading posts established along the Mediterranean coast; Trojan War (1250)
1200	The Iron Age; Dorian tribes invade Greece
1150	Dorians invade Minoans on Crete
700	Assyrian imperial influence from Iraq to Egypt
500	Persian Wars: Cyrus (d. 529) establishes Persian Empire through conquest; Cambyses (d. 521) conquers Egypt, extending empire from Pakistan to Libya; Darius (d. 486) defeated at Marathon (490); Xerxes (d. 465) defeated at Salamis (480); Athens establishes Delian League, an alliance against Persia
431–404	Peloponnesian War (Athens versus Sparta)
356–323	Alexander the Great (Aristotle's student) establishes Macedonian Empire through conquest
264–146	Punic Wars between Rome and Carthage (Tunis), leading to defeats of Carthaginians (Phoenicians) and establishment of Roman Empire

Dates are approximate; present-day country or city names are used for locational purposes.

if there is no record of them. This is not to say that civilizations leaving few records were somehow inferior to those that did. It is only to say that we cannot know much about them.

Historical Context

Our purpose here or elsewhere in this book is not to present a comprehensive history of the period under study. It is appropriate, however, to touch upon important historical events and sketch the nature of the international system within which the authors lived. The first period, which stretches from Homer to Thucydides, was a time of turmoil in which the security of the Greek city-states and empires were central issues. We can hardly be surprised, then, that realist notions of power and balance-of-power politics prevailed among ancient writers. Security, if not an obsession, was at least a preoccupation for them.

One can distinguish between the world depicted by Homer and the world in which he lived. The *Iliad* and the *Odyssey,* epic poems attributed to Homer, were written about 750–700 B.C. Supposedly taking place in the thirteenth century B.C., Homer's tales depict a world in which aristocratic warrior-chiefs ruled over loosely united and defined territories and only the earliest forms of state government are evident. Towns existed, but life was essentially rural, with wealth a function of flocks and herds. Kingship was not so much an office with certain duties as it was a social position. Extensive bureaucracies had not been created, and what little peaceable contact existed was on the basis of hospitality or friendship among noble families, not formal diplomatic relations. Hence, when Paris of Troy carried off Helen, wife of King Menelaus of Sparta, his act was as much an insult to private hospitality as it was a political outrage. Although the *Iliad* takes place in the later Mycenaean world, we know from archaeological findings that the states depicted by Homer were in reality much more complicated and developed. His description is more characteristic of the "dark age" that fell between the Mycenaean age and the time of Homer.[1]

Thucydides also provides interesting evidence of this part of the world during the time of the Trojan War. He argues that "these various Hellenic states, weak in themselves and lacking communications with one another, took no kind of collective action before the time of the Trojan War. . . . Indeed, my view is that at this time the whole country was not even called 'Hellas.'" Populations shifted regularly, and pirates played a role almost as important as kings' armies. Thucydides notes how pirates would "descend upon cities which were unprotected by walls and indeed consisted only of scattered settlements." Aristotle similarly characterizes this ancient period, describing the village as a union of families and a city as a union of villages.[2] In other words, society at this time was a long way from the modern state and even from the more integrated Greek city-state or *polis* of future centuries.

As for the time in which Homer was actually writing, the self-sufficient and insular communities of the dark age had given way to hundreds of separate city-states. A city-state typically consisted of an urban center and the surrounding agricultural land within several miles. Populations were small, numbering only in the thousands. As some families acquired larger plots of land, the size of the nobility increased. Over time, hereditary monarchs often gave way to collective governments by the nobles from which an *archon* or chief magistrate was chosen. Nascent bureaucracies were formed, with councils of leading men appointed to advise the rulers. By the time of Homer's death, the domination of cities by families—so prevalent in the *Iliad*—was weakening. One reason for their decline was the introduction of a simple alphabet in the eighth century B.C. that encouraged laws to be written down and hence strengthened the rights of citizens. For the Greeks, the importance of law distinguished them from the barbarians and was a defining characteristic of the *polis*.[3]

As the population of Greece grew, resources were stretched to the point where groups left to found colonies. As early as the eighth century B.C., Greek colonies were established in Italy and Sicily and on the coast of the Black Sea. The colonies were established according to the principles of the city-states in Greece, with each colony being supported by an existing *polis*. Increased contact with the wider world brought increased trade, but also warfare. Inevitably, many strong states preyed on weaker neighbors. This development had an impact on Greek warfare, and toward the end of the eighth century the hoplite phalanx—heavily armed infantrymen working closely together—came to be the basic form of military organization. The appearance of the hoplites encouraged the development of the *polis* in two ways. First, it devalued the role of Homer's warrior-chieftain who heroically engaged in single combat. Instead, steadfastness among the ranks was key. Second, the creation of a phalanx required a communal effort and drew on the dedication and courage of all male citizens.[4] As seen in the work of Herodotus, such courage is enhanced if the soldier believes he is fighting for his liberty and the continuation of his way of life. Although power was widely dispersed among a number of city-states in this Greek international system, one in particular, Sparta, gained renown for its military prowess and martial spirit. This is the setting within which Homer recorded the *Iliad* and the *Odyssey*.

Homer

Unfortunately, we know virtually nothing about Homer as a person. The Greeks attributed the *Iliad* and the *Odyssey* to this single poet, with tradition suggesting he lived on the island of Chios. In these two works, Homer creatively recorded the story of the Greek triumph over Troy and the fantastical adventures of Odysseus on his return home from the war. Historical accuracy was not Homer's purpose so much as telling a good story. The importance of his works, then, is not so much for their contribution to history as such and certainly not for any direct contribution to thinking about international relations. Rather, Homer's influence on later Greek writers—all of whom were familiar with the *Iliad* and *Odyssey*—stemmed from the fact that for the Greeks history and epic poetry were closely associated. Indeed, the manner in which Greek history was written and its depiction of many historical events as tragic drama can be directly traced to Homer and other Greek epic poets.[5] Furthermore, many of the same questions Homer raised about the ability of individuals to control their fates and about the nature of cause and effect in politics and international relations would be dealt with by Herodotus, Thucydides, Plato, Aristotle, Polybius, and later Roman historians (even though their answers would be different and certainly less entertaining).

Determinism and Voluntarism

The *Iliad* presents a vivid and tragic view of the world and depicts both the human and the divine impact on events. The first line reflects this interaction between mortals and gods: "Sing, goddess, of the anger of Achilles, son of Peleus, the accursed anger which brought uncounted anguish on the Achaians and hurled down to Hades many mighty souls of heroes, making their bodies the prey to dogs and the birds' feasting: and this was the working of Zeus' will."[6] Throughout the narrative, choices by individuals have dramatic consequences, such as the war between the Greeks and Trojans, which was caused by the seduction and abduction of Helen by Paris. Such individual actions, as opposed to factors so familiar to the modern world— divergent ideologies, militaristic societies, or extreme nationalism—are critical. Even the depictions of the battles often come down to combat between individuals whose bravery and other virtues decide the outcome rather than the superiority of weaponry, so important in modern warfare.

The humans, however, share center stage with the gods. As powerful as an Agamemnon or Odysseus may be, the gods ultimately, and very often capriciously, determine matters of life and death. Their constant intervention places limits on the ability of humans to control their fates. As Achilles says to Priam, who has come to plead for the body of his dead son, "This is the fate the gods have spun for poor mortal men, that we should live in misery."[7] Notwithstanding these supernatural interventions, human will still can be decisive in Homer's epics. In the *Iliad,* for example, Achilles takes the leading role in subduing the Trojans, even though his vulnerability subsequently will result in his death. The important point here, however, is not the death of Achilles, but what he was able to accomplish in life. To Homer, human beings are not merely or always the captives of fate, the gods, or even human nature; individuals can have a decisive effect on the initiation, conduct, and outcome of wars because human volition or free will is possible.

This belief that gods or other supernatural forces play a role in human affairs is an early example of the determinist mode of thought and also emphasizes the chance phenomena or uncertainty that surrounds human events. Even biblical references in the Judaic-Christian tradition (as at Jericho, where God gives Joshua the tactical guidance instrumental to producing a victory) are consistent with this *deus ex machina* way of thinking. Coping with uncertainty or fortune and the issue of volition or free will are also recurrent themes in writings on international politics. As part of the Greco-Roman revival in Western thought, for example, Machiavelli raised

Writing About a Turbulent Ancient World:
Greek Thinking About International Relations

Date (B.C.)	Historical Developments	Commentators and Writers
1250	Greeks destroy city of Troy on Turkish coast	
800		Homer writes *Iliad* and *Odyssey* (c. 750–700) about defeat of Troy and aftermath
500	Persian wars: Persians lose at Marathon (490) and Salamis (480); Athens establishes Delian League against Persia; Peloponnesian War (431–404) between Athens and Sparta	Herodotus (484–430) writes about Persian wars
		Socrates (466–399) teaches Plato and others; Thucydides (460–406) writes about Peloponnesian
400		War, an effort continued by Xenophon (434–354); Aristophanes (448–385) writes
300	Alexander the Great (356–323), Aristotle's student, establishes Macedonian Empire through conquest	about war versus peace; Plato (427–347) and Aristotle (384–322) deal briefly with international relations; Zeno (334–262) and other Greek Stoics lay foundation for development of a more cosmopolitan world view
200	Punic Wars (264–146) between Rome and Carthage (Tunis), leading to defeat of Carthaginians (Phoenicians) and establishment of Roman Empire	Polybius (200–120) writes about the Punic wars and the rise of Rome

Dates are approximate; present-day country or city names are used for locational purposes.

this ancient theme in his discussion of how to deal boldly with *fortuna*, a concern that would be echoed still later in Clausewitz's treatment of the "friction" and uncertainty that obtain in the "fog of war."

The importance of physical, moral, and intellectual strength in allowing humans to prevail in their competition with external forces is underscored in Homer's *Odyssey*. Although he has the goddess Athena's backing and moral support, in adventure after adventure Odysseus, a veteran of the Trojan War, extricates himself and others from danger through application of human skill, particularly his mental agility and cleverness in dealing with often life-threatening situations.

While the *Iliad* is essentially a tragedy, the *Odyssey* is a romance. Taken together, these two great epic poems raise some of the most basic issues concerning the nature of human existence. As a result, they have had great effect on not only the subsequent course of Western literature, but on thinking about politics as well.[8]

Herodotus

Writing several hundred years after Homer, also known for his exaggerations, and sometimes presenting supposition as fact, Herodotus (about 484 to 430 B.C.) nevertheless is often referred to as the "father of history." Just as Homer had chronicled the Trojan wars, Herodotus detailed the Persian wars of Cyrus the Great (d. 529 B.C.), Cambyses (d. 521 B.C.), Darius (d. 486 B.C.), and Xerxes (d. 465 B.C.) and in the process took many entertaining diversions that enlighten the reader on such matters as the Egyptian mummification process and the gruesome methods of sacrifice carried out by the Scythians.[9] The first half of his work concerns the rise of Persia, the second half focuses on the great conflict between Persia and Greece. As he states, his purpose was to "set down to preserve the memory of the past by putting on record the astonishing achievements both of our own and of other peoples; and more particularly, to show how they came into conflict."[10]

Herodotus was particularly well suited for this role. Born in a town on the southern Aegean coast of Asia Minor, he was a subject of the Persian empire. This is perhaps why he was able to travel so far and wide, to Egypt, Babylon, and up to the Black Sea. As a young man he apparently lived on the island of Samos, and later he exhibited respect and fondness for Periclean Athens, a city he obviously knew quite well. By the time of his death in an Athenian-founded state in southern Italy, the Peloponnesian War of 431 B.C. had broken out. The deterioration in Athenian-Spartan relations was probably an impetus for Herodotus to remind the Greeks of their collective heroism in twice repelling Persian invaders at Marathon and Salamis.

Herodotus is of interest to students of international relations for at least three reasons. First, conflict among different city-states, empires, and peoples is the pervasive theme throughout his work. Second, the primary interest of leaders has historically been the realist one of maintaining the security and autonomy of the state through the marshalling of a state's internal resources or by its participation in alliances—policies quite evident throughout *The Histories*. Finally, like Homer, Herodotus was interested in how fate or the gods tended to frustrate the aspirations of statesmen and military leaders.

Conflict and War

Compared to Thucydides, Herodotus' *The Histories* places more emphasis on the description as opposed to the analysis of events. He does not lay out a basic argument, for example, about the underlying cause of war between Persia and its neighbors. Like Homer, Herodotus saw war as simply a fact of life, an occurrence as natural and inevitable as the changing of the seasons. Familiarity with other cultures, states, or empires did not mean acceptance of them, much less any notion that there could be a community of humankind among them. For example, Herodotus notes, "Like the Egyptians, the Scythians are dead-set against foreign ways, especially against Greek ways."[11] As a result, warring among the ancient peoples was the dominant mode of international relations, in which defeat very often meant the destruction of a city, the death of all male adults, and the selling of women and children into slavery.

In describing the outbreak of various wars, Herodotus gives particular emphasis to what would be called today the individual level of analysis. The desire of a ruler to secure power, glory, wealth, or revenge is very often all that is required to plunge a state or empire into war. Croesus, king of Lydia, for example, had a "craving to extend his territories."[12] Similarly, following the conquest of Egypt, Xerxes called a conference of the leading men of his country and addressed them as follows:

> Do not suppose, gentlemen, that I am departing from precedent in the course of action I intend to undertake. We Persians have a way of living, which I have inherited from my predecessors and propose to follow. I have learned from my elders that ever since Cyrus deposed Astyages and we took over from the Medes the sovereign power we now possess, we have never yet remained inactive. This is God's guidance, and it is by following it that we have gained our great prosperity. Of our past history you need no reminder; for you know well enough the famous deeds of Cyrus, Cambyses, and my father Darius, and their addition to our empire. Now I myself, ever since my accession, have been thinking how not to fall short of the kings who have sat upon this throne before me, and how to add as much power as they did to the Persian empire. And now at last I have found a way to win for Persia not glory only but a country as large and as rich as our own—indeed richer than our own—and at the same time to get satisfaction and revenge.[13]

His plan was to invade Greece and destroy Athens.

Security

Given the desire of such leaders to expand their power and the resultant conflicts, it is only natural that the key interest of all states was to maintain their security and autonomy. In a typical aside, Herodotus states, for example, that although "in most respects I do not admire" the Scythians, they "have managed one thing, and that the most important in human affairs, better than anyone else on the face of the earth—I mean their own preservation."[14] Interest defined in terms of security was the criterion to be applied in any number of circumstances. Thus, in determining whether Athens would have command of a combined fleet from several Greek city-states, Herodotus notes that the proposal for Athenian command "had not been well received by the allied states." As a result, the "Athenians waived their claim in the interest of national survival" because they understood "the danger attendant upon a lack of unity." The Athenians reasoned that "a quarrel about the command would certainly mean the destruction of Greece" at the hands of the Persians. Herodotus comments that in this the Athenians were "perfectly right" in trying to avoid "internal strife."[15]

This realism also admits to use of deception as a means of survival in such a world. In a line of reasoning adopted later by Machiavelli, Herodotus notes how the Persian Darius uses deception as an act of self-interest. Darius is quoted as saying:

> If a lie is necessary, why not speak it? We are all after the same thing, whether we lie or speak the truth: our own advantage. Men lie when they think to profit by deception, and tell the truth for the same reason—to get something they want, and to be the better trusted for their honesty. It is only two different roads to the same goal. Were there no question of advantage, the honest man would be as likely to lie as the liar is, and the liar would tell the truth as readily as the honest man.[16]

It should be noted that for Herodotus the security of the Greek *polis* was of special concern because the *polis* was a special sort of polity. Similar to Plato and Aristotle, Herodotus believed that the highest reward for an individual was to be honored and respected by citizens of the *polis*. Conversely, the worst possible fate was to be exiled. To fight bravely for one's city-state was particularly commendable, and death would bestow upon the individual a certain immortality through the honoring of his children. This emphasis on the state as the object of one's loyalty and devotion is expressed in a mythical conversation between Croesus, the wealthy king of Lydia, and Solon of Athens. Croesus asks Solon to name the happiest man he has ever met, assuming Solon will name the king. But Solon states it is Tellus of Athens, because besides living in a prosperous city and having fine sons and enough wealth to live comfortably, "he had a glorious death. In a battle . . . he fought for his countrymen, routed the enemy, and died like a soldier; and the Athenians paid him the high honor of a public funeral on the spot where he fell."[17]

Herodotus' narrative repeatedly describes two basic approaches leaders can follow to maintain a state's security—marshalling internal resources or creating an alliance. If states cannot deter an aggressor through the establishment of a balance of power, then sufficient internal resources would have to be available to repel the invader. Herodotus underscores the importance of a state controlling economic and military capabilities, key elements of power. Thus, he comments that "Darius, having an immense revenue in money and an unlimited number of men to draw upon in his Asiatic dominions" felt strong enough to take on his enemies.[18] Similarly, in order to conduct a war against Aegina, Athens utilized "a large sum of money from the produce of the mines at Laurium" to construct two hundred ships. With the threat of the Persian invasion, Athens had to "expand this existing fleet by laying down new ships."[19] This emphasis on tangible capabilities has traditionally dominated works in the field of security studies.

But superior economic and military capabilities are not enough to guarantee victory. Herodotus also sees the nature of a social–political system as a potentially important factor. Whether a function of unbiased historical analysis or his personal admiration for Periclean Athens, he presents one of his few explicit propositions when he observes that fighting capabilities were greater when Athens was in a democratic period with freedoms assured than "while they were oppressed under a despotic government" and thus "had no better success in war than any of their neighbors." But once freed, "they proved the finest fighters in the world. This clearly shows that, so long as they were held down by authority, they deliberately shirked their duty . . . but when freedom was won, then every man amongst them was interested in his own cause."[20] The same point is made in a conversation between Xerxes and a Greek exile, Demartus, prior to the Persian invasion. Xerxes asks, "Will the Greeks dare to lift a hand against me?" Demartus notes that "Poverty is my country's inheritance from of old, but valor she won for herself by wisdom and the strength of the law." Speaking of the Spartans in particular, "they will not under any circumstances accept terms from you which would mean slavery for Greece." Xerxes finds this hard to believe, believing that free men could not fight as well as those of his army who are made courageous due to a fear of their own generals and king. Demartus responds that "They [Spartans] are free—yes—but not entirely free; for they have a master, and that Master is Law, which they fear much more than your subjects fear you. Whatever this master commands, they do."[21] For Herodotus, this emphasis on the rule of law sets the Greeks apart from the Persians and other "barbarians."

Herodotus, therefore, clearly thinks that the nature of a political–social system is not only a potential source of power, but that it more generally influences state behavior. In the debate among Persian leaders on the relative merits of democracy, oligarchy, and monarchy (the first time, it should be noted, that this basic typology appears in Western literature) the advocate of democracy points to "envy and pride" as the "typical vices of a monarch" that "are the root cause of all wickedness: both lead to acts of savage and unnatural violence." By contrast, the democratic argument is that when the people hold power they "do none of the things that monarchs do." Or is it correct, as Darius is said to have argued, that "in a democracy, malpractices are bound to occur" and that oligarchies tend toward "violent personal feuds" and quarrels that "lead to open dissension, and then to bloodshed"?[22] Whatever the truth in the matter, the importance point, as Herodotus has constructed the debate, is that all agree on one thing—the constitution or political structure and associated norms of a state affect significantly the behavior exhibited by a state and its statesmen.

Does Herodotus suggest that democracies, oligarchies, or monarchies are more peaceful in terms of their foreign and military policies? No, he does not. Given the violent world of international relations at the time, Herodotus was simply making the narrower point that democracies are best able to ensure the security of the state because the citizens have something to lose—their liberty. As we will see, Livy and Machiavelli addressed this theme at some length, arguing that republican regimes in which people have some degree of influence in the government were the most secure, but not necessarily peaceful.

As for the second means by which a state can meet a threat to its security—joining an alliance—Herodotus notes a number of instances in which the threat was severe enough that various tribes or states joined together to repulse the invader. The Scythians, for example, realized "they were unequal to the task of coping with Darius in a straight fight," so they "sent off messengers to their neighbors, whose chiefs had already met and were forming plans to deal with what was evidently a threat to their safety." The Scythian envoys asked for their support, pleading for a "common plan of action." Failure to do so would have affected them as much as the Scythians because "this invasion is aimed at you as much as at us, and, once we have gone under, the Persians will never be content to leave you unmolested."[23]

There is, therefore, strength in unity. Lack of unity undercuts the capability to provide for defense. Herodotus observes how the Greeks had the "hope of uniting, if it were possible, the whole Greek world" against a Persian invasion led by Xerxes. After sending spies to observe the Persian forces and gather intelligence, diplomats were dispatched to conclude alliances with other Greek city-states in an effort to bring "all the various communities to undertake joint action in face of the common danger." A common external threat, however, does not always lead to a countervailing alliance. As Xerxes' forces moved to conquer Greece, "various Greek communities . . . viewed the coming danger with very different eyes. Some had already made their submission, and were consequently in good spirits." This band-wagoning effect, however, was offset by the decision of Athens to commit its full military capabilities—particularly its navy—to an alliance with its rival, Sparta, in an attempt to defeat the Persians. Herodotus argues that "one is surely right in saying that Greece was saved by the Athenians. It was the Athenians who held the balance—whichever side they joined was sure to prevail."[24] The Greek naval victory at Salamis against Xerxes' Persian forces would seem to bear this out.

Unity against an external security threat is enhanced if the threatened states have developed some sense of common identity. Herodotus relates how Spartan envoys arrived in Athens, concerned that the Athenians might ally with the Persians against Spartan and other Greek interests. The envoys were assured by the Athenians that they would not betray the Greek cause, least of all to the Persians. Indeed, Athens would support "the Greek nation—the community of blood and language, temples and ritual; our common way of life."[25] But in the absence of an external threat, such common bonds may not be enough to unite peoples sharing a common identity. Herodotus tells us that "the population of Thrace is greater than any country in the world except India." Thus, he comments that "if the Thracians could be united under a single ruler, or combine, they would be the most powerful nation on earth, and no one could cope with them."[26] At the time Darius was moving toward Greece, however, the Thracians were not unified and hence were conquered. Similarly, according to one Persian observer, in the absence of external threats the Greeks tended to "start fights" among themselves "on the spur of the moment without sense or judgement to justify them." Somehow it was difficult for the Greeks even though "they all talk the same language . . . to be able to find a better way of settling their differences by negotiation, for instance, or an interchange of views—indeed by anything rather than fighting."[27]

Fate

As for the issue of determinism versus voluntarism and the ability of statesmen to control and predict international events, like Homer's presentation, Herodotus's account includes a great deal of the metaphysical. Oracles and prophecy matter and heavily influence, if not determine, decisions and outcomes—the oracle is taken as truth-teller. Thus, Herodotus relates how the Euboeans were warned by the oracle of Bacis, but "this warning they ignored; and the result was great suffering."[28] In yet another place, Herodotus asserts that "the prophecy of the oracle was fulfilled."[29] Cambyses, son of Cyrus, concedes "that it is not in human power to avert what is destined to be," but it is not clear that Herodotus himself always accepted such determinism.[30] In some cases he merely describes these influences on decision making. Thus, Xerxes could be misled when his cousin would only tell him good news: "Any prophecy which implied a setback to the Persian cause he would be careful to omit."[31] At other times, advice from the oracles would be ignored. Concerning the Athenians, Herodotus tells us that "not even the terrifying warnings of the oracle at Delphi could persuade them to abandon Greece; they stood firm and had the courage to meet the invader."[32] Sometimes fate seems to seal events and at other times not to predestine them. In such circumstances, human will or volition may prevail.

Conclusion

Homer's subsequent influence on thinking about international relations stems from his framing of his epic poems in the context of determinism versus voluntarism or free will. Individuals matter, not only in terms of the onset of the Trojan War, but also with regard to how it was fought and its outcome. Physical, moral, and intellectual strength have an effect. Nevertheless, gods and oracles can dominate events, making it difficult for mere humans to foresee the outcomes of their actions.

As for Herodotus, his history is also a tale of conflict, although with less emphasis on the intervention of gods in the affairs of man. Concern for the security and autonomy of tribes, cultures, and city-states is a dominant theme. Individuals and their thirst for power and glory, however, very often initiate conflicts. Concerning the ability of countries to withstand aggressors, Herodotus makes it quite clear that the success of the Greeks against Persia was to a great extent a function of the nature of the Greek city-state and its ability to command the loyalty of its citizens. Consistent with contemporary works on national security, the marshalling of internal resources or joining an alliance are two basic ways to defend a state's autonomy. Herodotus, however, essentially observes such behavior without analyzing systematically the relation between a polity (the state–societal level of analysis) and the impact of external threats (the international system level of analysis) on a state's foreign policy behavior.

In examining these two authors, one might be left with the impression that all of the writing in ancient Greece contributed in one way or another to the realist tradition and its attendant preoccupation with security. Contrary to this tide, however, the playwright Aristophanes (about 448–385 B.C.) raised antiwar themes in his farcical comedy *Lysistrata*, in which the women agree to deny their favors to the soldiers until the latter finally renounce warfare and make peace. But while the destruction and human pain of war was recognized throughout Greek literature, the "make love, not war" notion originated by Aristophanes was hardly a major theme in Greek thought. The heroism and glory displayed in the *Iliad* and *Odyssey* and Herodotus' focus on conflict were the more enduring values and concerns. This viewpoint was also evident in the work of Thucydides, who is responsible for writing the centerpiece of ancient Greek thinking about international politics—*History of the Peloponnesian War*.

Notes

1. P.J. Rhodes, *The Greek City-States: A Source Book* (London and Sydney: Croom Helm, 1986), 1; W. Warde Fowler, *The City-State of the Greeks and Romans* (London: Macmillan, 1893), 66–67.

2. Thucydides, *History of the Peloponnesian War*, trans. Rex Warner (Harmondsworth, Eng.: Penguin Books, 1954), I: 3, 5; *The Politics of Aristotle*, trans. Ernest Barker (London: Oxford University Press, 1958, 1971), I:2.

3. Rhodes, *The Greek City-States*, ix–x.

4. Donald Kagan, *The Great Dialogue: History of Greek Political Thought from Homer to Polybius* (New York: The Free Press, 1965), 17–18.

5. Michael Grant, introduction to Tacitus, *The Annals of Imperial Rome* (Harmondsworth, Eng.: Penguin Books, 1971), 10.

6. Homer, *The Iliad*, trans. Martin Hammond (Harmondsworth, Eng.: Penguin Books, 1987), I:1–34.

7. Homer, *The Iliad*, XXIV:491–537.

8. Hammond, introduction to *The Iliad*, p. 16.

9. For the interested reader, see Herodotus, *The Histories*, trans. Aubrey de Selincourt and A. R. Burn (London: Penguin Books, 1954, 1972), II:83–90; IV:59–71. All subsequent citations are to this book.

10. Herodotus, *The Histories*, I:1.

11. IV:76.

12. I:73.

13. VII:8a. In support of Darius' goal, a Persian general states: "It would indeed be an odd thing if we who have defeated and enslaved the Sacae, Indians, Ethiopians, Assyrians, and many other great nations for no fault of their own, but merely to extend the boundaries of our empire, should fail now to punish the Greeks who have been guilty of injuring us without provocation." VII:9b.

14. IV:46.

15. VIII:1.

16. III:71–75.

17. I:30, as noted by Kagan, *The Great Dialogue*, 24–25.

18. IV:1.

19. VII:143.

20. V:81.

21. VII:103–7. Pericles, in his famous funeral oration, makes a similar statement concerning how obedience and respect for laws strengthen Athens. Thucydides, *History of the Peloponnesian War*, trans. Rex Warner (Harmondsworth, Eng.: Penguin Books, 1954), II:37.

22. Herodotus, *The Histories*, III:79–85.

23. IV:105, 119. Of course, an aggressor can also form alliances to further imperial aims. Hence Croesus, in invading Persia, called "upon the Egyptians to assist him according to the pact which he had concluded with King Amasis before the treaty of alliance with Sparta; he meant also to summon the Babylonians (for with them too, under their king, Labynetus, he had previously formed an alliance)." I:77.

24. VII:139, 143.

25. VIII:142–44.

26. V:1–3.

27. VII:8–9.

28. VIII:15–22.

29. IX:61–67.

30. III:63–65.

31. VII:3–8.

32. VII:136–39.

4
Thucydides and the Peloponnesian War

T hucydides' *History of the Peloponnesian War* is an account of the first twenty years of the fifth-century struggle (431 to 404 B.C.) between two alliances dominated by Athens and Sparta. An Athenian of what we would call today the upper middle class, Thucydides (c. 460–406 B.C.) was a naval officer who was stripped of his command and banished from Athens in the seventh year of the war for failing to arrive in time to prevent the fall of the city of Amphipolis to the Spartans. His failure as a military leader was history's gain. Thucydides made the most of his circumstances by traveling throughout Greece, witnessing or faithfully recording events. In effect, his writings pick up where Herodotus left off. He diverged from his predecessor, however, in that his work has no role for gods, oracles, and omens. The result of Thucydides' efforts was the foremost work of the ancient era on international relations.

As we will see, a major reason for such an accolade is that Thucydides exhibits an intellectual characteristic common to international relations theorists—the use of actual events to illustrate underlying patterns of world politics. Shedding light on recurrent behavior and trends is a major goal of his work. Not only does this history of the war move beyond a simple recounting of campaign strategies and battle tactics to the illumination of trends, but moral issues are intimately intertwined with his analysis of the war. Specifically, Thucydides was interested in highlighting the difficulties of what could be termed the morality of power.

We begin by briefly reviewing events of the hundred years prior to this period to set the stage for the discussion of the *History of the Peloponnesian War*. Such a review is useful because it allows us to describe the nature of the international system in that part of the world and provides a benchmark to which we can compare later systems.

Historical Context

As was discussed in chapters 2 and 3, the Hellenic world of the fifth century B.C. was composed of a variety of political entities that today we call city-states. Their small populations, limited control of territory beyond city walls, and their proximity to other city-states made them more akin to the Italian Renaissance city-state system than to modern states which, compared to the Hellenic world, usually consist of large populations and vast territorial expanses. The political forms of city-states, as discussed by Plato and Aristotle, included monarchies that often degenerated into despotism. Both monarchy and despotism involved rule by a powerful individual. Other forms of rule ranged from enlightened aristocracies to exploitative oligarchies (rule by the few), and, in some cases, rule by the many (democracies, in which participation generally was limited to those deemed worthy of the title "citizen"). These democratic polities, such as Athens at the time of Pericles, came closest to the idea of an integrated, organic relation between state and society—the *polis*. At the same time, however, slavery was an accepted institution throughout the Hellenic world, even in the democratic city-states that excluded slaves from their citizenry. Within this Greek system of city-states, some city-states were naturally more powerful than others; these dominated weaker city-states and, perhaps, extracted tribute in return for military protection. Diplomatic practices were rudimentary, generally consisting of delegations traveling to other city-states in order to present demands, resolve disputes, or negotiate trade agreements.[1]

In the middle of the sixth century B.C. the city-state of Sparta was ruled by an aristocracy, which was considered by the Spartans to be an excellent form of government compared to the many tyrannies and oligarchies that ruled elsewhere. Aristocracy depended upon the participation of the upper classes, accountability on the part of the individuals chosen to preside over the city-state, and a strong warrior caste. The latter was particularly important because the vast majority of the population consisted of an underclass known as the helots who were excluded from the political system. The expansion of Spartan power was confined principally to the Greek peninsula south of Athens known as the Peloponnese, and the primary goal was to assure that neighboring states would not be in a position to stir up trouble among the helots. This concern for domestic security tended to limit the extent of Spartan ambitions beyond the Peloponnesian peninsula because the Spartan leadership did not wish to have its military forces in foreign lands should a helot revolt break out. City-states allied with Sparta were allowed to conduct their own affairs and were assured Spartan military protection, but were pledged to support Sparta in time of need.[2]

As a result of being generally content to be the dominant power in the Peloponnese, the Spartans played a minor role in repelling the Persian invasion of northern Greece in 490 B.C., which ended with the spectacular Greek victory at the battle of Marathon described by Herodotus. Ten years later, however, the Spartans reluctantly agreed to accept command of combined Greek forces to repel the second Persian invasion of King Xerxes in 480 B.C. Spartan forces were unable to hold back the Persians at Thermopylae and proposed to make a final stand at the Isthmus of Corinth, the gateway to the Peloponnese and the Spartan heartland. Not surprisingly, this trading of space for time was not acceptable to city-states located in the path of the advancing Persian army. The city-state of Athens, known for its navy as well as its democratic form of government, which placed a great deal of power in the hands of its citizens, argued for a naval confrontation and, at the battle of Salamis, the Persian fleet was defeated. The following year the Spartan army routed the Persians at the battle of Plataea, and Xerxes' forces retreated.

With the repulse of the Persians, Sparta returned to its traditional concerns and more limited sphere of influence on the Peloponnese. At this point Athens came to the fore and championed the cause of keeping the Persians deterred from launching another invasion of Greece. The institutional expression of this policy was the creation of the Delian League, comprised principally of the city-states most vulnerable to Persian pressure, including those along the west coast of Asia Minor (present-day Turkey) and the islands in the Aegean. As a result of a need to protect these city-states and sweep the Persians out of northern Greece, Athens continued to expand the size of its navy and other military forces. In the process it became a major military power. Aside from the military build-up, the Athenians also reconstructed what were known as the "long walls," which provided a defensive perimeter designed to protect Athens from invaders.

After a series of further victories against Persian forces, the Delian League totaled some two-hundred members. But as so often happens in alliances once the foreign threat has been neutralized, problems among the member city-states soon began to appear. This disharmony was in part due to resentment and fear of Athenian domination. In many cases, the city-states controlled by democratic factions remained faithful to Athens, while those ruled by aristocracies began to look to Sparta. Attempts at defection resulted in Athenian military and political intervention so that the Delian League eventually began to look more like part of an Athenian empire than an alliance of independent city-states. These states, although formally autonomous polities, were forced to pay tribute to Athens, which determined not only their foreign policies but also important domestic policies.[3]

A deterioration in relations between Athens and Sparta led in 457 B.C. to the outbreak of war. Athens dominated central Greece and was easily the supreme sea power, while Sparta controlled the Peloponnesian peninsula and was the dominant land power. By 454 B.C. direct conflict died down, and a truce finally came into effect in 451 B.C. As a result, the Athenians could turn their attention to keeping their erstwhile Delian League allies in line. League resources were used by Athens to extend its power in campaigns against Corinth and Aegina, campaigns that had little to do with the League's avowed purpose of repelling the Persians.

Following a peace treaty between the Greeks and Persians in 449, the Athenian leader Pericles invited all Greek city-states to attend a conference at Athens in order to improve relations. The offer was rejected by the city-states in the Peloponnese and was viewed with suspicion by other city-states subject to Athenian rule. Unrest supported by the Spartans in the region known as Boeotia was put down by the Athenians and threatened to renew direct conflict between Athens and Sparta. Thereafter Athens and Sparta negotiated another peace treaty that was supposed to last thirty years. In return for allowing a number of reluctant city-states to leave the Delian League, Athens received Spartan recognition of Athenian rule over its remaining allies. The treaty in effect recognized spheres of influence and the virtue of the two city-states being roughly balanced in terms of power. The ensuing peace allowed the two rivals to consolidate their control in their respective spheres. It is at this point, in 435 B.C., that Thucydides takes up the story in detail and discusses specific events that led to the outbreak of the second Peloponnesian War. While the Greek international system is generally viewed by most scholars to have been bipolar in the distribution of capabilities, other states such as Corcyra, Thebes, Argos, and Corinth also had significant capabilities that distinguished them from the vast majority of city-states. Hence, structure of the Greek international system at this time was rather complex.[4]

History of the Peloponnesian War: The Work Itself

Thucydides' *History of the Peloponnesian War* is an easily accessible work that does not require the reader to have any background knowledge of Greek philosophy, Hellenic myths, or the artistic brilliance of Greek sculptors and poets. One can simply enjoy it as an extraordinarily gripping account of war in all its manifestations. Thucydides presents us with vivid and timeless portraits of prudent statesmen and grasping politicians, heroic officers and short-sighted generals, and the moral dilemmas facing all states throughout history. While his prose is generally straightforward and without rhetorical flourishes, the cumulative effect of many of his descriptions at times can be overwhelming. This power is evident, for example, in his moving account of the effect upon Athenian society of a plague that almost led to the complete social disintegration of this renowned city-state. Similarly, his harrowing account of the civil war in Corcyra—which literally set brother against brother and father against son—accurately captures the essence of this most devastating type of war. Nor is it possible to be unmoved by his detailed account of the destruction of the Athenian military expedition to Sicily, an account that creates in the mind of the reader the impression that he or she is actually on the scene as Athenian officers desperately attempt to rally their troops to avoid brutal death or slavery.

Aside from the enjoyment of a fascinating story, there are other reasons a student of international relations might wish to become familiar with the *History of the Peloponnesian War*. First, the work provides numerous analytical insights into world politics that are useful to anyone interested in understanding the dynamics of international relations.

Second, the work offers cautionary tales for statesmen engaged in the conduct of foreign policy; it is one of the best examples of "learning from history." While the particulars of the war were certainly of interest to Thucydides, he hoped to reveal larger truths about the human condition and to highlight certain situations he expected to recur throughout the ages. As he stated: "My work is not a piece of writing designed to meet the taste of an immediate public, but was done to last for ever."[5] He succeeded admirably.

Finally, the *History of the Peloponnesian War* is a prime example of what has come to be known as the realist perspective, an image of international relations that traditionally has dominated the halls of power as well as the halls of academe. In the remainder of this chapter we will examine each of Thucydides' contributions to the study of international relations: analytical insights, cautionary tales for statesmen, and the realist image of international politics.[6]

Analytical Insights

We begin this section with a discussion of Thucydides' answer to the basic question of what caused the outbreak of the Peloponnesian War. As noted earlier, Thucydides was not simply interested in describing what happened during the war. The purpose of his narrative was to draw larger lessons about the general phenomenon of war that would stand the test of time. In doing so he made a crucial distinction that can be applied to any war—the difference between the *underlying* and the *immediate* causes of a given war. For Thucydides, the underlying cause involved factors that had developed over a long time. Immediate causes included specific events or more recent developments that made war more likely or accounted for the timing of its outbreak. As will be discussed in subsequent chapters, Polybius, Montesquieu, and Kant also differentiate types of causes.

Underlying Cause of War

What was the underlying cause of the Peloponnesian War? Thucydides' answer is straightforward: "What made war inevitable was the growth of Athenian power and the fear which this caused in Sparta."[7] To put it another way, Sparta feared its relative decline compared to Athens. The explanatory emphasis is on the overall changing distribution of power or balance of power in the Greek system of city-states, and how this shift generated suspicion and distrust. Thucydides mentions, for example, that the fortification of Athens and the building of the protective long walls made the Pelopon-

MAP I. *Eastern Mediterranean*

Thracia
Amphipolis
Tharos
Chalcidice
Samothrace
Potidaea
Imbros
Lemnos
Hellespont
Aegean Sea
salia
Lesbos
Mytilene
Euboea
Chios
Attica
Athens
Andros
Samos
Tenos
rgos
Delos
aconica
Paros
Naxos
Melos
Kythera
Byzantium
Chalcedon
Phrygia
Mysia
Pergamon
Lydia
Sardis
Ephesus
Caria
Miletus
Persian Empire
Rhodos
Mediterranean
Sea
Crete

und 5th Century B.C.

nesians uneasy, with the worst possible interpretation placed upon the actions.[8]

Thucydides' emphasis on the changing distribution of power in an international system characterized by anarchy is viewed by modern scholars as a hypothesis on a critical, underlying cause of war that has applicability down through the ages. In what has come to be known as power transition theory, the argument is that when a rival begins to gain on the dominant or hegemonic state, the probability of war increases.[9] As with a rear-end auto collision, the dynamics of the process may vary: State A (the challenger) may be increasing in power while state B (the hegemon) remains static; or state A may be increasing in power faster than state B; or state A is only gradually increasing in power while state B is losing power. Whatever the particular dynamics may be, power transition theory has been applied by modern scholars to analyze major wars. Despite differences among them, these scholars all owe an intellectual debt to Thucydides, who deserves credit as the first to articulate the basic elements of power transition theory.[10]

Would war have broken out if the situation had been the reverse, if it had been the Athenians who were afraid of the growth of Spartan power? Power transition theory suggests this would have been very likely. Feeling fear and being afraid of the consequences of a relative decline in power vis-à-vis another state is something all leaders can experience, no matter what the nature of the regime. If one theme dominates Thucydides' narrative, it is how fear time and again is the basic reason a city-state takes a particular action in the hope of safeguarding its security and independence.[11]

If the anarchic nature of the international system and the shift in the balance of power or capabilities are the critical factors in explaining the outbreak of the Peloponnesian War, what about other levels of analysis— the nature of the system's political units and human nature? Differences in the Spartan and Athenian societies, for example, are emphasized in a speech by the Corinthians, and Pericles' famous funeral oration praised the unique aspects of Athenian society that would supposedly aid Athens in winning the war.[12] While Thucydides would agree with Herodotus' general observation that the type of political system or society may influence a state's foreign policy behavior, he did not see such factors as underlying causes of the Peloponnesian War. In other words, he did not emphasize the internal makeup of Greek city-states. He did not say war was inevitable because Sparta was a society glorifying martial virtues or because Athens was a limited democracy.

As for human nature, Thucydides' view is best revealed in his discussion of the horrors of the Corcyraean civil war and reflects the traditional realist pessimism. He argues that "love of power, operating through greed and through personal ambition, was the cause of all these evils." People engaged in "savage and pitiless actions," and were "swept away into an internecine struggle by their ungovernable passions. Then, with the ordinary conventions of civilized life thrown into confusion, human nature, always ready to offend even where laws exist, showed itself proudly in its true colors." No one was deterred "by the claims of justice nor by the interests of the state." But while human nature is generally portrayed in a negative light, Thucydides did not argue that human nature in and of itself accounted for these acts—interstate war and the desire of aristocratic and democratic factions to enlist outside support destroyed the constraints of law and "forced [people] into a situation where they have to do what they do not want to do."[13]

Immediate Causes of War

Thucydides observes that two disputes were immediate causes of the war. First, there was the matter of Corcyra, today known as Corfu. Corcyra had been founded as a colony of Corinth, but as it prospered Corcyra took an increasingly independent stance. These two city-states became involved in a struggle over the colony of Epidamnus, and after being defeated in a naval battle by Corcyra, the Corinthians planned a major military operation. This alarmed the Corcyraeans who went to Athens and asked for an alliance. After a lengthy debate among its citizens, Athens agreed, stating it would be for "defensive" purposes only. There was a general feeling that war with the Peloponnesian states was bound to come sooner or later, and the Athenians did not want the Corcyraean navy to fall into the hands of the Corinthians. Subsequently thwarted in its desire to conquer Corcyra because of the intervention of an Athenian naval force, Corinth charged Athens with breaking the truce between the Spartan and Athenian leagues and began to plot its revenge.

The second incident involved the city of Potidaea, whose citizens were colonists of Corinth yet were tribute-paying allies of Athens. The Athenians feared Potidaea would be induced to revolt by Corinth and hence demanded that the city fortifications be torn down and hostages sent to Athens. In response to a plea from Corinth and the Potidaeans, Sparta pledged to come to their aid if they were attacked. Potidaea and other cities then revolted from Athens. By this point, Thucydides notes, both Athens and Sparta had grounds for complaints against each other.[14]

Eventually the Spartans voted that the Athenians had broken the peace treaty and war was declared. Almost a year went by, however, before full-scale fighting broke out. As Thucydides observes, Sparta and its allies spent their time preparing for the upcoming conflict and making various charges against the Athenians "so that there should be a good pretext for making war."[15] Athens did the same. While the events involving Corcyra and Potidaea were the immediate causes of the war, Thucydides concludes his account of these incidents by once again arguing that Spartan fear of the further growth of Athenian power was the underlying cause of the conflict.[16]

Similarly, historians have argued that the underlying cause of World War I was the rise to power of Germany and the fear this caused in Great Britain and other major powers of the day. Among the immediate causes of the war, the most important was the August 1914 assassination in Sarajevo of the Austro-Hungarian Archduke Ferdinand. While his assassination touched off the fuse, no one would claim that this was the major or underlying cause of World War I, anymore than Thucydides claimed that events in Corcyra or Potidaea in and of themselves were the reason for the second Peloponnesian War. It should be noted, however, that despite the emphasis Thucydides places on the underlying cause of the war, he does not say that the more immediate factors are somehow less important; both underlying and immediate causes must be taken into account in explaining why the Peloponnesian War occurred and why it broke out when it did.

In answer to the question posed in chapter 2, therefore, concerning the relative importance of the international system, the international system's political units, and human nature, Thucydides emphasizes what is called a systems-level explanation—the increase in Athenian power relative to Sparta and other city-states. By placing such explanatory weight on the structure of the system, Thucydides' narrative seems to have a rather deterministic cast. Statesmen apparently have little control over international events in the face of such basic trends as changes in the balance of power.

One of the reasons the *History of the Peloponnesian War* is such a fascinating work, however, is that Thucydides' own narrative seems to undercut the deterministic, "war was inevitable due to the rise of Athenian power" thesis.[17] First, as a number of historians have noted, war broke out in 431 B.C., some twenty-five years after Athenian power had peaked. In 454 the Athenian military expedition to Egypt was destroyed at a cost of some 250 ships and forty to fifty thousand men. Revolts within the Athenian empire in 452 and a military defeat at Coronea in 446 further weakened Athens. Such setbacks encouraged Athens to seek peace with Persia in 449, and in 446 it concluded a thirty years' peace agreement with Sparta. This treaty cost Athens much of its continental empire and required it to withdraw from the Megarid, which was the strategic land route between Attica and the Peloponnese.[18]

Secondly, much of Thucydides' work contains extended debates among various participants concerning what policies a state should follow. The fact that a Corinthian delegation did a masterful job in buttressing the Spartan war party's position did not mean the declaration of war with Athens was inevitable—the cautions of the Spartan King Archidamus were quite compelling. Conversely, participants in the Athenian debate on how to deal with Mytilene following its failed revolt did not necessarily have to conclude that it was in Athen's self-interest to avoid bloody retribution.[19] Different decisions were possible, and hence different outcomes could have occurred.

Finally, Thucydides obviously wished to warn future decision makers about making the sorts of strategic miscalculations committed by many of the participants. If shifts in the balance of power made war inevitable, what would be the purpose in providing cautionary tales to statesmen? Nevertheless, this was undoubtedly one of Thucydides' goals.

Cautionary Tales

Be Wary of Wars in Distant Lands

The launching of the Sicilian campaign by Athens is a classic example of how pride, prejudice, impatience, and ignorance can result in a disastrous foreign policy decision. The Athenians, their war against Sparta stalemated, decided the deadlock could be broken if the Sicilian states allied with Sparta could be subdued. As Thucydides notes, the Athenians "were for the most part ignorant of the size of the island and of the number of its inhabitants," yet this did not dissuade them from declaring war on Syracuse, Sicily's principal city-state.[20] Thucydides' position is quite clear: Be wary when making the decision to engage in wars in distant lands.[21]

The Athenian desire to break the military stalemate parallels the German desire during World War II to break the stalemate on the western front by invading the Soviet Union in June 1941. Furthermore, in the public debate prior to the launching of the Athenian military expedition, a number of arguments are made that sound eerily similar to those concerning American involvement in Vietnam as well as to analyses of the Soviet invasion of Afghanistan in 1979. One is also reminded of General MacArthur's warning that the United States should be wary of engaging in a land war in Asia. In fact, much of the discussion in Thucydides appears applicable to any power contemplating going to war far from home.

A principal player in this drama is Nicias, one of the Athenians chosen to head the expedition. Personally against the Sicilian campaign, he favored a policy of nonintervention. Specifically, he felt that Athens should not trust its supposed allies in Sicily who had their own reasons for seeing that Athens got "drawn into a war which does not concern us." This was "the wrong time for such adventures." Athens should not divide its forces, run risks, and grasp "at a new empire before we have secured the one we have already," nor should Athens underestimate the difficulties associated with governing rebellious foreigners living at the edge of the Hellenic world. Sometimes, Nicias believed, the best foreign policy decision is to do nothing. Putting its reputation to the test against a distant power could have disastrous consequences if anything went wrong by encouraging other powers to test Athens' will. Athenians, he observed, should "spend our new gains at home and on ourselves" instead of on those "begging for assistance and whose interests it is to tell lies" and "leave all the dangers to others." He was wary of those who spewed patriotic platitudes but wished to go to war for their "own selfish reasons" and ran the risk of "endangering the state in order to live a brilliant life."[22]

The response is made by Alcibiades, also chosen by the citizenry to be one of the commanders. He is certainly one of the more intriguing and colorful characters in history. The argument he made in favor of the expedition is clever—alternatively sarcastic and cajoling. Alcibiades denigrates the Sicilians and disparagingly refers to their cities as having "swollen populations made out of all sorts of mixtures." They were supposedly not patriotic and lacking in "the feeling that they are fighting for their own fatherland"[23] and hence would most likely submit without much of a struggle once faced with Athenian power. This optimism was tempered by the warning that not intervening risked losing the entire existing empire. Alcibiades claimed that Athens was virtually forced by the circumstances "to plan new conquests," otherwise "we ourselves may fall under the power of others." He went on to make the case for expansionism, arguing that "the city, like everything else, will wear out of its own accord if it remains at rest."[24] According to this image, state and society are virtually a living organism that is impelled to expand or else wither and die. The Athenians embraced the arguments of Alcibiades and, in a classic case of wishful thinking, dismissed the cautionary words of Nicias, thus committing Athens to a two-front war.

The expedition set forth, and very little went as planned. City-states they expected to aid them preferred to remain neutral. The Athenians "sailed down the Italian coast, finding that the cities would not provide them with a market or even allow them inside their walls." When the expedition reached the southern tip of Italy, the Athenians assumed that their ethnic ties to the people of Rhegium would mean support for Athens. Instead, the leadership of Rhegium preferred to sit on the fence, stating that "they would not join either side, but would wait for a general decision from all the Greeks in Italy and would then act in accordance with it." At the same time, three Athenian ships that had gone to Egesta seeking financing for the expedition arrived at Rhegium and announced that "the promised sums of money did not exist and only thirty *talents* were available."[25]

Lamachus, one of the Athenian generals, argued that the fleet should sail straight to Syracuse and begin the war because "it is at the beginning . . . that every army inspires most fear; but if time is allowed to pass before it shows itself, men's spirits revive." He also claimed that if the Athenians attacked immediately with overwhelming force, "the rest of the Sicilians would at once be less inclined to ally themselves with Syracuse and would be more likely to come over to the Athenians without waiting to see which side was going to win."[26]

The Athenians did, however, delay in mounting military operations, and thereby allowed the Syracusans to gain confidence. Even Athenian victories in battles did not seem to translate into concrete progress toward winning the war. Morale began to deteriorate, and Nicias sent a letter to Athens stating "the time therefore has come for you to decide either to recall us, or else to send out another force, both naval and military, big as the first, with large sums of money."[27] Athens decided to send reinforcements because its Corinthian and Spartan rivals had escalated their commitment to the war effort in Sicily. This step required total mobilization on the part of Athens and an increase in the draft, but further military setbacks "produced a feeling of bewilderment in the army and a decline in morale."[28] The economic costs of the war began to be felt in Athens as taxes were raised. The Athenians, a proud naval power, were eventually faced with the imperative of winning the most important battle of the entire war in the great harbor of Syracuse. If they failed, the army would be cut off from a retreat by sea. It is worth quoting Thucydides' powerful description of the scene:

> For the Athenians everything depended upon their navy; their fears for their future were like nothing they had ever experienced; and, as the battle swung this way and that, so, inevitably, did their impressions alter as they watched it from the shore. . . . As the fight went on and on with no decision reached, their bodies, swaying this way and that, showed the trepidation with which their minds were filled, and wretched indeed was their state, constantly on the verge of safety, constantly on the brink of destruction. So, while the result of the battle was still in doubt, one could hear sounds of all kinds coming at the same time from this one Athenian army—lamentations and cheering, cries of 'We are winning' and of 'We are losing,' and all the other different exclamations bound to be made by a great army in its great danger.[29]

The Athenians were utterly defeated. Forced to try to escape overland, the army was systematically cut to pieces. Those who survived as prisoners of war were held in stone quarries and suffered from disease, hunger, and thirst. The generals (including Nicias) were put to death, although by this time Alcibiades had defected to the Spartans. Thucydides concludes his account by stating that the Sicilian campaign was, in his opinion, "the greatest action that we know of in Hellenic history—to the victors the most brilliant of successes, to the vanquished the most calamitous of defeats; for they were utterly and entirely defeated; their sufferings were on an enormous scale; their losses were, as they say, total; army, navy, everything was destroyed, and, out of many, only few returned. So ended the events in Sicily."[30] On the home front, the public greeted this news with disbelief. Recriminations immediately began over who was to blame for this disaster.[31]

The Dangers of a Punitive Peace

A recurrent question raised by Thucydides is how the victor should deal with the vanquished, the powerful with the weak. Although it seems the phrase he uses most often in his narrative is "laid waste the land," neither side always engaged in completely ruthless actions. Such restraint is not a function of pity for the opposition, but is generally the result of a pragmatic calculation that showing mercy is in the long-term interest of the state.

Ten years before the Sicilian campaign, for example, an Athenian force landed at a place known as Pylos, only forty-five miles from Sparta. The Athenians began to fortify the desolate headland, actions the Spartans viewed as a threat to their vital interests. A Spartan force soon took up positions on the mainland, on an island opposite Pylos, and in the harbor. An Athenian fleet arrived to relieve its men at Pylos and in the ensuing battles defeated the Spartan navy and cut off the Spartan troops on the island. During an armistice, Spartan representatives were sent to Athens, where they suggested a treaty be signed to end the war. In making their case to the Athenians, two insightful observations were made that have since become conventional wisdom.

The first observation directly addresses the question posed in chapter 2: Why is it so difficult to predict the course of international events? The Spartans argued that no matter how carefully one calculates, the course of war is impossible to predict. Today's winner may be tomorrow's loser, with the fruits of victory quickly turning sour. True wisdom is recognizing that things will change. As the Spartans noted, intelligent leaders know that war is "governed by the total chances in operation and can never be restricted to the conditions that one or the other of the two sides would like to see permanently fixed."[32] Thucydides makes numerous references throughout the book to the uncertainty that Clausewitz would later call the "fog of war," whether referring to either the conduct or final outcome of specific battles. The best-laid plans too often go awry, while, at other times, sheer luck can save the day. Hence, it is in one's own interest to imagine how one would wish to be treated in a similarly disadvantageous position.

Secondly, the Spartans warn Athens against pursuing the Athenian advantage at Pylos "to the bitter end" by destroying the Spartan troops beseiged on the island. In another insight relevant throughout history, Thucydides states, "Where great hatreds exist, no lasting settlement can be made in a spirit of revenge." If an opponent is forced "to carry out the terms of an unequal treaty," a thirst for revenge will result. Hence it is better for the victor to make "peace on more moderate terms than his enemy expected," reducing the desire for revenge and instead placing the vanquished "under an obligation to pay back good for good."[33] The best modern example of this line of thinking concerns the handling of a defeated Germany after the two world wars. The punitive Versailles Treaty of 1918 fueled a spirit of revenge in Germany and contributed to the rise of Adolf Hitler and the Nazis, who capitalized on this public discontent. Conversely, the American, British, and French treatment of what came to be known as West Germany following World War II, particularly the provision of economic aid through the Marshall Plan, did much to stabilize the country, undercut political extremism, and encourage the development of democracy. For Thucydides, statesmen are those who recognize that the long-term interests of the state are often better served by not pursuing short-term advantages to the bitter end.

War Fever and a Fickle Public

Another catalyst to conflict noted by Thucydides is the initially strong public support for war that all too often quickly turns to dismay and a search for scapegoats. The Spartan king, Archidamus, notes that the older generation "are not likely to share in what may be a general enthusiasm for war."[34] Pericles observes that the "enthusiastic state of mind in which people are persuaded to enter upon a war is not retained when it comes to action, and that people's minds are altered by the course of events."[35] As Thucydides comments, "At the beginning of an undertaking the enthusiasm is always greatest, and at the same time both in the Peloponnese and in Athens there were a number of young men who had never been in a war and were consequently far from unwilling to join in this one."[36] Such attitudes not only provide an impetus to war, but they also foster overconfidence and a belief that the war will be short. A classic case of war fever and jingoism involved the initial Athenian enthusiasm for the Sicilian expedition:

> There was a passion for the enterprise which affected everyone alike. The older men thought they would either conquer the places against which they were sailing or, in any case, with such a large force, could come to no harm; the young had a longing for the sights and experiences of distant places, and were confident that they would return safely; the general masses and the average soldier himself saw the prospect of getting pay for the time being and of adding to the empire so as to secure permanent paid employment in [the] future. The result of this excessive enthusiasm of the majority was that the few who actually were opposed to the expedition were afraid of being thought unpatriotic if they voted against it, and therefore kept quiet.[37]

Initial public enthusiasm for a war is a common phenomenon in international politics. World War I provides a classic example. Even the European social democratic parties and trade unions that had expressed pacifist tendencies got caught up in the war fever of 1914. It had been assumed that, if the vast working classes of all the countries refused to fight, war would be impossible because the requisite cannon fodder would not be available. Instead, young men hurried to join the military, motivated by patriotism or merely afraid of missing out on the great adventure. In sum, while Thucydides did not view public war fever to be an underlying cause of war, it was an important domestic contributor to an aggressive foreign policy, and such behavior was not restricted to any single type of political system.

Thucydides and Realism

Thucydides' narrative would seem to be consistent with the realist assumptions discussed in chapter 2. Although influenced by Homer and Herodotus, he went well beyond both in his attempt to generalize about international relations. Indeed, his work has been viewed by many scholars as the foundation of the realist perspective on international relations.

One is hard pressed to find in Thucydides suggestions of alternatives to realism. The globalist emphasis on class conflict is apparent in Thucydides' observation of the internal and international ramifications of the Corcyraean civil war: "practically the whole of Hellas was convulsed, with rival parties in every state—democratic leaders trying to bring in the Athenians and oligarchs trying to bring in the Spartans."[38] Pluralism is certainly not a central theme in Thucydides' work, although in his funeral oration Pericles does refer to a transnational phenomenon when he notes that "the greatness of our city brings it about that all the good things from all over the world flow in to us, so that to us it seems just as natural to enjoy foreign goods as our own local products."[39] Even this claim to openness is probably more sentiment than fact, particularly since Athens was at the time engaged in major warfare—hence the need to have a funeral oration to honor the war dead. Nevertheless, Thucydides' contribution to the contemporary realist image of international politics is, upon closer examination, not so self-evident.

First Assumption: State as Principal Actor

The major actors in Thucydides' tale are Athens and Sparta. Along with their allies, they dominate the story. Nonstate actors such as mercenaries or the oracle at Delphi are mentioned only occasionally, and they do not play a significant role when compared to the city-states that are at center stage. The importance of states is further reflected in the fact that for Thucydides it was the shift in relative power between the two most powerful states that accounted for the outbreak of the Peloponnesian War.

Second Assumption: State as Unitary Actor

As for the idea of the state as a unified or unitary actor, most of Thucydides' famous dialogues involve debates among representatives of various states. The arguments presented reflect the point of view of Athens, Corinth, Syracuse, or Thebes. Some of the more extraordinary debates, however, involve domestic arguments over what policy the state should follow. For example, it has already been noted that the Athenians disagreed among themselves on how to treat the rebellious state of Mytilene.[40] Some advocated making a brutal example to show clearly that any revolt would be punished by death. Others argued that showing leniency and mercy would better serve Athens' future interests. But despite such lively domestic differences of opinion, however, one could argue that the notion of the unified state is preserved because, once the decision is taken on such issues, the state speaks with one voice to the outside world.[41] Moreover, Thucydides tells us that although Athens "was nominally a democracy" and thus allowed its citizenry to be free, in fact "power was really in the hands of the first citizen," Pericles. In relation to the people, "it was he who led them, rather than they who led him."[42] In short, one could argue that to Thucydides even democratic Athens was a unitary city-state, so that one could speak of an "Athenian policy."

Having stated this, however, it is impossible to deny the impact of fractious domestic politics—particularly civil wars—on the Greek international system; the two are inextricably linked and Thucydides dramatically highlights this linkage in the course of his narrative. Hence, Thucydides' work differs from much of the behavioral literature of the 1960s and 1970s, which essentially black-boxed the state and focused on state interactions in order to uncover the causes of war. Similarly, current "neorealists" who treat state actors as "functionally similar units" differ somewhat from Thucydides on this point.[43] The genesis of the realist emphasis on the unitary state, therefore, is not to be found as clearly in the work of Thucydides as in the work of later scholars in the realist tradition.

Third Assumption: Rationality

Rational Reconstruction. Thucydides, like other educated Greeks, believed people were essentially rational beings. Hence much of his work consists of recounting arguments and debates on the assumption that through this process a state can reach the decision that is in its best interests. This weighing of opposites is consistent, of course, with the Socratic method used by Plato in *The Republic*. (See the discussion in chapter 5.) Thucydides obviously was not present at all of the debates he "recorded." He relied on other accounts, reconstructed the arguments, and judged which words were appropriate for the situation. To put it another way, his reconstruction of the essence of an argument in the form of a dialog is what a *rational* person would argue in such circumstances.

Thucydides also argues that political leaders must be able to imagine themselves in the shoes (or sandals) of rival statesmen in order to anticipate what they might do. The question to ask is this: Given a certain situation with various constraints and opportunities, what would I do? As a Syracusan leader states, "When dealing with the enemy it is not only his actions but [also] his intentions that have to be watched."[44] In a classic summation of the rational reconstruction perspective, the Syracusan notes that one should be wary of taking intelligence reports at face value and should not use them "as a basis for calculating probabilities, but instead will consider what a clever and a widely experienced people, as, in my view, the Athenians are, would be likely to do."[45] As the realist writer Hans Morgenthau stated some 2,400 years later:

> We put ourselves in the position of a statesman who must meet a certain problem of foreign policy under certain circumstances, and we ask ourselves what the rational alternatives are from which a statesman may choose . . . and which of these rational alternatives this particular statesman, acting under these circumstances, is likely to choose."[46]

The rationality assumption is central to the work of many present-day realists.[47]

Limitations of the Rationality Assumption: Outcomes. Thucydides not only shows us the practical utility of the rationality assumption when one wishes to divine the intentions of a rival. His reconstructed debates also illustrate foreign policy decision-making processes that generally consider the pros and cons of various suggested actions. As another Syracusan leader puts it concerning a state's decision to go to war: "The fact is that one side thinks that the profits to be won outweigh the risks to be incurred, and the other side is ready to face danger rather than accept an immediate loss."[48] This seems to be common sense.

An obvious question arises: Does such rational calculation guarantee a good outcome? Of course not. Thucydides presents us with a number of instances where sound calculation still leads to a poor outcome. A prime example involves the decision of Chios to revolt against Athens. Thucydides notes that the Chians were sensible people and that their decision to revolt was not the result of overconfidence. Indeed, they first secured allies to share the risk and calculated that the time was ripe, as the destruction of the Athenian expedition to Sicily had occurred and many states believed (erroneously) that Athens was near collapse. Chian calculations were incorrect, and they suffered the consequences.[49]

Limitations of the Rationality Assumption: Perception. Thucydides' contribution to the international relations discipline as a result of his emphasis on the rationality assumption has been noted by a number of scholars.[50] Indeed, he seems to have been granted paternity of this idea. But it would be more precise to state that Thucydides intended *History of the Peloponnesian War* to be an illustration of the *limits* of rationality, as opposed to a paradigmatic case study of rationality at work.[51] Thucydides presents us with numerous examples of not only the problem of translating intentions into desired outcomes, but also the cognitive limitations on rational decision making. There are, in other words, psychological pitfalls in attempts to achieve a rational decision-making process, and even when the process works to virtual perfection there is a disjuncture between the psychological milieu of statesmen and the operational milieu in which decisions are actually implemented.[52]

We have already noted how, because of anarchy and the security dilemma, attempts by a state to enhance its own security breed suspicion and can result in an unanticipated and unwelcome outcome: other states may follow a similar logic so that the level of tension and suspicion throughout the international system increases. Within the psychological milieu, a number of possible perceptions held by decision makers reinforce the implications of international anarchy. Three types of faulty perceptions are discernible in the narrative of the *History of the Peloponnesian War*:

1. Decision makers perceiving the enemy to be more centralized and coordinated in its decision making than it actually is.
2. Statesmen experiencing "cognitive closure," as evidenced by a belief that few if any alternatives are open to them.
3. Leaders engaging in wishful thinking.

Social scientists interested in the cognitive processes of decision makers claim all three contribute to flawed assessments of rivals, undercut rational decision making, and increase the possibility of war during a crisis. We will briefly illustrate these three phenomena by referencing Thucydides' text and the contemporary literature.

Perception of Centralization. As has been noted, by adopting the logic of rational reconstruction, one attempts to place oneself in the mind of an opponent in order to discern what is his most likely course of action. There is an obvious utility in this exercise in that it provides some basis upon which a response can be planned. The trade-off, however, is that one may end up perceiving the opponent's decision making as being more centralized, coordinated, and integrated than it actually is. Potential divisions or bureaucratic politics might be downplayed and an excessive amount of omniscience ascribed to the rival, who comes to be viewed as clever, resourceful, and in complete control of his decision-making system. Furthermore, coincidences, accidents, and unintended consequences are either viewed with suspicion or dismissed. Former U.S. Secretary of State John Foster Dulles may have been correct when he noted, "the Russians are great chess players and their moves in the world situation are . . . attempted to be calculated as closely and carefully as though they were making moves in a chess game."[53] The question, though, is how typical is such behavior? Contemporary research has provided an impressive array of examples illustrating the tendency of decision makers to assume a high degree of coherence and consistency in events that in fact lack these qualities. The greater the fear and suspicion one has of the adversary, the more likely this cognitive distortion is to occur. Perceptions of centralization, therefore, are the down side of attempts to discern an adversary's intentions through rational reconstruction. The corollary is that if one is divining the intentions of an ally, it is more likely that one will give him the benefit of the doubt, downplaying volition and instead emphasizing environmental factors beyond the allies' control in order to explain his behavior.[54]

This psychological phenomenon is illustrated throughout Thucydides' narrative. The confidence with which various speakers assume to have divined the intentions of rival states is quite striking; they attribute to these states some sort of strategic game plan that is being implemented. During the revolt of Mytilene, for example, ambassadors from that country go to Olympia to secure the support of Sparta and its allies. The Mytileneans argue that Athens has all along had a strategic plan for seizing control of all of Greece. They claim that "the only reason why we were left with our independence was because the Athenians, in building up their empire, thought that they could seize power more easily by having some specious arguments to put forward and by using the methods of policy rather than of brute force."[55] Prior to the initial Spartan declaration of war, we also find the Corinthians claiming that Athens has been scheming to deprive states of their freedom and "has for a long time been preparing for the eventuality of war."[56] Perhaps. But certainly a more benign interpretation could be placed upon Athenian actions with regard to Corcyra, Potidaea, and Megara that emphasizes a prudent concern for Athenian national security in the event war did break out with Sparta and an incremental decisionmaking process as opposed to slavish devotion to some sort of imperial game plan.

Cognitive Closure. Given Thucydides' belief that Athens and Sparta were compelled toward war, it is not surprising that he is pessimistic about the ability of humans to control their fates. Assuming he accurately recorded the gist of the debates, it is striking the number of times leaders made the basic assumption that there were few, if any, choices open to them. When Pericles tells his countrymen, for example, why Athens must stand firm against Spartan demands, he concludes his argument by bluntly stating "this war is being forced upon us."[57] Similarly, Sparta also believed the situation had reached a point that was "no longer tolerable."[58] This same thinking is also evident in the decision to launch the Sicilian expedition. At one point Alcibiades states, "We have reached a stage where we are forced to plan new conquests and forced to hold on to what we have got."[59] Choices and alternatives seem to be lacking. The situations seem to be characterized more by determinism than one in which free will or voluntarism can be exercised effectively. In certain circumstances this may indeed be the case, or choices may be severely circumscribed, such as when the Athenians delivered their ultimatum to the Melians—capitulate or be destroyed. At other times, however, particularly in those cases involving the decision to go to war, one suspects Thucydides has recorded examples of what scholars term "premature cognitive closure," which involves a failure to search seriously for alternative policies. Decision makers exhibit a certain air of resignation, if not fatalism.

This psychological phenomenon is particularly dangerous during crisis situations involving stress and time pressure. Several studies of the July 1914 crisis bear this out. As in the case of ancient Greece, there was a sense that war was inevitable. Once the armies of Russia, France, Germany, and Britain began to mobilize, military leaders told the politicians it was impossible to stop the process. Events seemed to take on a terrible logic of their own that was unable to be arrested by mere human beings. When German Chancellor Bethmann Hollweg stated, "We have not willed war, it has been forced upon us," he was echoing the sentiments of Pericles and other statesmen before and after him.[60]

During the Corinthian speech designed to goad Sparta into war with Athens, Thucydides records a related psychological phenomenon. Modern scholars call it the "inherent bad faith model"—no matter what a state may do, its actions are interpreted in the worst possible light because images, once developed, are highly resistant to change.[61] Even conciliatory actions are viewed by a decision maker as a ruse to get him to drop his guard. Evidence that may undermine this hostile image is rejected. Hence, in claiming that Athens was preparing for war and bent on imperialist expansion, the Corinthians, with their own axe to grind, rhetorically asked the Spartans, "Why otherwise should she have forcibly taken over from us the control of Corcyra? Why is she besieging Potidaea? Potidaea is the best possible base for any campaign in Thrace, and Corcyra might have contributed a very large fleet to the Peloponnesian League."[62] Such actions were viewed as aggressive in intent as well as part of a carefully conceived strategic plan by which Athens would pursue its imperialistic objectives; everything Athens did was viewed in this light. The corollary to this phenomenon is the tendency of decision makers to assume that their own benign intentions are self-evident to an adversary. Hence, when the rival fails to respond favorably to a supposedly mutually beneficial initiative, the assumption of bad faith is reinforced. This is a recurrent event throughout Thucydides' narrative.

Wishful Thinking. Thucydides also makes it clear that wishful thinking and self-delusion may undercut attempts at achieving a rational decision-making process. After the Spartan capture of Amphipolis that cost Thucydides his job, other cities decided to revolt against Athenian rule. Such a decision was too often "based more on wishful thinking than on sound calculation . . . for the usual thing among men is that when they want something they will, without any reflection, leave that to hope, while they will employ the full force of reason in rejecting what they find unpalatable."[63] Thucydides records a number of instances in which leaders exhibit the tendency to reject unsettling information. For example, when Athens was suffering from the plague, the Athenians at first refused to believe that Lesbos, with its powerful navy, had revolted because this would have meant a dramatic increase in the military might of the opposition alliance at a most inconvenient time.[64] Similarly, the Syracusans refused to believe initial reports that the Athenians were planning to launch an expedition against Sicily, despite the fact that "news of the expedition arrived from many quarters."[65] The classic case concerning the dangers of wishful thinking is presented to the Melians by the Athenians: "Hope, that comforter in danger! . . . Do not be like those people who, as so commonly happens, miss the chance of saving themselves in a human and practical way, and, when every clear and distinct hope has left them in their adversity, turn to what is blind and vague, to prophecies and oracles and such things which by encouraging hope lead men to ruin."[66] The Melians put their faith in Sparta and were severely disappointed.

Wishful thinking, however, is not reserved for those who are in fear or in deadly straits. Confident powers may also engage in wishful thinking by drawing on inappropriate historical analogies. Japan, for example, thought a limited war with the United States was possible in 1941 in part because the Japanese recalled how Russia had settled for a limited defeat earlier in the century rather than risk a long war. Similarly, Hitler assumed that France and Great Britain would not fight for Poland as they had not fought for Austria or Czechoslovakia.[67] As noted earlier, perhaps the best example of wishful thinking based on arrogance involves Alcibiades' defense of the Sicilian expedition. He dismisses Nicias's concerns over enemies closer to home by stating that "our fathers left behind them these same enemies when they had the Persians on their hands."[68] This questionable historical analogy helped to sway the Athenian citizens, who eventually approved the expedition.

In sum, while Thucydides may have believed people were essentially rational and able to perceive alternative courses of action, it can be argued that he also recognized the limitations of rational discourse as well as the fallibility and foibles of human beings. Current research has provided ample evidence of how, because of either extreme emotional stress or certain cognitive processes, it is difficult for a rational decision-making process to be achieved consistently.[69]

Fourth Assumption: Security as the Most Important Interest

Given that his work deals with war, Thucydides is obviously preoccupied with security issues, the prime interest of all states. For realists, security means primarily the protection of state and society from both external and internal threats. Hence, during the Athenian debate over how to deal with rebellious Mytilene, both Cleon and Diodotus state the Athenians should come to a decision based on "your interests."[70] While security is usually viewed by realists in terms of defense considerations (with the armed services playing the critical role), it also may include such factors as a productive economy and a society with a strong will to resist foreign subversion or other intrusion—for example, Herodotus's characterization of the Greeks— or what one scholar has termed the "social dimensions" of strategy.[71] As also noted in our discussion of Herodotus, for realists a state essentially can enhance its security in one of two ways—by internal efforts to increase its capabilities and by joining an alliance. By pooling resources, it is assumed that the security of each state will be enhanced at a lower cost than if each state attempted to provide its own security on a unilateral basis. This latter option is a constant theme in Thucydides' work, and hence is worthy of discussion.

Alliances. Contemporary research on alliances focuses on two major questions: How are they formed, and what is their relation to the onset of war? Thucydides notes that states may join one alliance or another because of compulsion, interest, moral principle, or cultural and racial affinity. Later scholars have not improved much upon this classification scheme. While Thucydides describes a number of instances in which decisions to join an alliance appear to be a function of complementary systems of government or society, the critical factor in alliance formation throughout Thucydides' narrative is national security interests.[72] There are two competing hypotheses in the international relations literature concerning how a state chooses its allies in attempting to maximize national security interests— balancing and bandwagoning.[73] According to the balancing hypothesis, states join an alliance in order to oppose other states that are perceived to be a threat. The greater the threat, the larger and stronger the alliance. The bandwagoning hypothesis suggests the opposite. Faced with an external threat, states will accommodate and ally with the threatening state either to avoid being attacked or to share in the spoils of victory.

Which of these hypotheses appears to be borne out by Thucydides' narrative? The evidence he presents suggests that fear of a rival made balancing the policy norm both before and during the Peloponnesian War, but fear of bandwagoning preoccupied the leaders of alliances once the war began. As for balancing as a policy to counteract a threat, a prime example involved Corcyra's seeking of protection from Athens against Corinth: "They [Corcyreans] had no allies in Hellas, since they had not enrolled themselves either in the Spartan or in the Athenian League. They decided therefore to go to Athens, to join the Athenian alliance, and see whether they could get any support from that quarter." In pleading their case, the Corcyreans admitted "We recognize that, if we have nothing but our own national resources, it is impossible for us to survive, and we can imagine what lies in store for us if they overpower us. We are therefore forced to ask for assistance."[74] Even stronger states or empires may pursue a policy of balancing in attempting to prevent the rise of a major power. This was quite evident in the case of Persia, whose leader was advised by the omnipresent Alcibiades "not to be in too much of a hurry to end the war. . . . It was better to have the two parties [Athens and Sparta] each in possession of its own separate sphere of influence, so that if the King had trouble with one of them, he would always be able to call in the other against it." Such advice reinforced the Persian policy of "keeping the two Hellenic forces in balance against each other."[75]

As for bandwagoning, there is some evidence of this occurring during the Peloponnesian War.[76] Of particular interest, however, is the fact that Thucydides' narrative provides evidence that in attempting to prevent alliance defections and the loss of neutrals to a rival's alliance, states may pursue counterproductive policies resulting in self-fulfilling prophecies. Athens was particularly preoccupied with possible defections from the Delian League. But it was not simply fear of losing the military capabilities of a league member that was of concern to Athens. Athens was also worried how such defections would be viewed by allies and enemies. The basic fear was that one defection might lead to others and that a stampede would begin as erstwhile allies attempted to get on board the rival's bandwagon. This especially concerned Athens given the nature of its alliance. As with the Soviet Union and the Warsaw Pact, the alliance was not simply directed against an external threat, but was the organizational expression of an imperialist power. As aptly stated by the Mytilenes, the Delian League was originally designed to liberate Hellas from Persia, not to be used to subjugate Hellas for Athens.[77] One by one the allies became either subject states or, as in the case of Mytilene, nominally retained their independence. Increasingly, compulsion instead of common interest held the alliance together. In the typically blunt words of Cleon to his fellow Athenians, "What you do not realize is that your empire is a tyranny exercised over subjects who do not like it."[78] Compulsion, therefore, became the primary reason for the continued existence of the alliance, and less feelings of loyalty or even fear of Persia. As a result, Athenian power was directed as much against subject states as it was directed against states outside the alliance, just as Red Army troops performed an internal policing function in Eastern Europe as well as deterred NATO forces.

In the case of the Delian League this compulsion made for a somewhat fragile alliance and the constant specter of defection. Mytilene, for example, had its own regional ambitions and revolted from Athens when the latter was suffering from the effects of the plague and war exhaustion. Mytilene joined the Peloponnesian League but soon returned to Athenian control. In the famous debate in Athens over what to do with Mytilene, Cleon clearly expresses the bandwagoning perspective, arguing that severe punishment is required. It is necessary to "make an example of them to your other allies," otherwise "they will all revolt upon the slightest pretext."[79] Reputation is critical.

Fear of defection is an understandable concern for leaders of alliances that are based more on compulsion than on common interest. Nevertheless, in an alliance leader's obsession with defection, he may pursue counterproductive policies that have the unintended effect of encouraging an ally to defect. The dispute over Potidaea is a case in point. Thucydides notes, "Athens feared that . . . Potidaea might be induced to revolt [by Corinth] and might draw into the revolt the other allied cities in the Thracian area."[80] To prevent this from occurring, the Athenians order the Potidaeans to pull down fortifications, provide hostages, and banish the Corinthian magistrates. If the goal was to keep Potidaea in the Athenian alliance and prevent its defection, the plan backfired. The Potidaeans sent a delegation to Athens in hope of having the orders rescinded, but at the same time the Potidaeans hedged their bets by sending representatives to Sparta to seek support. The Spartans pledged to invade Attica if Potidaea was attacked. What they failed to realize was that this pledge was an incentive for the Potidaeans to revolt. They did so, and Athens was compelled to go to war against them.

If fear of defection is a principal concern of states leading alliances based more on coercion than common interest, all types of alliances can be adversely affected by the decisions of neutrals. In certain circumstances, the very existence of a neutral state can be viewed as a threat. In the Melian Dialogue, for example, Athens expresses a concern over alliance defections resulting from a perception of Athens as weak and indecisive.[81] It is interesting to compare the Athenian decision involving Melos with the earlier decision on Mytilene's revolt. In the case of Mytilene, an Athenian ally, the Athenians eventually rejected Cleon's advice. Harsh measures, however, were taken against Melos when it was not even an ally but rather a neutral state. Why the different decisions? It can be argued that events in Melos took place during the seventeenth year of the war, by which time Athens had suffered a number of setbacks. The events in Mytilene took place some eleven years earlier and at that time Athens could afford to consider the possible payoffs of being magnanimous. The same logic applies to the Spartans. The Spartan king Archidamus could initially offer Plataea the neutrality option because it was only the second year of the war and Spartan capabilities and confidence were high.[82]

The most obvious case in which neutrals pose a threat is when they abandon their neutral status. In Thucydides' narrative, neutrals would appear to be particularly susceptible to bandwagoning once it is clear which way the wind is blowing. Thucydides records a number of instances in which neutral states join an alliance as soon as it is clear who is going to be the winner. Following the Athenian defeat at Plemmyrium, Syracusan entreaties to previously neutral states such as Camarina led to the provision of troops, and hence "practically the whole of Sicily . . . instead of just watching how things would go, as they had been doing, came in with Syracuse against the Athenians."[83] Following the destruction of the Athenian expedition, "the whole of Hellas, after the great disaster in Sicily, turned immediately against Athens. Those who had not been allied with either side thought that . . . they ought not to keep out of the war any longer."[84]

While states may join alliances in order to enhance their security, the leader of the alliance (whether the latter is based on common interest, compulsion, or societal–ideological affinities) has to be wary of manipulation by smaller allies who may have a different national security or internal security agenda. As so often seems to be the case throughout history, wars begin in small places, whether an Epidamnus or a Sarajevo. In an attempt to settle a regional dispute, states call upon their alliance leaders for support. Corinth, for example, had its own selfish reasons to goad Sparta into declaring war on Athens. In the case of Sicily, the Silinuntines called for Syracusan support in their conflict with the Egestaeans over "marriage rights and a piece of disputed territory."[85] The Egestaeans, in turn, appealed to their long-time Athenian allies for aid and in the process presented the possibility of the domino effect if Athens did not favorably respond to their entreaties.

In sum, leaders of alliances are faced with two potential tradeoffs. Fear of either bandwagoning or loss of an ally might lead to a policy of capitulation or confrontation with the ally. If the leader attempts to illustrate his willingness to back an ally, the ally may be tempted to use this guarantee in pursuit of its regional ambitions. Conversely, a leader's worries about his state's reputation and subsequent attempts to coerce allies into remaining in the alliance could encourage the very result the leader seeks to avoid—alliance defections.

This discussion on the formation and dynamics of alliances is not to suggest that Thucydides believed the *only* concern of leaders should be security interests; throughout the *History of the Peloponnesian War* Thucydides quotes numerous leaders on the need to balance justice, honor, and state interests. In the revolt of Mytilene against Athens, ambassadors from Mytilene try to convince the Spartans of the importance of "justice and honesty" and the importance of obligations among allies: "there can never be a firm friendship between man and man or a real community between different states unless there is a conviction of honesty on both sides and a certain like-mindedness in other respects."[86]

The relation between justice and power is a major theme of the Melian Dialogue.[87] This exchange between Athens and Melos, the small island city-state that wanted to be neutral in the conflict between Athens and Sparta, is a wellspring of normative international relations theory. Do states have rights, or is power ultimately always the decisive factor? Is the world little more than a jungle in which, as the Athenians argue, "the standard of justice depends on the equality of power to compel and that in fact the strong do what they have the power to do and the weak accept what they have to accept."?[88] Is it in fact "a general and necessary law of nature to rule whatever one can."?[89] Or are the Melians correct when they argue that the Athenians should not destroy a principle that is to the general good of all men— "namely, that in the case of all who fall into danger there should be such a thing as fair play and just dealing" if for no other reason than one day Athens may find itself in a similar predicament?[90] In any event, there is no doubt in Thucydides' mind that security should be the primary interest of statesmen. Yet, it is also apparent that for Thucydides questions of morality and power should not be divorced from one another. E.H. Carr, among others, came to the same conclusion in the twentieth century, arguing for a balance or blend of power and moral considerations in international relations.[91]

Conclusion

The *History of the Peloponnesian War* is of interest today to scholars of international relations because it provides analytical insights, offers a number of important cautionary tales concerning matters of war and peace, and has contributed to the development of certain aspects of the realist image of international politics. In terms of the questions outlined in chapter 2, Thucydides placed his primary emphasis on the overall nature of the international system, particularly on how a shift in the balance of power exacerbated the security dilemma and increased the chances of war. Furthermore, as with other realists, Thucydides held a pessimistic view of human nature. If anything, war brought out the worst in people. As he astutely observed, "In times of peace and prosperity cities and individuals alike follow higher standards, because they are not forced into a situation where they have to do what they do not want to do. But war is a stern teacher; in depriving them of the power of easily satisfying their daily wants, it brings most people's minds down to the level of their actual circumstances."[92] Nevertheless, Thucydides' narrative seems to mute this rather deterministic cast by illustrating how within states (the domestic level of analysis) options other than war or confrontation were seriously discussed and debated by leaders and citizens of both Athens and Sparta. Other policies could have been pursued. Hence, Thucydides makes allowance for voluntarism or free will on the part of statesmen. Who is leading a country can make a great deal of difference. For example, in his overview of Persian–Greek relations, Thucydides praises the Athenian Themistocles, who "was particularly remarkable at looking into the future" and who "through force of genius and by rapidity of action . . . was supreme at doing precisely the right thing at precisely the right moment." Similarly, under Pericles Athens "was wisely led and firmly guarded, and it was under him that Athens was at her greatest."[93]

As for the difficulty in predicting the course of international events, this was a reality commented upon by Thucydides rather than explained. Whether in politics or war, it is extremely difficult to foresee how various factors may come together to produce a certain outcome. The important point, however, is that whatever the outcome, it is the result of the actions taken by human beings, not destiny or the gods, as occasionally invoked by Homer and Herodotus. In terms of the relation between morality and power, Thucydides claims the Melians suggested that the two should not be divorced from one another. This should hold even during times of war, if for no other reason than a state may later be in a disadvantageous position and wish to be treated with compassion. As for the relation between the international economy and the international political system, Thucydides had little to say, but political considerations are of critical importance throughout his work.[94]

It is tempting to believe that everything written in the past 2,400 years on international relations is merely a footnote to Thucydides, that his work is a veritable Rosetta stone that can unlock the complexities of world politics. As one contemporary scholar has remarked: "In honesty, one must inquire whether or not twentieth-century students of international relations know anything that Thucydides and his fifth-century compatriots did not know about the behavior of states."[95] In point of fact, however, Thucydides was very much a man of his times. As one historian noted, "For classical Greeks, the fundamental metaphor of social relations was mastery. Life appeared to be a choice between dominating and being dominated, between ruling and being ruled. Politics was often treated as a zero-sum game, in which one man's victory required another man's defeat."[96] Such a perspective would only be reinforced during times of war. But suppose Thucydides had lived in a more peaceful international system. Had he any desire to chronicle events, he might have described a very different world, one in which balances of power and war did not play such an overwhelming role. As a result, he might have drawn other lessons about the nature of international relations, or at least modified his realist perspective.

There is no doubt that some of the best writing on international relations has been done during times of crisis and war among states—Thucydides, Machiavelli, Hobbes, E.H. Carr. Much less, by comparison, has been written on the ways and means of peace. It is interesting to speculate whether Thucydides, had he lived in a later period (such as after the weakening of the Hellenic world by internal strife and incorporation into the Macedonian Empire), might have devoted more effort to understanding the dynamics of empires instead of competitive city-states. The competitive city-state system that Thucydides observed does not exhaust the list of ways to organize international political life.

Notes

Multiple citations within notes are listed in the order in which the quotations appear in the text.

1. For an in-depth discussion of the elements of the Greek city-state system, see Martin Wight, *Systems of States* (Leicester, Eng.: Leicester University Press, 1977), Ch. 2. See also Sir Frank Adcock and D.J. Mosley, *Diplomacy in Ancient Greece* (New York: St. Martin's Press, 1975).

2. Given the fact that Sparta, compared to other powerful states throughout history, seemed relatively unconcerned with imperial ambitions, one author prefers to speak of Spartan "hegemony" as opposed to a Spartan empire. Michael W. Doyle, *Empires* (Ithaca, N.Y.: Cornell University Press, 1986), 59.

3. Doyle, *Empires*, 59.

4. At various times during the second Peloponnesian War, states increased in power relative to Athens and Sparta. As Thucydides notes, in 413 Syracuse was "as big as Athens" (VII:28), and in 421 powerful Argos "was very well off in every direction, having taken no part in the Attic war, indeed having profited greatly from her position of neutrality" and hoping "to gain the leadership of the Peloponnese" (V:28). All references are from the Rex Warner translation of Thucydides' *History of the Peloponnesian War* (Harmondsworth, Eng.: Penguin Books, 1954). The first number refers to the book or chapter, the second number the section within the book.

5. Thucydides, III:22. On the utility and pitfalls of historical comparisons, see Ernest R. May, *Lessons of the Past: The Use and Misuse of History in American Foreign Policy* (New York: Oxford University Press, 1973); Richard E. Neustadt and Ernest R. May, *Thinking in Time: The Uses of History for Decision-Makers* (New York: Free Press, 1986).

6. The *History of the Peloponnesian War* has also been of interest to military strategists. See, for example, F.E. Adcock, *The Greek and Macedonian Art of War* (Berkeley: University of California Press, 1962); W. Kendrick Pritchett, *The Greek State at War* (Berkeley: University of California Press, 1976); A.J. Holladay, "Ath-

enian Strategy in the Archidamian War," *Historia,* 27, no. 3 (1978): 399–427; Thomas Kelly, "Thucydides and Spartan Strategy in the Archidamian War," *American Historical Review,* 87, no. 1 (Feb. 1982): 25–54; John Wilson, "Strategy and Tactics in the Mytilene Campaign," *Historia,* 30, no. 2 (1981): 144–63; Borimir Jordan, *The Athenian Navy in the Classical Period* (Berkeley: University of California Press, 1975); David Blackman, "The Athenian Navy and Allied Naval Contributions to the Pentecontaetia," *Greek, Roman, and Byzantine Studies,* 10 (1969): 179–216; A.W. Gomme, "A Forgotten Factor of Greek Naval Strategy," *Journal of Hellenic Studies,* 53, no. 1 (1933): 16–24; Chester G. Starr, "Thucydides on Sea Power," *Mnemosyne,* 31, no. 4 (1978): 343–50.

7. Thucydides, *History of the Peloponnesian War,* I:23.

8. I:89–90.

9. For examples of this work, see A.F.K. Organski, *World Politics.* 2d ed. (New York: Knopf, 1968); A.F.K. Organski and Jacek Kugler, *The War Ledger* (Chicago: Chicago University Press, 1980); Charles F. Doran, "War and Power Dynamics: Economic Underpinnings," *International Studies Quarterly,* 27, no. 4 (Dec. 1983): 419–41; Charles F. Doran and Wes Parsons, "War and the Cycle of Relative Power," *American Political Science Review,* 74, no. 4 (Dec. 1980): 947–65; Robert Gilpin, *War and Change in World Politics* (Cambridge: Cambridge University Press, 1981).

10. For a critique of the power transition thesis in the context of Thucydides' work, see Mark V. Kauppi, "Contemporary International Relations Theory and the Peloponnesian War," in *Hegemonic Rivalry: From Thucydides to the Nuclear Age,* ed. Richard Ned Lebow and Barry S. Strauss (Boulder, Col.: Westview Press, 1991), 101–24.

11. Thucydides provides numerous examples. Why did the Athenians claim they initially increased their power? Because their chief motive was fear of Persia. Why did the Thessalians and Magnetes prepare for war? Because they were afraid that the army of Sitalces, allied with Athens, might descend upon them. Why did the Athenians send a fleet of ships to Mytilene? Because they were afraid Mytilene would form an alliance with a neighboring state. Why did the Athenians tell the Melians they had to side with Athens and could not be neutral? Because the Athenians feared they would look weak in the eyes of other states.

12. Thucydides, *History of the Peloponnesian War,* I:68–71; II:35–46.

13. III:82–84.

14. I:66.

15. I:126.

16. I:88.

17. For an argument that the basic assumptions and arguments presented by Thucydides at the outset of his work are designed to create certain expectations in the mind of the reader and then later purposely subverted, see W.R. Connor, *Thucydides* (Princeton, N.J.: Princeton University Press, 1984).

18. Richard Ned Lebow, "Thucydides, Power Transition Theory, and the Causes of War," in *Hegemonic Rivalry,* ed. Lebow and Strauss, 127–29, citing F.E. Adcock, *Thucydides and His History* (Cambridge: Cambridge University Press, 1963), 90–91; and Donald Kagan, *The Outbreak of the Peloponnesian War* (Ithaca, N.Y.: Cornell University Press, 1969), 189, 373–74.

19. Thucydides, *History of the Peloponnesian War,* I:66–71; III:36–50.

20. VI:1.

21. As one scholar has noted, Pericles' original strategy was "to abstain from attempts to extend Athenian domination and to avoid involvement in dangerous enterprises, to keep firm control of the allies, and to maintain seapower and to avoid land-conflicts with the main forces of the enemy." It is argued that the Sicilian campaign and other military operations in Aetolia, Pylos, Megara, and Boeotia violated this Periclean strategy and reflected the views of Demosthenes and Cleon after the death of Pericles. A.J. Holladay, "Athenian Strategy in the Archidamian War," *Historia*, 27, no. 3 (1978): 399 passim.

22. Thucydides, *History of the Peloponnesian War*, VI:9–12.

23. VI:17.

24. VI:18.

25. VI:44–46.

26. VI:49.

27. VII:15.

28. VII:24.

29. VII:71.

30. VII:87.

31. One should be wary of pushing historical parallels too far. The Sicilian expedition, for example, differed from the American Vietnam experience in a number of ways. First, due to an earlier military expedition, the case can be made that the Athenians were not as ignorant of Sicily as Thucydides' narrative would lead us to believe. Second, despite Thucydides' statement that the Sicilian campaign failed in part because of a loss of public support, his narrative shows the Athenian public to be enthusiastic for the war effort and quite willing to send reinforcements. Finally, tactical and strategic mistakes by Nicias in the field may well have cost Athens an early and relatively inexpensive victory; the expedition was perhaps not necessarily doomed from the start.

32. IV:18.

33. IV:19.

34. I:80.

35. I:140.

36. II:8.

37. VI:24.

38. III:82.

39. II:38.

40. III:36–50.

41. An exception to the concept of the unified state, however, is the prevalence of "fifth columns," factions or groups of citizens who sell out to enemy states.

42. Thucydides, *History of the Peloponnesian War*, II:65.

43. Kenneth Waltz, *Theory of International Politics* (Reading, Mass.: Addison-Wesley, 1979), 97. For a discussion of where Thucydides fits into the realist tradition, see Michael Doyle, "Thucydides: A Realist?" in *Hegemonic Rivalry*, ed. Lebow and Strauss, 169–88.

44. Thucydides, *History of the Peloponnesian War*, VI:38.

45. VI:36.

46. Hans J. Morgenthau, *Politics Among Nations*, 4th ed. (New York: Knopf, 1966), 5.

47. See, for example, Waltz, *Man, the State and War* and *Theory of International Politics;* Robert Gilpin, *War and Change in World Politics* and *U.S. Power*

and the Multinational Corporation (New York: Basic Books, 1975) and *The Political Economy of International Relations* (Princeton, N.J.: Princeton University Press, 1987). In Graham Allison's study of the 1962 Cuban Missile Crisis between the United States and the Soviet Union, the rational actor model (Model I) portrays the decision-making process as stating objectives, weighing alternatives, and choosing the optimal course. Notwithstanding a large chance of error in such an approach, when facts are uncertain or not available (as was true in this study, particularly in the Soviet case), rational reconstruction may be the only practical alternative available to the theorist who still wants to say something, however qualified, about the process leading to a particular decision or outcome. It should be noted, however, that Allison finds the rational-actor model insufficient and introduces two other models to take organizational processes and bureaucratic politics into account. Graham Allison, *Essence of Decision: Explaining the Cuban Missile Crisis* (Boston: Little, Brown, 1971). See also the attempt at historical reconstruction in James G. Blight and David A. Welch, eds., *On the Brink: Americans and Soviets Reexamine the Cuban Missile Crisis* (New York: Hill and Wang, 1989).

Bruce Bueno de Mesquita's causal explanation of war faces some of the same data problems in the testing of propositions or hypotheses derived from his theory. Nevertheless, his "expected utility" theory as a means to construct a general theory of conflict rests fundamentally on the same assumption of rationality as one finds in Waltz, Gilpin, or in Allison's rational actor Model I. Bruce Bueno de Mesquita, *The War Trap* (New Haven, Conn.: Yale University Press, 1981). For a useful discussion on different ways to conceive of rationality, see Frank C. Zagare, "Rationality and Deterrence," *World Politics*, 42, no. 2 (Jan. 1990), 238–43.

48. Thucydides, *History of the Peloponnesian War,* IV:59.

49. VIII:24. An example from World War II, sometimes used by present-day game theorists, is a sea battle in 1943 between the United States and Japan near New Guinea. American aircraft succeeded in sinking much of the Japanese fleet even though the Japanese commander chose what for him was the optimal course of action. O.G. Haywood, Jr., "Military Decision and Game Theory," *Journal of the Operations Research Society of America,* 2 (1954): 365–85, as cited in Samuel B. Richmond, *Operations Research for Management Decisions* (New York: Ronald Press, 1968), 506–8.

50. See, for example, Robert O. Keohane, "Theory of World Politics: Structural Realism and Beyond," in *International Relations Theory: Realism, Pluralism, Globalism,* ed. Paul R. Viotti and Mark V. Kauppi, (New York: Macmillan, 1987), 132.

51. At least in this regard, Thucydides seems to be a realist more in the vein of Arnold Wolfers, Martin Wight, Raymond Aron, and Stanley Hoffmann than more recent neorealists such as Kenneth Waltz and Robert Gilpin who utilize microeconomic assumptions of rationality in constructing their theories. Doyle, "Thucydides: A Realist?", 170, note 10.

52. Harold Sprout and Margaret Sprout, "Environmental Factors in the Study of International Politics," *Journal of Conflict Resolution,* 1 (1957): 309–28.

53. Robert Jervis, *Perception and Misperception in International Politics* (Princeton, N.J.: Princeton University Press, 1976), 320.

54. This tendency has been particularly prevalent in the case of the United States and the Soviet Union. See, for example, Richards Huer, "Analyzing the Soviet

Invasion of Afghanistan: Hypotheses from Causal Attribution Theory," *Studies in Comparative Communism*, 13, no. 4 (Winter 1980): 347–55.

55. Thucydides, *History of the Peloponnesian War*, III:11.

56. I:68.

57. I:144.

58. I:118.

59. VI:18.

60. Richard Ned Lebow, *Between Peace and War: The Nature of International Crisis* (Baltimore: Johns Hopkins University Press, 1981), Ch. 5; and Ole R. Holsti, "Theories of Crisis Decision Making," in *Diplomacy: New Approaches in History, Theory, and Policy*, ed. Paul Gordon Lauren (New York: Free Press, 1979), 99–136. On the impact of stress, see Alexander L. George, "Adaptation to Stress in Political Decision Making: The Individual, Small Group, and Organizational Contexts," in *Coping and Adaptation*, ed. George V. Coelho, et al. (New York: Basic Books, 1974); and Irving Janis and Leon Mann, *Decision Making: A Psychological Analysis of Conflict, Choice, and Commitment* (New York: Free Press, 1977). See also Miriam Steiner, "The Search for Order in a Disorderly World: Worldviews and Prescriptive Decision Paradigms," *International Organization*, 37, no. 3 (Summer 1983): 373–413.

61. Jervis, *Perception and Misperception*, 310–11; and the classic article by Ole R. Holsti, "Cognitive Dynamics and Images of the Enemy: Dulles and Russia," in *Enemies in Politics*, ed. David Finley, Ole Holsti, and Richard Fagin (Chicago: Rand McNally, 1967), 25–96.

62. Thucydides, *History of the Peloponnesian War*, I:68.

63. IV:108.

64. III:3.

65. VI:32.

66. V:103.

67. Jervis, *Perception and Misperception*, 278–79, 365–72. See also D. Clayton Jones, "American and Japanese Strategies in the Pacific War," in *Makers of Modern Strategy: From Machiavelli to the Nuclear Age*, ed. Peter Paret (Princeton, N.J.: Princeton University Press, 1986), 703–8.

68. Thucydides, *History of the Peloponnesian War*, VI:17.

69. See, for example, James G. Blight, "The New Psychology of War and Peace," *International Security*, 11, no. 3 (Winter 1986–87): 175–86; Stanley Hoffmann, "On the Political Psychology of War and Peace: A Critique and an Agenda," *Political Psychology*, 7, no. 1 (March 1986): 1–21.

70. Thucydides, *History of the Peloponnesian War*, III:40, 44.

71. Michael E. Howard, "The Forgotten Dimensions of Strategy," *Foreign Affairs*, 57, no. 5 (Summer 1979): 975–86.

72. A Syracusan, Hermocrates, argues that it is in the collective interests of the states in Sicily to repel Athenian aggression and that such unity should take precedent over societal and cultural differences among them. "We should make friends, man with man and city with city, and should set out on a united effort to save Sicily as a whole. No one should have the idea that, while the Dorians among us are enemies to the Athenians, the Chalcidians are quite safe because of their Ionian blood. Athenian intervention has nothing to do with the races into which we are divided; they are not attacking us because they hate one or the other; what they

want is the good things of Sicily which are the common property of us all." Thucydides, *History of the Peloponnesian War,* IV:61.

73. Stephen M. Walt, *The Origins of Alliances* (Ithaca, N.Y.: Cornell University Press, 1987); Deborah Welch Larson, "Bandwagon Images in American Foreign Policy: Myth or Reality?" in *Dominos and Bandwagons: Strategic Belief and Superpower Competition in the Eurasian Rimland,* ed. Robert Jervis and Jack Snyder (New York: Oxford University Press, 1990), 85–111.

74. Thucydides, *History of the Peloponnesian War,* I:31.

75. VIII:46, 57.

76. For examples, see Barry S. Strauss, "Of Balances, Bandwagons, and Ancient Greece," in *Hegemonic Rivalry,* ed. Lebow and Strauss, 198–201.

77. Thucydides, *History of the Peloponnesian War,* III:10.

78. III:37.

79. III:39, 40.

80. I:56–57.

81. V:95.

82. II:72.

83. VII:33.

84. VIII:2.

85. VI:6.

86. III:10.

87. V:84–116.

88. V:89.

89. V:105.

90. V:90.

91. Edward Hallett Carr, *The Twenty Years' Crisis, 1919–1939* (London: Macmillan, 1962).

92. Thucydides, *History of the Peloponnesian War,* III:82.

93. I:138; II:65.

94. Thucydides, for example, has little to say about Pericles' Megarian Decree, which forbade neighboring Megara from the ports of the empire and the market at Athens (I:67, 139). Furthermore, during the Persian wars, "The Athenian economy was increasingly dependent on trade, a large part of it in the Aegean and in the Hellespontine region. A significant part of the grain eaten by the Athenians came from the Ukraine through the Hellespont and the Aegean. It was in large part for these reasons that Athens had planted colonies on the Chersonese in the sixth century. She could not allow the Hellespont and northern Aegean to remain in Persian hands or under threat of Persian control." Kagan, *The Outbreak of the Peloponnesian War,* 39–40.

95. Gilpin, *War and Change in World Politics,* 227. Similarly, Bruce Bueno de Mesquita states, "Despite the attention of such intellectual giants as Spinoza, Rousseau, Kant, and Clausewitz, we know little more about international conflict today than was known to Thucydides four hundred years before Christ." *The War Trap,* 2.

96. Strauss, "Of Balances," 202.

5

After Thucydides: Plato, Aristotle, and Polybius

We turn in this chapter to the writings of Plato, Aristotle, and Polybius. All three carried forward the realist tradition already developed by Herodotus and Thucydides, but with important elements that set their works apart. Beyond conceiving of the politics of city-states and empires as contests among competing powers or coalitions of powers, they can be found discussing concepts consistent with pluralist and globalist images of international relations that would be advanced by later writers. Because of their influence on epistemology and the development of theory, of particular interest are the use of dialectical reasoning by Plato, the comparative method employed by Aristotle, and the discussion of the nature of causality in international relations by Polybius.

Historical Context

The Peloponnesian War that began in 431 B.C. lasted until 404 B.C., two years after the death of the war's principal historian, Thucydides. Xenophon—a student, along with Plato, of Socrates—attempted to complete Thucydides' work on the Peloponnesian War. Unfortunately, Xenophon's exaggeration of fact and return to Herodotus' approach of incorporating supernatural explanation into his account, however enjoyable, clearly departed significantly from the approach used by Thucydides. As a result, with the passage of time Xenophon's work became less influential with scholars than it might have been.

The defeat of Athens and the subsequent peace treaty of 404 B.C. did not usher in a long period of stability in the Hellenic world. Sparta's domination was rather short-lived, because it did not have the resources to maintain its hegemony. Athens soon began to plan its comeback and Sparta also had to deal with the ambition of Thebes, its erstwhile ally.[1] Because of the destructiveness of the Peloponnesian War, the power of the Greek world as a whole to resist outside pressures was weakened. While throughout much of the fifth century B.C. Persia represented an imperial threat, Philip, king of the growing Macedonian Empire centered north of Greece, became a new cause of concern in the fourth century. His son, who came to be known as Alexander the Great (356–323 B.C.), as a youth had been taught by Aristotle and hence exposed to Hellenic thinking. In 342, however, he was a commander in the army of his father, Phillip, which defeated the allied Greek city-states. Following the assassination of his father, Alexander claimed the throne. When it was rumored that he had died in battle, Thebes revolted from Macedonian control, supported by other city-states and urged on by Athens. Within two weeks, Alexander's armies marched to Thebes. When the city refused to surrender, the city was destroyed, 6,000 citizens were killed, and the survivors were sold into slavery. This intimidated the rest of the Greek city-states, and modest garrisons were left in three cities as Alexander turned his attention to the Persian Empire to the east. His armies eventually conquered territory from Egypt to India and brought with them aspects of Greek culture. Following Alexander's death, however, rivalries among his successors and rebellions within the sprawling empire led to a weakening of central control.[2]

Notwithstanding the defeat of Athens in the Peloponnesian War and the eventual end of Hellenic independence, it was a golden age of Athenian scholarship in ancient Greece. As well as making his contributions as an historian, Thucydides had marked a watershed in the development of thinking about international relations. He had set a model for the study of international relations that others would emulate. His realism was not challenged by two of the most famous Greek philosophers who wrote after him—Plato and Plato's student, Aristotle.

Much later, when Greece clearly had gone into decline in relation to the rising power of Rome, Polybius (c. 200–120 B.C.) tried to emulate Thucydides in his attempt to find causes for events as well as in his objectivity and secularism as an historian. Thus, the gods and their oracles do not play a role in the histories written by Polybius. When possible, he used primary sources and took a critical view of the data he collected. The result, though of course still subject to human error, was a somewhat more reliable, if less entertaining, chronicle of events and account of causes in history than the work of Herodotus and Xenophon. Polybius was preoccupied with explaining the rise of the Roman Empire that effectively displaced Greek power. But Greek decline was really only in imperial terms. Its culture and civilization influenced the Romans directly. Through the Romans and those who followed, Hellenic ideas have survived to the present day.[3] We now turn to a discussion of these Greek scholars and those of their views that relate directly or indirectly to international relations.

Plato

Plato was born in 427 B.C., approximately four years after the beginning of the Peloponnesian War and a year after the death of Pericles. He came from a distinguished family interested in politics, and during the war years he witnessed the tendency of political leaders such as Cleon to pander to the public and undertake such actions as the Sicilian expedition, which ended in disaster in 412 B.C. As a result of that ill-fated adventure, oligarchic control was established the following year and power invested in the Council of Four Hundred. A year later this was succeeded by the Government of Five Thousand, which the following year succumbed to the democratic opposition forces that initiated six years of what could be termed democratic terror. In 404, when Plato was twenty-three, Athens was defeated by Sparta, leading once again to an oligarchic revolution that resulted in political and personal vendettas. This regime lasted only eight months. Democracy was restored, but in 399 the generally moderate leadership did something Plato could never forgive—they ordered the death of Socrates on the grounds of impiety and corruption of the young. Although friends and family had expected Plato to go into politics, his experiences as a youth helped to turn him to a life of philosophy and a belief that a new type of politician could be trained. This hope was translated into action in 386 with the establishment of the Academy.[4]

Plato had very little to say about international relations. He is a prime example, however, of a political philosopher whose indirect effect on thinking about world politics has been profound. In a number of Plato's dialogues, for example, we find dialectical reasoning—dealing with opposites—as the key method used by the great teacher Socrates. Hegel would find dialectics useful in the development of theory, as would Marx. Beyond the more formal Hegelian and Marxian uses of dialectics to consider contrary possibilities, hypothetical opposites or conflicting analyses are at the core of the critical and creative thinking that is so essential to theorizing, whether in international relations or other fields of inquiry. More generally, Plato and Aristotle deserve credit for beginning systematic thinking about politics and the function and nature of the state, and hence they influenced those scholars who followed them. Indeed, to this day the state has remained the key unit of analysis in not only comparative politics, but also in realist thinking about international relations. Although tangential to his primary focus on the domestic aspects of the state, the following questions that Plato touches on are of interest to scholars of international relations: How does the state come into being? How can its security be enhanced? What is the primary cause of war among states? Do different types of states exhibit different types of foreign policy behavior? What is the relation between power and justice? Each will be addressed in turn.

The State and Security

In the course of Plato's famous dialogue on the nature of justice in *The Republic,* one of his participants in the discussion, Glaucon, presents his view on the origins of the state that anticipates the social contract theories of the seventeenth and eighteenth centuries. He argues that conventional wisdom assumes that "according to nature" it is "a good thing to inflict wrong or injury, and a bad thing to suffer it." But after experiencing both, people decide that "as they can't evade the one and achieve the other, it will pay to make a compact with each other by which they forgo both. They accordingly proceed to make laws and mutual agreements, and what the law lays down they call lawful and right." Given the selfishness of human nature, people must be "forcibly restrained by the law and made to respect each other's claims."[5] Later social contract theorists such as Thomas Hobbes would use the myth of the social contract as a means by which to distinguish and justify the civil order found within states as compared to the anarchy of international politics. It should be noted, however, that while Hobbes, Locke, and Rousseau were interested in the problem of sovereignty—who should be the final authority and why should the individual citizen obey it?—Glaucon is concerned with establishing a morally justifiable as well as political basis of mutual obligation.

But Socrates, more closely reflecting Plato's own views, states that "society originates . . . because the individual is not self-sufficient, but has many needs which he can't supply himself." It is interesting to note, however, that when Socrates proceeds to enumerate these needs in order of importance—food, shelter, and clothing—personal security is not mentioned. This, as we will see, was one of the prime motivating factors for justifying the state by later social contract theorists such as Hobbes, but for Socrates the security dimension comes to the fore only after the state begins to expand.[6]

As Socrates and his compatriots proceed further to discuss the elements of this mythical state and its development and enlargement, Socrates suggests that eventually "the territory which was formerly enough to support us will now be too small." As a result "we shall have to cut a slice off our neighbors' territory." He assumes, however, that if they, too, are growing in size they will also want a slice of our territory, and "that will lead to war." At this point Socrates states that the concern is not with the effects of war, but rather to note that "we have found its origin to be the same as that of most evil, individual or social"—acquisitiveness. In order to defend the property and possessions of the citizens, an army is required. Glaucon asks if a citizen army would be sufficient, but Socrates replies that "it is surely of the greatest importance that the business of war should be efficiently run." Hence those in the military require "complete freedom from other affairs and a correspondingly high degree of skill and practice." We now have the primary justification of the "auxiliaries" of Plato's guardian class, which he compares to a watchdog: of "utmost gentleness to those it is used to and knows, but to be savage to strangers."[7] As Plato observes in *The Laws*, "no better or more powerful or efficient weapon exists for ensuring safety and final victory in war" than the "combined and united action" of soldiers.[8]

This suspicion, if not hostility, to the world beyond the city-state is typical of Plato as well as Aristotle, who viewed the *polis* as the supreme form of organization because it was created by man acting in accordance with his own nature. It is in *The Laws* where an older Plato describes in great detail his utopian state, which is to be insulated from the outside world as much as possible. In terms of foreign visitors, "good care" needs to be taken lest any "of this category of visitor introduces any novel custom"; contact with foreigners is to be kept "down to the unavoidable minimum." Consistent with this principle, "no young person under forty is ever to be allowed to travel abroad under any circumstances; nor is anyone to be allowed to go for private reasons, but only on some public business, as a herald or ambassador or as an observer of one sort or another." Those who do go abroad for such purposes are obligated when they return to "tell the younger generation that the social and political customs of the rest of the world don't measure up to their own."[9]

The State and Foreign Policy

In *The Republic*, Plato's discussion of justice leads to the conclusion that in the "perfect state" people "should be governed by those of their number who are best at philosophy and war." In one of the major contributions to the study of comparative government and politics, Plato has Socrates describe four other "imperfect" types of states that are inferior to the one he is proposing—timarchy, oligarchy, democracy, and tyranny. Plato's discussion focuses on the nature of these types of states and how they degenerate or evolve one from the other. Very little is said about how the type of political system affects the foreign policy behavior of a state.

He does note, however, that a timarchy—a military aristocracy similar to Sparta—prefers "simpler, hearty types" as rulers "who prefer war to peace." Its citizens "will admire the tricks and stratagems which are needed in war, which will be its constant occupation." An oligarchy, on the other hand, exhibits an "inability to wage war" because of a fear of arming the people or a desire to avoid the heavy expenses associated with war. As for a democracy, Plato perhaps has the Corcyraean civil war in mind when he discusses the transition from oligarchy to democracy, defining the latter in terms of the individual being free to do what he likes. "It [democracy] will fall into sickness and dissension at the slightest external provocation, when one party or the other calls in help from a neighboring oligarchy or democracy." Once democracy triumphs, individual liberty means "you needn't fight if there's a war, or you can wage a private war in peacetime if you don't like peace." Tyranny emerges from the chaos and excesses of democracy. A tyrant arises who leads a class war against owners of property. Once in power and having defeated foreign enemies, "he will in the first place continue to stir up war in order that the people may continue to need a leader." In other words, real or imagined external threats can be used to enhance one's domestic political position.[10]

Power and Justice

Analyzing the relation between power and justice is, of course, one of Plato's primary concerns. Furthermore, by arguing that justice consists of individuals each doing the job for which he or she is naturally suited, Plato begins the tradition of class analysis that informs much of the work of present-day scholars influenced by the globalist tradition. But as for justice, it is not Plato's definition that is of greatest interest to scholars of international relations, but rather that of Thrasymachus, whom Plato has present what could be termed the conventional wisdom of the day, very often propounded by the Sophists. He bluntly states, "I say that justice or right is simply what is in the interest of the stronger party."[11] This perspective is reasserted by the character Callicles in Plato's *Gorgias*. According to Callicles, nature "demonstrates that it is right that the better man should prevail over the worse and the stronger over the weaker. . . . Right consists in the superior ruling over the inferior and having the upper hand." He then gives the examples of Darius invading Scythia and Xerxes invading Greece, noting such actions "are in accordance with natural law."[12]

Such "might makes right" arguments are not those of Plato, but would seem closer to those of the Athenians who argue in the course of Thucydides' Melian dialogue that "it is a general and necessary law of nature to rule whatever one can." It should be noted, however, that the Athenians actually argue that the question of "right" is divorced from that of power. They tell the Melians that they must submit to the power of Athens, not because "we have a right to our empire because we defeated the Persians," but rather, as stated by the Melians themselves, one should "leave justice out of account and to confine ourselves to self-interest."[13]

Plato has justifiably been characterized as an idealist, and his emphasis on the philosopher king in *The Republic* and the utopia depicted in *The Laws* would seem to reflect an optimistic, voluntarist predilection to assume that wise leadership can ensure the security of the city-state and, most importantly, a just and well-ordered society. But two cautions are in order. First, his teleological view of the development of the state—meaning there are purposes apart from, as well as greater than, the will of individual human beings—is an obvious example of determinism. In other words, it is nature that wills a particular end, not the will of man or woman.[14] Secondly, and perhaps in contradiction, there is a strong undercurrent of pessimism in his work. While he hopes that a philosopher king can be nurtured through the right sort of education, he doesn't seem to have found many likely role models. In a portrayal of the rather bitter debate between the advocates of political oratory and Socrates in his defense of philosophy in the *Gorgias,* Plato denigrates the achievements of such noted Athenians as Pericles, Cimon, Miltiades, and Themistocles. In the words of Socrates, no one "has been a good statesman in this country."[15] Hence, while a ruler should strive to achieve perfection in conduct and policies, attaining the Platonic ideal of state and constitution appears to be highly unlikely. The works of Aristotle, however, seem to be not only more practical than those of Plato's, but also more optimistic about what statesmen can achieve.

Aristotle

Aristotle was born in Chalcidice, part of the dominions of Macedonia. At age seventeen he went to Athens and enrolled as a student in Plato's Academy. He remained there for some twenty years, and after Plato's death he traveled to Asia Minor and conducted scientific studies. In 343 B.C. he returned to his native land to teach King Philip's son Alexander for about two years, but eventually he returned to Athens in 336 B.C. Two years before that, Philip had grouped most of the Greek states into a federation under Macedonian control. In 336 B.C., after ascending to the throne, Alexander led his combined armies in an invasion of Asia. As Alexander was conquering the East, Aristotle established his famous school, the Lyceum. With the death of Alexander in 323 B.C., anti–Macedonian feeling intensified, and Aristotle—always a foreigner in Athens—felt it was prudent to move to nearby Euboea, where he died at age sixty-two.

For Greeks and Romans in general, Plato's *Republic* was of more interest than Aristotle's *Politics.* After the Fall of Rome, Aristotle's works were lost to scholars until the Middle Ages. The real impact of his *Ethics* and *Politics* is not apparent until the twelfth century, when such religious scholars as Thomas Aquinas studied them closely. In the fourteenth century Dante was also heavily influenced by Aristotle, and the latter's works were also essential reading for Machiavelli, Jean Bodin, and Thomas Hobbes.[16]

As with Plato's *Republic* and *The Laws,* Aristotle's *Politics* is essentially about domestic politics—the search for the ideal constitution. This concern is rather interesting in that Aristotle lived at a time when militarily and politically the Greek city-states were progressively being overshadowed by the Macedonian Empire. Despite events unfolding around him, Aristotle had little to say about empires or international relations in general—an absence that should be a necessary caution against assuming that a scholar's life work is overly determined by the times within which he or she lives. Nevertheless, Aristotle's writings influenced later scholars interested in international relations in at least three ways: through his conceptual and empirical approach to political phenomena, his detailed examination of different types of state constitutions and the causes of instability, and his writings on economics. In the course of our discussion of states and stability, we will also discuss what little Aristotle had to say about security.

Epistemology

While Aristotle, like Plato and other Greeks, was interested in determining the ideal state and constitution, his approach was more analytic and scientific. Plato believed that all objects have a perfect form or ideal that has an independent existence and that such perfection can never be achieved but only approximated. Aristotle, while sharing Plato's teleological perspective, believed that things are continually moving toward their full completeness and that through this natural process perfection can be achieved. Hence, in discussing the origins of the state, he, like Plato, does not adopt a social contract perspective; as with the family and then the village, the development of the city-state is a natural follow-on:

> While the state came about as a means of securing life itself, it continues in being to secure the *good* life. Therefore every state exists by nature, as the earlier associations too were natural. This association is the end of those others. . . . It follows that the state belongs to the class of objects which exist by nature, and that man is by nature a political animal.[17]

Perfection is not some unattainable goal, floating among the clouds, but is a kernel residing in individuals or political communities that has the potential to achieve completeness. A desire to lend credibility to this perspective contributed to Aristotle's fascination with rigorous empirical observation, reflected in his studies in the natural sciences as well as those focusing on human institutions. Hence, in conjunction with his students at the Lyceum, he collected information on some 168 constitutions, classified them based on conceptions of the just distribution of political power, and analyzed them in terms of their respective causes of instability.[18] While not denying the normative and metaphysical appeal of Aristotle's works down through the ages, it is his interest in classifying, conceptualizing, and engaging in empirical research that has had the largest effect on the social sciences, including international relations as a field of inquiry.

Constitutions, Stability, and Security

As noted previously, Aristotle was particularly interested in how states organized themselves internally, and hence he made a major effort to collect as many constitutions as possible. In *The Politics* he classifies constitutions in several ways. For example, he first classifies states based on the number and aim of the rulers—monarchy is rule by one, aristocracy rule by a few, and polity rule by the mass of the populace. What all have in common, however, is a concern for the common interest. The "corresponding deviations" are tyranny, oligarchy, and democracy. He goes on to argue, however, that the key criterion for classification is economic. In a discussion with what we would now term Marxist overtones because of the emphasis on property, he argues, for example, that "oligarchy occurs when the sovereign power of the constitution is in the hands of those with possessions, democracy when it is in the hands of those who have no stock of possessions and are without means." Finally, he suggests that another possible criterion that can be used to differentiate constitutions is the division of political power based on what is viewed by a particular society as being "just."[19]

What is of interest for our purposes, however, is that in Aristotle's detailed examination of various states and constitutions—which includes discussions of how to preserve these political systems—the reasons he offers for their downfall almost always stem from internal factors. External or international factors generally play little if any role at all. When they are mentioned, they tend to be of secondary importance. For example, in Aristotle's discussion of the rise of factions within an aristocracy, five contributing factors are listed. Only one, the disparity of wealth between rich and poor, is related to the international environment; Aristotle notes such disparity is "particularly likely to come about in time of war." Similarly, in democracies "the most potent cause of revolution is the unprincipled character of popular leaders," and in oligarchies it may result "when the oligarchs wrong the multitude" or arise "out of the oligarchs' own rivalry."[20] This almost exclusive emphasis on internal factors as a means to understand domestic political stability is not unique to Aristotle. Indeed, it is primarily since World War II that political scientists have engaged in systematic and comparative studies of the international determinants of domestic politics.[21]

In discussing Plato's *Laws*, Aristotle quotes his mentor's belief that "in framing the laws a legislator ought to have regard both to the territory and to the population," but he criticizes Plato by noting "but surely we should add that he ought to take note of the neighboring territories too," as a state "must provide itself with such arms for warfare as are serviceable not merely internally but also against the territories beyond its border."[22] Therefore, in describing his ideal state in *The Politics*, Aristotle discusses basic security matters for essentially the first and only time. He obviously does not think much of those city-states or peoples who engage in war for reasons of aggrandizement—the Scythians, Persians, Thracians, Celts. He notes "how completely unreasonable it would be if the work of a statesman were to be reduced to an ability to work out how to rule and be master over neighboring peoples."[23] For him, war should only be a means to defend the good life.

Security, therefore, is essentially in the realm of defense, in which it is necessary to have "sufficient armed force to give the laws protection" and "to repel attempts at wrongdoing coming from outside."[24] In one passage,

Aristotle goes into considerable detail describing appropriate defense preparations and emphasizing the need "to secure the greatest degree of protection that strong walls can afford." This is "the best military measure" when "the superiority of the attackers is too much for the valour" of the defenders, particularly in light of "all the modern improvements in the accuracy of missiles and artillery for attacking a besieged town." Adversaries likely will be deterred from attacking well defended city-states. In Aristotle's words: "An enemy will not even attempt an attack in the first place on those who are well prepared to meet it."[25] This is one of the first statements of the military-strategic view *si vis pacem, para bellum*—if you seek peace, prepare for war.

Consistent with the observations of nineteenth- and twentieth-century realist geopolitical strategists, Aristotle argues that a city-state's power or capabilities are affected directly by a number of other factors. For example, its location in relation to "both sea and land" is important, the objective being to make it "hard for a hostile force to invade, easy for an expeditionary force to depart from." Furthermore, "if it is to play an active role as a leading state, it will need naval as well as land forces large enough for such activities."[26]

It is apparent, however, that for Aristotle good government, the theme of this book, is the really critical source of security. He contends that "a state's purpose is also to provide something more than a military pact of protection against injustice, or to facilitate mutual acquaintance and the exchange of goods." It must "ensure government under good laws" and promote civic "virtue" among the citizenry.[27] A good constitution—for Aristotle a mixed one, or polity, with a large middle class that blends elements of oligarchy and democracy—contributes to security and good living. Unity within the state under a system of good and effective laws is also important to the security of any city-state.[28]

Economy

Finally, more so than the other ancient writers we have surveyed, Aristotle explicitly deals with the relation between economics and politics. His contributions to both domestic and international political economy provided a foundation upon which later writers would build. Like Plato, Aristotle employs class analysis, an approach with both domestic and international (or transnational) applications in present-day scholarship. He asserts that "a division of the state into classes is necessary."[29] Indeed, he provides a defense of slavery and the master–slave relationship as integral to the political economy of his times. Class formation, however, is not due solely to economic exigencies, but also to security threats stemming from possible slave revolts or foreign powers. Hence, just as Plato elevated warriors to an important class unto themselves, Aristotle claims the two critical parts of the state are the military and deliberative elements.[30] Furthermore, in his extensive survey of constitutions, he notes that "the reason for the plurality of constitutions lies in the plurality of parts of every state." He initially defines this plurality in terms of economic classes—"some must be wealthy, others poor, others in the middle." But he also notes that "in addition to wealth there are other *differentiae*, of family, virtue, and any other similar feature we described as 'part' of a state."[31]

Such writings certainly influenced the domestic and world views of Adam Smith, David Ricardo, Karl Marx, and the other classical economists who found in Aristotle the basis for what would become their labor theory of value. In particular, Marx would combine the class analysis and political economy of the ancients, transposing their view through history to the nineteenth-century circumstances he observed. Marx's classic phrase in the *Communist Manifesto* that all history is the history of class struggles, beginning with the master–slave relationship, seems really to be a distant echo of Aristotle's notion of the rule of "master over slave."[32] Indeed, Marx characterized the dominant mode of production of the ancients as slavery and differentiated it from the successive historical and global modes of feudal and capitalist production that could not have been known to Plato and Aristotle.

On property rights, Aristotle argues that "while property should up to a point be held in common, the general principle should be that of private ownership."[33] It is the same Aristotle, however, who expresses hostility toward "the practice of charging interest" for the loan of money, a sentiment also central to the thinking of the Middle Ages, when all interest charges, however small, were regarded as the sinful practice of usury. Aristotle's reasoning, similar to that of the medieval church, is that interest earnings are not the outcome of productive labor; instead, "the gain arises out of currency itself."[34] This idea would have a long shelf life through the Middle Ages and after, inhibiting financial transactions of the market place that we now view as essential to a capitalist mode of production.

Trade, an important consideration for later writers influenced by what have been termed the pluralist and globalist perspectives, derives, according to Aristotle, from "men having too much of this and not enough of that," an observation that would be repeated by the eighteenth- and nineteenth-century classical economists. Aristotle argues that "exchange" effectively is "carried on far enough to satisfy the needs of the parties." Moreover, Aristotle extends this logic to international trade and finance when he observes how "the import of necessities and the export of surplus goods began to facilitate the satisfaction of needs beyond national frontiers" and, consequently, that traders "resorted to the use of coined money."[35]

While commerce may have brought contact with foreigners, such awareness did not mean acceptance of diversity. Ethnocentric rejection of foreign ways was the common response among most Greek writers, who contrasted themselves with the "barbarians." Aristotle seems to have shared these prejudices, perhaps in part because he was no fan of foreign trade and coined money, which encouraged such contacts; he was concerned that foreigners and their ideas would undermine the unity of the state. Hence Aristotle suggests that one should deal differently with foreigners when their disputes involve one's own citizens. He argues, for example, that there should be two judicial courts, "one for foreigners disputing with foreigners" and "the other for foreigners disputing with citizens."[36] The suggestion that mankind is really a human family that extends beyond the borders of any given tribe, city-state, or set of city-states clearly was not the dominant image in ancient Greece. Such thinking was foreign to Plato, Aristotle, and their contemporaries.

Aristotle's student, Alexander the Great, however, spread Aristotle's— and, more broadly, Greek—political ideas well beyond Athens and the other Greek city-states. A new cosmopolitanism that departed significantly from the ethnocentrism of Plato, Aristotle, and other Greeks was reflected in Alexander's policy of encouraging soldiers to marry with the local populations conquered by force of arms. In a larger sense, Alexander's conquests effectively spread Hellenic ideas throughout the world of his time. The development of the idea of the unity of mankind, however, would have to await Greek Stoicism, which developed in the century after Alexander and spread to Rome and elsewhere in the world.

Polybius

The work of the Greek historian Polybius is not often read or even cited by most present-day political theorists. This omission is a mistake. Such obscurity is unwarranted. Indeed, the influence Polybius had on political philosophers as diverse as Machiavelli, Montesquieu, and the writers of the U.S. Constitution is striking. Polybius took a very rational approach to his study of politics by relating observations to theory. Following the example set by Thucydides and relevant to the development of international relations theory, he sought causal explanations for the phenomena he observed. More than other historians of his time, he was a theorist in the modern meaning of the term. His work is more than just a history of the Punic wars between Rome and Carthage. Polybius focused on the transformation of world politics—the rise of the Roman empire—and sought explanatory variables for the phenomenon at what today would be termed the international, domestic, and individual levels of analysis.

Polybius was born in Greece in the city of Megalopolis on the Peloponnese. The son of a wealthy landowner, he was attracted to history and political theory, but his talents and family connections led him to be elected a cavalry leader in the Achaean League, to which Megalopolis belonged.

During his life the Greeks were caught between the rival ambitions of the Macedonians and the Romans, but with the defeat of the former at Pydna in 168 B.C., Rome moved to purge any Greek notables whom they suspected they could not trust. Polybius was one of a thousand Greeks sent to Italy for cross-examination, and he remained there for sixteen years without ever being tried or even accused of any crime. He was, however, fortunate to be housed in Rome, where he became close friends with Publius Scipio, son of the Roman general who had defeated the Macedonians at Pydna. Polybius became acquainted with many of Rome's leading families. He accompanied Scipio when he volunteered for service in Spain and also visited north Africa, where he queried the aged king of Numidia about Hannibal. On his return to Italy he detoured through the Alps to see where Hannibal's famous crossing had occurred nearly seventy years earlier.

Eventually those Achaean detainees who were still alive were allowed to return to Greece, but Polybius returned to Carthage at Scipio's request to witness, if not advise, the Romans in their siege of the city. Following the capture and burning of Carthage, he traveled beyond Gibralter and down the coast of Africa. He then returned to Greece and spent two years (146–144 B.C.) acting as an intermediary between the Romans and the Achaeans. When the league was disbanded and Roman troops removed, Polybius began a continuous effort to resolve disputes among the cities. During the last part of his life he visited Alexandria and probably returned to Spain for a time with Scipio. He died at age eighty-two as a result of a fall from a horse. His work influenced, among others, Livy, Plutarch, and Cicero during the Roman era and found a receptive audience at Constantinople. It was not until the fifteenth century, however, that his writings reappeared in Italy, and his discussion of the Roman constitution clearly influenced Machiavelli and, in the eighteenth century, particularly Montesquieu.[37]

Polybius tells us at the very outset why he wrote *The Rise of the Roman Empire:*

> There can surely be nobody so petty or so apathetic in his outlook that he has no desire to discover by what means and under what system of government the Romans succeeded in less than fifty-three years in bringing under their rule almost the whole of the inhabited world, an achievement which is without parallel in human history.[38]

He was particularly interested in enlightening his fellow Greeks as to why and how the vaunted city-state system had come under Roman domination. This work should be of interest to students of international relations for at least four reasons. First, Polybius' epistemology, or approach to knowing about the world, sounds quite modern to contemporary scholars. Second, his explanation of the rise of Rome takes into account the relative importance of different causes and external and internal factors; it is, in the language of contemporary international relations theory, a multilevel approach. Third, more so than any other writer discussed in this book, Polybius addressed the role of fate or chance in aiding or frustrating the political and military designs of leaders. Finally, he has contributed to both the realist and pluralist images of international relations.

Epistemology

Thucydides provided Polybius a model for historical research. This is clear from the criticism Polybius directs toward Timaeus and other historians who wrote after the time of Thucydides. Consistent with Thucydides, Polybius states that his purpose is "to write a history of actual events"—"not so much to give pleasure to my readers as to benefit those who devote their attention to history." To Polybius the best education for dealing with the vicissitudes of life comes from the study of serious history. In the opening statement of the work, Polybius emphasizes that his efforts are intended also to be policy relevant: "Mankind possesses no better guide to conduct than the knowledge of the past."[39]

Polybius lays out in some detail his views on the appropriate epistemological assumptions historians should adopt and the scholarly norms to which they should adhere. For him, history is much more than a collection of facts—explanation is the goal. He asserts that "the mere statement of a fact, though it may excite our interest, is of no benefit to us." It is only when "knowledge of the cause is added" that "the study of history becomes fruitful."[40] A theorist in the present-day meaning of the term, he contends "that by far the most important part of historical writing lies in the consideration of the consequences of events, their accompanying circumstances, and above all their causes." Aside from explanation for its own sake, better prediction may also result. When we can "draw analogies between parallel circumstances of the past and of our own times," we may be able "to make forecasts as to what is to happen." At the very least, "comparing and evaluating" these "parallel occurrences" provides "a far more reliable general picture than is possible if everything is judged in isolation."[41] Such thoughts on how we understand or know about politics in general—or international relations in particular—seem rather commonplace today. However, this is because writers such as Polybius and Thucydides made causal explanation and prediction their principal tasks and their example was followed.

Polybius also addresses the empirical research enterprise itself and favors original or what we might call field research. Confining oneself to documentary or library sources is not enough. Although it "demands much greater exertion and expense," he favors "personal investigation" and use of original and what we now refer to as primary sources. According to Polybius, it is "the business of making first-hand inquiries which is the historian's most important duty." Moreover, as much as is humanly possible one must be an impartial observer: "Now in other spheres of human life we should perhaps not rule out such partiality. A good man ought to love his friends and his country, and should share both their hatreds and their loyalties. But once a man takes up the role of the historian he must discard all considerations of this kind."[42] While Polybius is addressing historians directly, in a broader sense he is addressing all theorists who attempt to explain what they observe and test their propositions or hypotheses with evidence derived from empirical data.

Not surprisingly, it follows that Polybius considers accuracy and honesty as imperatives in the scholarly enterprise. More specifically, he condemns plagiarists who "commit the disreputable act of claiming as one's own what is really the work of others." Beyond giving credit where it is due, telling the truth about what one observes is essential. In this regard, he notes "that there are two kinds of falsehood, the one being the result of ignorance and the other intentional." Although we may "pardon those who depart from the truth through ignorance," we must "unreservedly condemn those who lie deliberately." Unintentional error "deserves kindly correction," whereas deception warrants "outright condemnation!" Indeed, as a general caveat, Polybius advises readers of history to be critical and cautions them "not to be misled by the authority of the author's name, but to pay attention to the facts."[43]

Explanation

In developing explanations, Polybius argues that one should differentiate "causes" from "beginnings" and "pretexts," distinctions reminiscent of Thucydides' "underlying" versus "immediate" causes of war. Polybius is principally interested in causes, which he defines as "those events which influence in advance our purposes and decisions, that is to say our conceptions of things, our state of mind, our calculations about them and the whole process of reasoning whereby we arrive at decisions and undertakings." The examples he gives of these three terms come from the war between Antiochus and the Romans. The cause of the war was "the anger felt by the Aetolians," the pretext for war was "the so-called liberation of Greece," and the beginning of the war was "Antiochus' descent upon Demetrias."[44]

Of interest to us here, of course, is not so much the correctness of the particular analysis as the way in which Polybius framed the question—differentiating causes from beginnings and pretexts. In order to do this effectively, one must take a longer view of history that contains antecedent causes.[45] In focusing only on "particular episodes" at the expense of the longer view one also runs the risk of being driven "by sheer lack of subject-matter to exaggerate the importance of trivial incidents and to write at length on matters which are scarcely worth mentioning at all."[46]

Polybius is also sensitive to what present-day international relations theorists call the level of analysis problem. What unit should one study? Does one focus on the whole or on the parts that make up the whole? How does one relate the general to the specific? In a particularly insightful passage, he notes how a "grasp of the whole is of great service in enabling us to master the details, while at the same time some previous acquaintance with the details helps us towards the comprehension of the whole."[47] This is a very clear expression of the dynamic relation between theory building and data gathering. Even more to the point, Polybius treats the occurrences he observes as part of "an organic whole: the affairs of Italy and of Africa are connected with those of Asia and Greece" and are all part of a larger causal explanation.[48] If one overlooks these relations and interrelations, explanation cannot be complete.

Following from the above, it is apparent that Polybius recognizes the importance of factors in the external environment that surrounds an empire, city-state, or other political unit. But domestic factors are also central to his explanation. He contends that "in all political situations we must understand that the principal factor which makes for success or failure is the form of a state's constitution." Thus, Rome's success in the wars with Carthage was related to "the perfection and strength of the Roman constitution," a position also taken by Titus Livy, the Roman historian.[49] Rome's "constitution contributed very largely not only to the restoration of Roman rule over the Italians and the Sicilians, but also to the acquisition of Spain, to the recovery of Cisalpine Gaul, and finally to the victorious conclusion of the war with Carthage and to the idea of attaining dominion of the whole world."[50]

Cohesiveness of a political unit—also emphasized by Herodotus and Thucydides—can be particularly enhanced if the constitution correctly allocates political power. In the case of Rome, "the result is a union which is strong enough to withstand all emergencies. . . . For whenever some common external threat compels the three [senate, consuls, and the people] to unite and work together, the strength which the state then develops becomes quite extraordinary." For Polybius, lack of unity is a particular problem for the Greeks, given numerous threats from foreign forces. One can hear Machiavelli when Polybius argues that "every state relies for its preservation on two fundamental qualities, namely bravery in the face of the enemy, and harmony among its citizens." When the customs, laws, and constitution are good, security is enhanced both internally and externally. Two other points emphasized by Polybius—the danger of placing the security of the state in the hands of mercenary troops and the role of religion as a means of keeping a political unit together—were to be further developed by Machiavelli. Of course, the idea of an integrating myth, if that is the way Polybius and Machiavelli both see religion, is also to be found in Plato's *Republic*.[51]

As for the role of the individual, Polybius leans toward the voluntarism that allows human will to be decisive in his causal explanation. As he argues, "the action of intelligent and far-sighted men" can make a difference, and he approvingly quotes the poet Euripides' saying that "one wise head can outmatch a score of hands."[52] More than 1,600 years later, Machiavelli would adopt essentially the same perspective. The importance Polybius attributes to human volition or choice in determining outcomes is underscored by his remark that it is "the choice of the right moment which controls all human action, and above all the operations of war."[53] Thus, Hannibal's strength as a commander stemmed from "calculating as he did" such that he "accurately plotted from experience the course he should steer." Polybius relates that "Hannibal, who had anticipated how" the Romans "would probably act, gave them neither the time nor respite to concert their plans." By contrast, Polybius criticizes the changes in the character and behavior of King Philip of Macedon that resulted in his loss of goodwill among his allies and the confidence of all Greeks.[54]

Fate

Polybius does not assume that everything is predetermined or the result of fortune or fate. He cautions against viewing outcomes merely "as acts of God." We should engage in causal analysis of "those events whose causes we can discover and give an explanation as to why they happen." Polybius comments that he has "criticized those writers who attribute public events" merely "to the workings of fate and chance" because they have taken the easy way out. It may appear reasonable when dealing with phenomena that are seemingly "impossible or difficult for a mortal man to understand" for one "to escape from the dilemma by attributing them in the work of a god or of chance." Scholars may confront problems that "baffle our intelligence" and confound our efforts "to discover any rational cause." In short, the "answer must remain in doubt" only "where it is impossible or difficult to establish a cause."[55]

At the same time, Polybius admits that some events seem to be affected by chance, if not fate. He starts his manuscript by referring to "the vicissitudes of Fortune" and "the element of the unexpected" in human events.[56] Much as Machiavelli would do centuries later, Polybius relates how some choose "to leave it to Fortune to decide whom she would honor." One particular turn of events may well "have been expressly designed by Fortune to demonstrate her power to mankind in general," and to underscore the fact that "we are no more than mortal men, and we should at all times make due allowance for the unexpected, and especially in time of war."[57] Fortune is "like a good umpire" who can bring about "an unexpected change in the context." For example, Polybius observes how "the first war which was fought between Rome and Carthage for the possession of Sicily" was profoundly influenced by "decisive changes of Fortune."[58] One can see clearly the influence of Polybius on Machiavelli's development of *fortuna* as a key concept in his own work.

In identifying causes for the events or outcomes he observes, therefore, Polybius tries to strike a balance between voluntarist explanations that depend on human volition or choice and determinist formulations in which events or outcomes are produced by external factors seemingly beyond the capability of individuals to control or affect significantly. Polybius adds a normative element by suggesting that as individuals we ought to control what can be controlled and accept what cannot:

> Human nature is always fallible, and to meet with some unpredictable mishap is not the fault of the victim, but rather of ill fortune, or of those who have inflicted it on him. But when we err with our eyes open and involve ourselves in great tribulations through sheer lack of judgement, then everyone agrees that we have nobody to blame but ourselves. It follows therefore that if a people's failures are due to ill-fortune, they will be granted pity, pardon and assistance, but if to their own folly, then all men of sense will blame and reproach them.[59]

Notwithstanding the presence of fortune as a confounding factor, Polybius does not abandon his effort to explain the rise of the Roman Empire in just half a century, the wars between Rome and Carthage, or lesser events such as the successes of King Philip of Macedon and the Achaean League over the Aetolian League. Whether his cause–effect analyses were correct or not, the important point is that he rejects as "inadequate explanation" any approach that relegates cause merely to the "work of chance." He argues forcefully that "we must rather seek a cause, since no chain of events, whether expected or unexpected, can reach its conclusion without a cause."[60] Putting aside David Hume's eighteenth-century empiricist critique of causality as purely abstract or metaphysical (after all, who has ever seen a cause?), it would be difficult to find in the ancients any clearer statement of the starting assumption for those engaged in international relations or other social science theorizing. We assume there are causes for what we observe and then seek to find them.

Realism and Pluralism

There is little doubt that the work of Polybius is well within the realist tradition. In his critique of the Athenian constitution, Polybius uses a ship as a metaphor for the state and emphasizes the importance of unitary and effective leadership in order to avoid instability and to keep the ship on course. In international relations, states "always reckon friendship or hostility in terms of advantage." Although one may enhance security by seeking allies, security is established most reliably when city-states do "not look to others for their safety, but [choose] to defend their cities and their territory with their own hands."[61] It is what in our own time has been termed a self-help system; one way or another, states provide for their own defense. Comments Polybius makes on spies, traitors, and treachery in international relations clearly influenced Machiavelli. Deception—when a leader is "obliged to act and speak in public in a way which was quite inconsistent with his real intention"—is another familiar and recurrent theme in realist thought.[62]

As has been discussed previously, Polybius places considerable emphasis on how a favorable constitution enhances the capabilities of a city-state or empire in relation to other political units, and his concern for political stability strikes a responsive chord in readers with a realist persuasion. Though it is a secondary or subordinate theme to realism, elements of pluralist thought can also be found in Polybius. The portrayal of Rome's constitution as a balance among the executive (Consul), legislature (Senate), and the people may not be entirely accurate because Polybius tended to idealize things Roman. Polybius is similar to Aristotle and other Greek writers in his advocacy of a mixed constitution that blends elements of kingship, aristocracy, and democracy. His discussion of the adverse forms of one-man rule (tyranny), minority rule (oligarchy), and mob rule, as well as the idea that there are cyclical shifts in constitutional type, are all consistent with mainstream ancient Greek thought.[63] What was new and what would be adopted by Montesquieu and others who followed was the idea of checks and balances among the branches of government. One hears Montesquieu (or James Madison in *The Federalist Papers*) in these words of Polybius:

> Whenever one of the three elements swells in importance, becomes overambitious and tends to encroach upon the others, it becomes apparent for the reasons given above that none of the three is completely independent, but that the designs of any one can be blocked or impeded by the rest, with the result that none will unduly dominate the others or treat them with contempt. Thus the whole situation remains in equilibrium since any aggressive impulse is checked, and each estate is apprehensive from the outset of censure from the others.[64]

Beyond its domestic application, one finds here an exposition of the logic of balance of power, which would be applied by later realists to the relations among states.

Although Polybius' idea of checks and balances was framed in a purely domestic context, his discussion of democratic ideas was also an important part of the corpus of ancient Greek political thought that would provide a foundation for liberal and pluralist formulations of both domestic and world politics during the Enlightenment of the seventeenth and eighteenth centuries. Consistent with Aristotle, Polybius sees human beings as social by nature. In particular, his version of the state of nature anticipates later use of the same metaphor (however different their interpretations) by such social contract theorists as Hobbes, Locke, and Rousseau to explain politics within a state or among states internationally. In looking for "the origins of a political society" he turns first to a state of nature composed of primitive human beings "herding together like animals and following the strongest and the bravest as their leaders." At a later stage of societal development (and because humans "differ from the other animals in that they are the only creatures to possess the faculty of reasoning"), the choice of rulers is not due any more to physical strength so much as to "the merits of their judgment and the power of their reasoning."[65] The important point for democratic theory and the liberal or pluralist perspective is that the choice of leaders is made by the people and the legitimacy of rulers stems from that process. Unless the people become dissatisfied, they are the ones who "ensure that the supreme power remains in the hands not only of the original leaders but of their descendants" as well.[66] To Polybius, although he is vague on precisely how they perform the role, the people are the ultimate check— a rather modern idea, indeed.

Market-oriented values—a normative economic orientation usually associated with liberal and pluralist thought on domestic and international political economy—are mentioned as characteristic of the inhabitants of the Mediterranean island of Crete:

> Their laws permit the citizen to acquire land without any restriction—the sky is the limit, as the saying is—and money is held in such high regard among them that the possession of it is regarded as not merely necessary, but also as most honourable. And indeed, avarice and greed are so much ingrained in the Cretan character that they are the only people in the world who consider no form of gain to be shameful.[67]

Because Polybius singles out the Cretans, it is clear that such notions, if not unique, were by no means universal, or even widespread. (Not until more recent centuries would work and commercial values—what Max Weber referred to as the Protestant ethic—become universalized.) Nevertheless, commerce was extensive among the ancient civilizations throughout the Mediterranean area. Indeed, an important provision in the Rome–Carthage treaty that followed the first Punic War was an agreement to establish normal trade relations.[68]

Commerce contributed in the long run to the development of broader conceptions of society beyond the borders of a given city-state or empire. Polybius comes close to developing such a concept when he refers to the development of such democratic values as "equality and freedom of speech" within the Achaen League and their successful transfer to various Greek city-states. He observes that these values spread because of a common "sense of humanity and of equality" that are "the foundation and the prime cause of the harmony which prevails in the Peloponnese, and hence of its prosperity."[69] Though only a glimmer in the writings of Polybius, this was an important theme that would be developed by others through the centuries. With the expansion of the Roman Empire, writers began to speculate on what are known today as transnational phenomena and the necessity to develop a set of universal values that can serve to unite disparate peoples.

Conclusion

The contributions made by Plato and Aristotle to thinking about international relations have been, at best, indirect. Their major impact has derived from four aspects of their work: their interest in thinking systematically about politics, Plato's analysis of the relation between power and justice, Aristotle's discussion of economics, and their inspiration to later theorists who have investigated the relation between the nature of a state and its foreign policy behavior. Even in their own time, however, they had an uphill struggle against prevailing attitudes, as exemplified by the Sophists who separated politics from morality and viewed the state as a mere convention, not in accordance with nature.

As for Polybius, it is apparent that his discussion of constitutions owes much to the classification devised by Plato, and he shares with Aristotle an interest in empirical observation and understanding causation. But he differed significantly from both Plato and Aristotle in his view of the purpose of the state. While his two predecessors argued that the ultimate purpose of the city-state was to make individuals virtuous and fulfill their potential as human beings, Polybius had a much more modest goal—political stability. By the time in which he was living, the *polis* was in demonstrative decline because the debilitating effects of the Peloponnesian War, followed by the military and political hegemony of first Macedonia and then Rome. Polybius did not see the purpose of the state as one of molding good men, and helping them lead a virtuous life. His dispassionate study of power, balanced appraisal of fate and human volition, and interest in the relative importance of internal and external factors to explain a state's power and status in the world means Polybius has more in common with Thucydides and such later theorists as Machiavelli than he does with Plato and Aristotle.[70]

Notes

1. Donald Kagan, *The Fall of the Athenian Empire* (Ithaca, N.Y.: Cornell University Press, 1987), 416–17.

2. "Alexander III," *Encyclopedia Britannica*, vol. 1 (Chicago: William Benton, 1973), 571–76.

3. See Peter Green, *Alexander to Actium: The Historical Evolution of the Hellenistic Age* (Berkeley: University of California Press, 1990).

4. Desmond Lee, introduction to Plato's *The Republic* (London: Penguin Books, 1955, 1987), 11–17.

5. Plato, *The Republic*, I:2: note 2, 104. Glaucon goes on to note that "no man is just of his own free will, but only under compulsion, and . . . he will always do wrong when he gets the chance."

6. II:2. In *The Laws*, however, Plato presents a different view of primitive man and his circumstances "after the flood," one which emphasizes man's innocence. Except for a few people at the early stages, there was enough food and clothing and "they were not intolerably poor, nor driven by poverty to quarrel with each other. . . . These men were *good* [and] innocent of the techniques of warfare peculiar to city-life." This image of what could be termed a state of nature is closer to Rousseau's than to Hobbes's. Plato, *The Laws*, trans. Trevor J. Sanders (London: Penguin Books, 1970, 1986), III:4.

7. Plato, *The Republic*, II:2, 3. Aristotle tends to disagree with this last statement: "Some say that to feel friendly at the sight of familiar faces and fierce at the approach of strangers is a requirement for the Guardians. . . . But what he [Plato] says about harshness to strangers is, I think, quite wrong; one ought not to behave thus to anyone, and fierceness is not a mark of natural greatness of mind except towards wrongdoers." Aristotle, *The Politics*, trans. T.A. Sinclair (London: Penguin Books, 1962, 1981), VII:7.

8. Plato, *The Laws*, XII.

9. XII.

10. Plato, *The Republic*, VIII:1–9.

11. I:3.

12. Plato, *Gorgias*, trans. Walter Hamilton (London: Penguin Books, 1960, 1988), 78–79.

13. *History of the Peloponnesian War*, V:89–90. As the Athenians go on to state: "This is no fair fight, with honor on one side and shame on the other. It is rather a question of saving your lives and resisting those who are far too strong for you." V:101.

14. Kagan, *The Great Dialogue*, 201.

15. Plato, *Gorgias*, 132.

16. T.A. Sinclair, introduction to *The Politics*. As an example of Aristotle's later influence, in a sentiment that would be repeated, although in modified form, by Machiavelli some two millennia later, the monarchical ruler needs to "give the impression of dignity, not of harshness, of being the kind of person who inspires not fear but respect in those who meet him." Of course, "this is not easy if he is readily despised." In such circumstances, when "he cannot manage to cultivate any of the other virtues, he should aim at least at valour in warfare, and establish for himself a military reputation." V:vi.

17. I:ii. There is a hint, however, of the idea of the social contract when Aristotle notes: "The point is that if a constitution is to have a good prospect of stability, it must be such that all sections of the state accept it and want it to go on in the same way as before." II:ix.

18. While much of this is found in *The Politics*, unfortunately only one such complete study survives. See *The Athenian Constitution* (London: Penguin Books, 1984, 1987).

19. Aristotle, *The Politics*, III:vii–ix.

20. V:vii, v, vi.

21. See, for example, Peter Gourevitch, *Politics in Hard Times: Comparative Responses to International Economic Crises* (Ithaca, N.Y.: Cornell University Press, 1986); Theda Skocpol, *States and Social Revolutions: A Comparative Analysis of France, Russia, and China* (London: Cambridge University Press, 1979).

22. Aristotle, *The Politics*, II:vi. Similarly, Aristotle criticizes Phaleas's ideal constitution for "disregarding, as he ought not to do, relations with neighboring and other foreign states." II:vii.

23. VII:ii.

24. III:xv; VII:viii.

25. VII:xi.

26. VIII:v, vi. See Halford Mackinder, *Democratic Ideals and Reality* (New York: Norton, 1962); Alfred Thayer Mahan, *The Influence of Seapower upon History, 1660–1783* (Boston: Little, Brown, 1897); James Fairgrieve, *Geography and World Power* (New York: Dutton, 1921); Nicholas J. Spykman, *American's Strategy in World Politics* (New York: Harcourt, Brace Jovanovich, 1942). For more recent efforts developed in the context of "long-cycles" theory, see George Modelski, ed., *Exploring Long Cycles* (Boulder, Col.: Lynne Rienner, 1987) and George Modelski and William R. Thompson, *Seapower in Global Politics, 1494–1993* (London: The Macmillan Press, 1988).

27. Aristotle, *The Politics*, III:ix.

28. IV:viii, ix, xi.

29. VII:x.

30. VII:ix.

31. IV:iii.

32. I:iii.

33. II:v.

34. I:x.

35. I:ix.

36. IV:xvi.

37. Introduction by F.W. Walbank to Polybius, *The Rise of the Roman Empire*, trans. Ian Scott-Kilvert (London: Penguin Books, 1979), 12–15, 35–37.

38. Polybius, *The Rise of the Roman Empire*, I:1.

39. IX:2; I:1.

40. XII:25b.

41. XII:32; III:25b; III:31.

42. XII:25e, 27a; XII:4c; I:14.

43. IX:2; XII:12; III:9.

44. III:6–7.

45. I:12–13.

46. VII:7.

47. III:1.

48. I:3.

49. VI:2, 56–58.

50. III:2.

51. VI:18, 46, 52, 56. Plato, *The Republic*, III:1.

52. Polybius, *The Rise of the Roman Empire*, XXXVI:9; I:35.

53. IX:15.

54. I:47; III:91, 93; VII:11–14.
55. XXXVI:17.
56. I:1.
57. II:2, 4.
58. I:103, 13.
59. II:7.
60. II:38.
61. II:47.
62. XVIII:13–15; II:47.
63. VI:5–10.
64. VI:18.
65. VI:5–6.
66. VI:7.
67. VI:46,
68. III:23–24.
69. II:38.
70. Kagan, *The Great Dialogue*, 266–67.

6

The Roman Empire and the Development of Greco-Roman Thought

oman influence on the development of international relations theory was profound. Writing in a realist tradition already established by the Greeks, Livy's historical work was read closely some fifteen centuries later by Machiavelli. A significant departure from realist premises, however, was the universalism of Stoic thought, a perspective quite influential in the eighteenth and nineteenth centuries among such writers as Immanuel Kant. Instead of a world fractured into mutually exclusive political communities, the Stoics offered an alternative vision of a unity in mankind that would transcend the borders of any city-state or other political unit. To the Stoics, as to pluralist writers centuries later, states and empires were not the only significant actors on the world stage; individuals exercising their will also mattered. Finally, the rule of law among nations, an idea directly traceable to Cicero, would influence Grotius and those who followed him, who looked to international law as a basis for order in international relations.

Historical Context

In his epic poem the *Aeneid*, Virgil (70–19 B.C.) tells how the Romans "wandered as their destiny drove them on from one sea to the next: so hard and huge a task it was to found the Roman people." It was the Roman destiny "to rule Earth's peoples." Rome was "to pacify, to impose the rule of law, to spare the conquered, to battle down the proud."[1] Beyond epic prophecies, any reader interested in the details of the development of the Roman Empire should consult the works of Polybius, Livy, and Plutarch. The Roman authors we discuss in this chapter lived between 106 B.C. and 180 A.D., and it is the nature of the international system to which they reacted that is of principal concern to us.

With the power of Carthage curbed by 201 B.C., the borders of the expanding Roman Empire suffered only occasional challenges. The Hellenistic monarchies to the east were weak, German and barbarian tribes to

Writing About Empire, Imperial and Civil Wars, and World Citizenship: Roman Thinking About International Relations

Date	Historical Developments	Writers and Commentators
B.C.		
753	Legendary date for founding of Rome by Romulus	
500	Roman republic established	
300	Alexander the Great (356–323) establishes Macedonian Empire	
200	Punic wars (264–146) between Rome and Carthage (Tunis), leading to defeat of Carthaginians (Phoenicians) and rise of Rome as empire	Polybius (200–120), a Greek, writes about the Punic wars and the rise of Rome as empire
100	Crassus, Pompey, and Caesar form triumvirate to rule empire (60); Caesar conducts Gallic wars, defeats Pompey in civil war, and emerges as singular leader (48), but is assassinated (44); Augustus is victor over opponents (31) and becomes emperor (27 B.C.–14 A.D.)	Cicero (106–43) writes with the universalism of the Stoics; J. Caesar (100–44) writes of Gallic and civil wars; Virgil (70–19) writes in epic style of Homer on Rome and its new empire; Livy (59 B.C.–17A.D.) writes Roman history
A.D.		
100	Period of Emperors Hadrian (117–38) and Marcus Aurelius (161–180)	Seneca (4 B.C.–65 A.D.) promotes Stoic cosmopolitanism; Paul of Tarsus (Turkey, d. 67 A.D.) advances Stoic universal view in Christianity; Plutarch (45–120) writes political-military biographies; Tacitus (55–117) writes about Roman imperial decline Marcus Aurelius (121–180), a late Stoic, promotes brotherhood of mankind as concept
300	Emperor Constantine (324–337) becomes Christian	St. Augustine (354–430) combines Greco-Roman ideas and Christian theology

the north could threaten the frontiers, and the emergent Parthian Empire beyond the Euphrates was watched with suspicion. To the west in Spain, southern Gaul, and Liguria, there was no organized state that could pose an effective challenge to Rome. As a result, following the defeat of Philip of Macedon, the major security preoccupations of Rome were to keep various tribes, states, and kingdoms within its sphere of influence under control and to guard the rather fluid borders of the empire. It is not surprising that Polybius, who died in 120 B.C., was so enamored of the rapid rise of Rome to imperial status.

Domestically, despite Polybius' characterization of a balance of power among the consuls, Senate, and people, the aristocrats in the Senate had effective control of the government. In 133 B.C., however, a tribune by the name of Gracchus challenged senatorial government when he proposed a bill that would distribute parcels of public land to the lower classes. The movement met with enough success—and enough aristocratic resistance—that within a century populist leaders came to the fore, leading to the triumvirate of Crassus, Pompey, and Julius Caesar and eventually to the civil war of 49 B.C. It was during this period that Cicero (106–43B.C.) made his mark as politician and historian, and the events he witnessed played a major role in his analyses.

Despite the assassination of Caesar by his opponents in the Senate in 44 B.C., Rome continued to enjoy military and political successes. After the period of turmoil and civil war, Augustus, the new "Caesar," assumed power in 27 B.C. By the time of his death in 14 A.D., he had managed to consolidate much of the empire and avoid a recurrence of civil war—no small achievement. It was during his reign that Titus Livy wrote much of his history of the Roman empire. In addition to less well known Roman emperors who succeeded Augustus, all of the other authors under consideration in this chapter—Seneca (4 B.C.–65 A.D.), Plutarch (45–120 A.D.), and Marcus Aurelius (121–180 A.D.)—lived during the reign of one or more of such diverse personalities as Tiberius (14–37 A.D.), Caligula (37–41 A.D.), Claudius (41–54 A.D.), Nero (54–68 A.D.), Trajan (98–117 A.D.), and Hadrian (117–138 A.D.). Marcus Aurelius, of course, was himself emperor from 161–180 A.D. All, to varying degrees, either expanded the empire, strengthened its frontiers, or put down revolts.

The term empire is derived from the Latin word *imperium,* and indeed the greatest empire of the ancient western world was certainly that of Rome. Roman administration of the various parts of the empire varied, with some provinces under the direct control of the emperor through proconsuls, others designated as senatorial provinces, and still others treated as client states. For two centuries beginning with Augustus, the Roman Empire provided internal stability, two common languages (Latin and Greek), and aided in the dissemination of Greek and eastern culture to western Europe. It was within such an international system that the authors under consideration in this chapter lived and worked.[2]

The teachings of Plato and Aristotle were an inadequate guide to this new age of territorially expansive bureaucratic empires. A new philosophy was required. It should be one that could provide a basis for individual action, now that the spiritual sustenance and intimate ties of the city-state were no longer available, but also could relate the individual to the world at large. The Macedonian and Roman empires housed a wide variety of peoples with different ethnic, religious, and political traditions. Hence the size and anonymity of empire required a subject to develop a philosophy that was self-sustaining at the level of the individual, but also allowed that individual to relate to the polyglot world of empire. No longer could one be content with restricting one's interests to the communal world of the city-state or even the Hellenic world. A more cosmopolitan outlook was required.

In the remainder of this chapter we first examine the thinking of Greek and Roman Stoics and their philosophical conception of the world. This is followed by a discussion of Livy's historical works on the Roman Empire and Plutarch's analysis of noble Greek and Roman lives. Despite their differences, all of these authors shared an interest in political communities that transcend the small city-state and the somewhat insular ancient Greek international system. This interest produced works that contributed, however indirectly, to the development of thinking about international relations.

The Greek Stoics

As noted, although militarily and politically in decline by the fourth century B.C., the Greek world continued to exert its cultural influence. A process of Hellenization of the "barbarians" continued for several centuries and transmitted Greek values to a wider audience. At the same time, the rise of bureaucratic empires increased individual mobility and allowed people of different regions and backgrounds to settle in Greece and infuse aspects of their own cultures into the Hellenic world. The best example of this cross-fertilization involved the philosophical school of thought known as Stoicism, founded around 300 B.C. by Zeno, a Cypriot of Phoenician background.[3] Although acceptance of one's circumstances and self-reliance are dominant elements in Stoic philosophy as it relates to individuals, its cosmopolitan notion that we are all part of a larger community of mankind is of particular relevance to international relations theory. Stoic ideas were very influential in Rome, and they anticipated the world views of the seventeenth-century Dutch legal writer Hugo Grotius and the nineteenth-century German scholar Immanuel Kant. Stoic philosophy is at the core of contemporary pluralist thought that sees the world as made up not only of states, but also of individuals, groups, and other nonstate actors who can influence events.

Stoicism did not develop a theory of the state or of state action. Rather, the emphasis was on the individual, not as a member of an organized political unit as was the case with Plato and Aristotle, but as an independent actor. Stoicism required the individual not to worship the laws or customs of one's political community, but rather to attempt to live in accordance with nature. The Stoic conception of nature was not that of Greek mythology, involving the antics of the gods. To the Stoics, nature involves certain goals and principles and processes by which these goals and principles are to be attained, with the supreme good being to lead a life of "virtue." It should be the duty of each individual to live according to nature and achieve in one's own life the harmony found in nature itself. In order to secure this good life, an individual must attempt to reduce elements of chance and circumstance.

According to the Stoics, the ability to reason is a quality shared by all humans. Reason was viewed as a divine spark, reflecting the God within us. Indeed, God was viewed as the author of these laws of nature and of the universe.[4] This universal ability to reason, plus the fact that laws of nature are of universal applicability, result in a Stoic emphasis on the equality of people and on what unites them as opposed to what divides them, whether those divisions be geographic, cultural, or political.

This emphasis on equality and the unity of humanity, which parallels later Christian thought, differs dramatically from Aristotle's view of the laws of nature. He, for example, did not see equality inherent in the laws of nature, as evidenced by his observations on the subordination of women to men in the city-states, slaves to citizens, and barbarians to the Hellenes as a whole. Similarly, although Thucydides was not a political philosopher and did not discuss laws of nature, the Stoic emphasis on the equality and unity of humanity is starkly at odds with the political world Thucydides depicted in the *History of the Peloponnesian War*. His narrative illustrated that even the common cultural heritage of the Greeks could not prevent the dynamics of interstate competition from leading to interstate war. Furthermore, in Thucydides' account, basic human nature is not cast in a particularly flattering light. The Corcyraen civil war, for example, was the result of a "love of power," "greed," and "personal ambition," with much of the destruction the result of a desire to settle personal scores. Similar civil wars led to a "general deterioration of character throughout the Greek world"— a comment reflecting Thucydides' view that civilization is a thin veneer covering more base human instincts that always threaten to burst through the surface.[5]

The Stoics, however, believed it was possible for human beings to discern through reason the laws of nature and live in accordance with them. To an extent, nature determines the course of an individual's life, but an individual has a certain amount of free will as well. Hence the Stoic philosophical tradition, as with other philosophies and religions, balances aspects of determinism and voluntarism. This is in contrast with Plato's notion in *The Republic* that what an individual does in life is almost wholly determined by heredity and environment, with the state playing a critical role in the socialization process.

The Stoic emphasis on the unity and equality of mankind had obvious political implications if one accepted the philosophical notion that the world is held together by laws of nature that transcend the laws of any

MAP II. *The Roman Empire*

Dacia

Upper Moesia

Lower Moesia

Thrace

Byzantium

Bithynia

Armenia Minor

Macedonia

Pergamum

Asia

Galatia

Cappadocia

Cilicia

Antioch

Syria

Epirus

Achaea

Cyprus

Damascus

Crete

Palestine

Jerusalem

Alexandria

Arabia

Cyrenaica

Memphis

Arsinoe

Oxyrhunchus

Hermopolis

Antinoopolis

econd Century A.D.

particular king or emperor. At best, manmade laws were derived from the laws of nature. Furthermore, the Stoics raised an issue that is debated to the present day: If everyone is part of humanity, to what extent do we have obligations to humanity as a whole as opposed to the more narrowly defined political community in which we live?

We can also credit the Stoics with one of the earliest secular justifications for a world state. Zeno wrote a tract that attacked Plato's *Republic* and the idea that an individual state should strive for the attainment of Plato's ideal community. Rather, the ideal state was a world state with universal citizenship and one system of law based on reason, as opposed to custom and convention. Again, the Stoic emphasis was on what unites humanity, not what divides it. Laws of nature bound the world together, transcending the laws of any particular state or empire. Through reason these laws could be known and provide a basis for the harmonious conduct of relations among disparate political communities until such time as reason might lead political leaders to create a world state.

Cicero and the Roman Stoics

Roman authors continued writing in the Greek tradition. Although Stoicism had its roots in the thought of Zeno and other late Greek writers of lesser renown, it was the Romans who developed these ideas and put them into practice within the empire. The writings of Cicero and the Stoics—Seneca and the emperor Marcus Aurelius—reflected central ideas in Roman thought. The organizing principle by which Rome managed imperial affairs was a universal image of mankind that transcended the boundaries of city-states and other small political units. Thus, Seneca, though born in Spain, could be a prominent Roman citizen. The same, of course, was true for St. Paul (Paul of Tarsus in Asia Minor), an early Jewish convert to Christianity. The catholicism of this new religion—open to all human beings regardless of origin—conformed to the universalism present in Roman thought even as it was a departure from the Judaic and other traditions that tended to support more exclusive communities. Because of his missionary work among non-Jewish peoples, Paul is often credited with assuring this "Romanization" of early Christianity.

Beyond the idea of common citizenship within the empire, for practical reasons considerable autonomy was given to local rulers in a time when transportation and communications within such a far-flung realm were difficult at best. At the same time, Stoic ideas provided legitimacy for such an approach. As the Roman Empire expanded its territorial scope, so did ideas central to Greco-Roman thought. Indeed, Roman legal precepts went well beyond laws binding only on residents of particular political communities. The idea of natural law *(jus naturale)* as well as of law commonly binding on all peoples (the *jus gentium*) were important Roman contributions that had profound influence on Western political thought in succeeding centuries.

Cicero

The orator and writer Marcus Tullius Cicero or, more commonly, Cicero, is one of the few philosophers to have attained high political rank—in his case, as consul of the Roman Republic. Son of a knight and educated in Rome and Greece, he served in the military and then made a reputation for himself as a lawyer. The age in which he lived was one of domestic turmoil, intrigue, and upheaval. In 91–89 B.C. economic devastation was wrought by the struggle between Rome and its neighboring allies, who demanded citizenship and the attendant privileges. Once this struggle ended, civil war broke out, and in 84 B.C. the military commander Sulla marched on Rome and seized power. Domestic unrest, including the slave revolt led by Spartacus, occupied the Senate and various rulers, including Cicero, who was elected consul in 63 B.C. By then a young senator, Julius Caesar, had gained a reputation as a popular leader, and in 60 B.C. he formed a triumvirate with Pompey and Crassus. Cicero had declined to join this political alliance and went into exile. He returned in 57 B.C. and agreed to align himself with the triumvirate, but turned to scholarship and completed *The Republic* in 52 B.C.

The power-sharing formula did not last, and in 49 B.C. Caesar crossed the river Rubicon with his veterans from the Gallic Wars. This second civil war consumed the entire empire, and after Caesar's assassination in 44 B.C., Cicero hoped to make political use of Octavian, Caesar's adopted son. However, he underestimated and offended Octavian. Following the formation of a triumvirate of Octavian, Lepidus, and Marc Antony, Cicero was arrested and killed, and his head and hands were placed on public display in Rome.[6]

Although rarely read today, Cicero greatly influenced the works of later writers, particularly up until the end of the eighteenth century. Machiavelli closely studied Cicero because of the Florentine's interest in republicanism, ancient Rome, and civic virtue. Cicero was revered by Jean Bodin and studied by Hugo Grotius, the father of international law. While Thomas Hobbes rejected Cicero's republicanism and support of mixed constitutions, the Englishman acknowledged his debt to Cicero in the introduction to his 1629 translation of the *History of the Peloponnesian War*. John Locke considered Cicero among the "truly great men." Such praise peaked during the eighteenth-century enlightenment. Voltaire, Montesquieu, and Diderot were all admirers, as were David Hume, Adam Smith, Edmund Burke, and Thomas Jefferson.[7]

Cicero was influenced profoundly by the ancient Greek writers. His major political works, *De Re Publica (The Republic)* and *De Legibus (The Laws)*, can be viewed as attempts to interpret Roman history in terms of Greek political theory. He even follows Plato's sequence of first writing about the ideal state and then turning to an ideal set of laws. Cicero also takes from Polybius directly (and Aristotle before him) the idea of a mixed constitution for the state and favors "a balanced combination of the three forms"—kingship, aristocracy, and democracy.[8] Cicero should be of interest to students of international relations, however, for his observations on three topics: his belief in laws of nature that allowed him to conceive of a community of humankind, his views on state and statecraft, and his observations on justice and war.

Laws of Nature

The influence of Stoic ideas led Cicero to conceive of one world ordered by laws of nature that were discoverable through the application of human reason. Perhaps because of the breadth of his thought, Cicero is not usually categorized as a member of the Stoic school of philosophy, given the more focused scope of its philosophical concern. Nevertheless, the influence of earlier Greek Stoics on Cicero and, in turn, his influence on later Roman Stoics are unmistakable. Cicero's inspiration was the notion that "as one and the same Nature holds together and supports the universe, all of whose parts are in harmony with one another, so men" ought also to be united.[9] Thus, one can speak beyond the civil law of a given commonwealth to a law among nations applicable to humanity as a whole (a *jus gentium*) and to people individually. Cicero proposes that we "conceive of this whole universe as one commonwealth." He refers to "man's fellowship and union with his fellow-men" and describes "citizenship" in a larger community of human beings. There can, therefore, be a law of nations.[10] Indeed, this concept of law common to all of humanity was a powerful idea that would prove central in the development of international law in the late Middle Ages.

Cicero saw law as "the bond which unites the civic association, and the justice enforced by law" as being the same for all.[11] Justice is associated with fairness, but "the origin of Justice is to be found in Law, for Law is a natural force; it is the mind and reason of the intelligent man, the standard by which Justice and Injustice are measured." As with law, one will find "the root of Justice in Nature."[12] According to Cicero, "True law is right reason in agreement with nature." Moreover, true law "is of universal application, unchanging and everlasting." As a part of our lives, law "summons to duty by its commands and averts from wrongdoing by its prohibitions." The universality of law assures that there ought "not be different laws at Rome and at Athens, or different laws now and in the future." Instead, Cicero argues that "one eternal and unchangeable law" should "be valid for all nations and all times."[13] Although some laws may be based on local customs, the law of nations and the laws of particular communities should be in conformity with what nature dictates uniformly.[14]

As noted, Cicero believed that law is based on rational principles and that human reason exercised rightly is the means by which one discovers the law in nature. It is important, however, that law should not be understood merely as "a product of human thought." It is instead "something eternal which rules the whole universe by its wisdom in command and prohibition." It has a divine quality: "This power" of law to compel nations "is not merely older than the existence of nations and States; it is coeval with that God who guards and rules heaven and earth."[15]

Thus, as in Stoicism in general, there is in Cicero a pluralist world view: individuals as well as states matter and law should play an important role in regulating relations among peoples and states. In economics he also takes an individually oriented position. He advocates moderation, saving money, and increasing one's wealth—a perspective, when accompanied by hard work, that would come to be known in Max Weber's work as the Protestant ethic and the spirit of capitalism.[16] Following Plato, Aristotle, and Polybius, who all addressed economic issues, Cicero makes economics, private property in particular, an important component of his political works. He follows the Stoic tradition of viewing the acquisition of wealth and material possessions as a natural activity. Centuries later, Cicero's economic individualism was not without influence on Adam Smith and on the social contract theorists, John Locke in particular.[17]

State and Statecraft

Cicero, however, also contributed to the realist image of international politics. His realism is reflected in two ways: the manner in which he conceptualizes the state, and his advice to statesmen. As we will see in later chapters, initial theorizing about the modern state is generally credited to such writers as Machiavelli, Bodin, Grotius, and Hobbes. Their views on the creation and nature of the state, however, were an expansion of the strain of ancient Greco-Roman thought that used social contract theory to explain and justify the creation of the state. Cicero sounds very modern in that for him the social contract is a result of individuals' natural quest for security. He asserts "that nature has implanted in the human race . . . a desire to defend the common safety." To attain this safety, a "commonwealth" comes into existence by mutual agreement. In Cicero's terms, a commonwealth is "an assemblage of people in large numbers associated in an agreement with respect to justice and a partnership for the common good." A "multitude" becomes "a body of citizens by mutual agreement." In order "to make human life safer and richer by our thought and effort," following our natural impulse we "increase the resources of mankind." As statesmen, we are urged "to increase our resources, to multiply our wealth, to extend our boundaries." Such realist sentiments, however, are tempered with the observation that justice requires us "to consider the interests of the whole human race."[18]

In a theme developed more than 1,500 years later by Sir Thomas More, Cicero argues that the affairs of state are so important that the "wise man," who might like to engage in loftier pursuits than statecraft, still can "not decline the duty if conditions force him to assume it." To Cicero, the noblest use of virtue, defined as "reason completely developed," is service to the "government of the State." Accordingly, one needs to study "this science of politics" if one is to be prepared to serve as a statesman, whenever called.[19] Even the best prepared person, of course, is still confronted by "the uncertainty of future events" and the vagaries of "fortune."[20]

Maintaining domestic order or stability is part of the overall responsibility statesmen have for security of the state. Like Polybius before him and Machiavelli to follow, Cicero sees law and a legal system as central to security. He observes that "laws were invented for the safety of citizens, the preservation of States, and the tranquillity and happiness of human life."[21] According to Cicero, "the two elements which most conspicuously contribute to the stability of a State" are "religion and the spirit of tranquillity."[22] With regard to the latter, Cicero relates how it was possible in Rome's earlier history to quench "the people's ardour for the warlike life to which they had been accustomed." Fighting enemies abroad is thus not necessary for domestic unity to prevail. Popular passions can be turned toward "markets, games, and all sorts of occasions for the gathering of large numbers." The net effect of these measures in the earlier Roman experience was to turn "toward benevolence and kindliness the thought of men who had become savage and brutish through their passion for war."[23]

Notwithstanding Cicero's intellectual orientation toward humanity as a whole, he acknowledges that for a particular state external influences may not be altogether salutary. It is a matter of fact to Cicero that a "certain corruption and degradation of morals" may stem from foreign influences. Maritime cities are particularly vulnerable in this regard, "for they receive a strange mixture of strange languages and customs, and import foreign ways as well as foreign merchandise, so that none of their ancestral institutions can possibly remain unchanged." Beyond crossing "the seas merely to gain knowledge and to visit other countries"—a cosmopolitan view—statesmen look abroad with the "more important task of defending our native land" from external danger.[24]

Justice and War

Just as law is critical to the maintenance of domestic stability, war should be subordinate to law. Cicero is the initiator of this important idea in Western political thought. Laying foundations upon which both Augustine and Aquinas would build centuries later, Cicero addresses the relation between justice and war. Cicero's discussion of what would become the just war doctrine is the first-known systematic treatment of this subject. Most present-day references to just war theory that acknowledge its intellectual roots cite Augustine, Aquinas, and Grotius—overlooking Cicero entirely. By contrast, Augustine gives Cicero the credit he is due.

Referring to the "law of war," Cicero claims that "in undertaking, carrying on, and ending a war, justice and good faith shall be supreme."[25] In other words, law and concern for justice through law apply not only to the decision to go to war (what would become known as the *jus ad bellum*), but also to the conduct of the war itself (the *jus in bello*) and to the restoration of peace. Moreover, war is to be waged for legitimate objectives: "A war is never undertaken by the ideal State, except in defence of its honor or its safety." Unjust wars are those "undertaken without provocation" because "only a war waged for revenge"—redress for having been wronged—"or defence can actually be just."[26] Moreover, just wars are waged by legitimate authorities: "The State shall have its official interpreters" of the law of war to guide its conduct and "no war is considered just unless it has been proclaimed and declared" by State authorities. Once declaring war, the authorities "shall wage just wars justly." Accordingly, because their orders are presumed to be just, commanders may expect absolute obedience from their troops on the battlefield. Finally, there are legal provisions for the diplomacy of both war and peace.[27]

Seneca and Marcus Aurelius

Like Cicero, both Seneca and Marcus Aurelius were statesmen and philosophers. Born in Cordoba, Spain at about the same time as Christ, Seneca was the son of an imperial procurator or commissioner for Rome. As a young man Seneca spent several years in Egypt where he gained experience in administration and finance. After studying law he entered the political scene in Rome, and when Caligula succeeded Tiberius in 37 A.D., Seneca was a leading figure in the senate and hence was viewed with suspicion by the new emperor. Caligula apparently ordered Seneca to be killed, but one version of the story says a woman close to the throne managed to have the order rescinded by claiming that Seneca, an asthmatic, was close to death from tuberculosis.

In 41 A.D., in the first year of the reign of Claudius, Seneca for unknown reasons again received a sentence of death, which was commuted to banishment on Corsica. This exile lasted eight trying years, whereupon the emperor's new wife, Agrippina, recalled him to Rome. Seneca received a high office and was made tutor to her son, who became the emperor Nero upon

Claudius' death by poisoning. In conjunction with an army officer, Seneca achieved supreme influence in Nero's court. Not surprisingly, he made a number of enemies who, perhaps justifiably, accused him of hypocrisy because of the large gap between his professed Stoic philosophy and his extravagant lifestyle. When he fell out of favor with Nero, Seneca retired from public life and devoted his last three years to philosophy and writing. In 65 A.D. a conspiracy against the emperor was foiled. Although it is not known whether Seneca was one of the plotters, he was ordered to commit suicide, a standard method of imperial execution.

Marcus Aurelius was born in 121 A.D. during the reign of Hadrian. After the death of his parents he was adopted first by a grandfather and then, at age seventeen, by his uncle by marriage, Aurelius Antoninus, who had recently become emperor. Upon the death of Antoninus in 161 A.D., Marcus Aurelius and another son adopted by the emperor ruled jointly. A difficult time for the empire ensued, with famine, plague, floods, and invasions by barbarians. Two years prior to his brother's death, Marcus Aurelius joined the Roman legions on the Danube. Most of the rest of this emperor's life was spent in the field, and during this period he wrote a series of reflections now known as *Meditations*. Marcus Aurelius died of disease in camp in 180 A.D. Because of his variable moods and bouts of melancholia, the emperor did not always meet the standard of the true Stoic, which emphasizes pride and self-sufficiency. Instead, his remarkable modesty seems more an anticipation of the Christian virtue of humility.[28]

We briefly discuss the works of these two writers in the context of three basic topics: the Stoic conceptions of humanity and reason, the state of nature, and the issue of causation and fortune.

Humanity and Reason

Seneca acknowledges the contributions of Zeno as the third-century B.C. founder of the Stoic school, which he describes as "a school with an unequalled record for courageous and saintly living."[29] Seneca is far removed from the realist perspective when he tells us that "the first thing philosophy promises us is the feeling of fellowship, of belonging to mankind and being members of a community" in which we live in conformity with nature. Philosophy is a beacon; it "does not set about constructing arms or walls or anything of use in war. On the contrary, her voice is for peace, calling all mankind to live in harmony." The Stoic concept of humanity, however, goes beyond individual human beings and their relationships. Indeed, "though human beings may perish, humanity in itself—the pattern on which every human being is moulded—lasts on, and while human beings go through much and pass away," humanity "itself remains quite unaffected."[30]

Values, therefore, transcend particular communities and embrace all of humankind. That universals exist and that they are discoverable by the exercise of human reason were powerful ideas that differentiated the Greek and Roman Stoics from the city-state focus of Plato, Aristotle, and other Greeks who wrote more about particular political communities. More important, this perspective influenced later scholars during the Middle Ages and buttressed the idea of universalism that was central to classical liberalism and strategies for universal peace. One can see striking similarities, for example, between the second-century comments of Emperor Marcus Aurelius and the thinking sixteen centuries later of Immanuel Kant. The emperor states:

> If the power of thought is universal among mankind, so likewise is the possession of reason, making us rational creatures. It follows, therefore, that this reason speaks no less universally to us with its "thou shalt" or "thou shalt not." So then there is a world-law; which in turn means that we are all fellow-citizens and share a common citizenship, and that the world is a single city. Is there any other common citizenship that can be claimed for all humanity? And it is from this world-polity that mind, reason, and law themselves derive.[31]

Marcus Aurelius argues in favor of a "community based on equality and freedom of speech for all." He sees individuals naturally as part of a social or human community and deplores the possibility of estrangement from it, of allowing oneself to be cut "off from the whole framework of society." We should always remember our close bond with the rest of mankind—"all of us were born for one another."[32]

The pluralism of his world view, which sees unity despite the wide diversity of individuals, is at odds with Platonic and Aristotelian thinking in which society is highly stratified and peoples beyond Greece are viewed as barbarians. Despite what may appear to be a chaotic universe, order and harmony can exist "when oneness of feeling exists between all parts of nature in spite of their divergence and dispersion." As human beings we enjoy citizenship in a "great world-city."[33] Speaking more personally he observes that

> the interest of every creature lies in conformity with its own constitution and nature. My own nature is a rational and civic one; I have a city, and I have a country; as Marcus I have Rome, and as a human being I have the universe; and consequently, what is beneficial to these communities is the sole good for me.[34]

Hence while Marcus Aurelius may start out with the Platonic assumption that each person should conform to his or her own nature, identity is not defined in class terms nor does it end at the gates of one's city or the borders of one's country—we are all citizens of the world.

State of Nature

How did Seneca and Marcus Aurelius reach such conclusions? As with other writers before and later, Seneca developed an image of the state of nature as the foundation for his political theory. He argued that fellowship has always been natural among human beings. "The first men on this earth . . . and their immediate descendants followed nature unspoiled. . . . It was an age in which the bounties of nature were freely available for the use of all without discrimination." The operative rule in this state of primitive communism was "share and share alike" as human beings enjoyed nature and there was "undisturbed possession of resources owned by the community."[35] One can see Seneca's influence on such seventeenth-century social contract theorists as John Locke and Jean-Jacques Rousseau, who also understood the state of nature as a metaphor with implications for both domestic politics and international relations.

Seneca does not argue that human beings in the state of nature were virtuous, but rather claims that their innocence was a result of ignorance. Because "they lacked the cardinal virtues of justice, moral insight, self-control and courage," they were vulnerable to having their happy world upset. According to Seneca:

> Virtue only comes to a character which has been thoroughly schooled and trained and brought to a pitch of perfection by unremitting practice. We are born for it, but not with it. And even in the best of people, until you cultivate it there is only the material for virtue, not virtue itself.[36]

For his part, Marcus Aurelius sees human beings as motivated to serve the common good. One acts in "regard for the common interest" and in "the service of the community." He exhorts us to "love mankind."[37] There is a glimmer of Rousseau's eighteenth-century concept of the *general will* and the realist concept of the unitary state in the argument that one ought to act consistently with the "general accord" in one's community. Marcus Aurelius contends that

> As a unit yourself, you help to complete the social whole; and similarly, therefore, your every action should help to complete the social life. Any action which is not related directly or remotely to this social end disjoints that life, and destroys its unity. It is as much the act of a schismatic as when some citizen in a community does his utmost to dissociate himself from the general accord.[38]

But particular communities also remain only parts of a larger whole. One needs to understand "the world as a city and himself its citizen." In this cosmopolitan world view, the common good or common interest goes beyond the confines of any given community. We need to "think often of the bond that unites all things in the universe, and their dependence upon one another. All are, as it were, interwoven, and in consequence linked." Indeed, to Marcus Aurelius "mutual integration is a universal principle."[39]

His extensive personal wealth notwithstanding, Seneca in the Aristotelian tradition adopts what could be called an antimarket bias when he asserts that he has "no respect for any study whatsoever if its end is the making of money." To Seneca "there is really only one liberal study that deserves the name—because it makes a person free—and that is the pursuit of wisdom."[40] As with Rousseau, Seneca believed it was the privatization of property that upset the harmony of interest in the state of nature:

> Into this ideal state of things burst avarice, avarice which in seeking to put aside some article or other and appropriate it to its own use, only succeeded in making everything somebody else's property and reducing its possessions to a fraction of its previous unlimited wealth. Avarice brought in poverty.[41]

As a result, human beings now live with "a feeling of insecurity" that contrasts sharply with the earlier happy state of life "in conformity with nature."[42]

In those days "to govern was to serve, not to rule." Wise leaders "kept the peace, protected the weak from the stronger, urged and dissuaded, pointed out what was advantageous and what was not." They were devoted to bringing well-being and prosperity to their subjects. According to Seneca, "That fellowship lasted for a long time intact, before men's greed broke society up." Unfortunately, with the passage of time "avarice and luxury split human beings up and got them to abandon partnership for plunder." He laments "that we can clothe ourselves without importing silks" and "we can have the things we need for our ordinary purposes if we will only be content with what the earth has made available on its surface." Although "we were born into a world in which things were made ready to our hands, it is we who have made everything difficult to come by through our disdain for what is easily come by." One needs to speak out against the love of money and extravagance, and the proper limit to a person's wealth should be restricted to what is essential. Although not a very precise formulation, it nevertheless addresses the distribution of wealth in human society, a theme that would echo in the writings of social contract and classical economic theorists centuries later.[43]

On another question concerning political economy and social justice, Seneca departs sharply from Aristotle's defense of slavery. He condemns slavery and its "harsh and inhuman behavior," specifically the abuse of slaves "as if they were beasts of burden instead of human beings."[44] As noted earlier, in the nineteenth-century, Marx identified slavery as an historically distinct mode of production found in the Egyptian, Greek, Roman, and other ancient societies. Slavery was accepted as a fact of life and thus had legitimacy among the ancients, Aristotle included. By contrast, Seneca diverged from the conventional wisdom of his day. Even if enslaving foreigners and others were a profitable form of ancient political economy, to Seneca it was wrong.

Causation and Fortune

Seneca also made a contribution to epistemology and helped lay the intellectual foundation for the development of the theoretical enterprise. Following Polybius, he argues that causation can be understood as "everything in the absence of which a thing cannot be brought into being"—in other words, those elements necessary for its existence or occurrence. Central to discovery is "the exercise of human reason."[45] Marcus Aurelius adds that "what follows is ever closely linked to what precedes; it is not a procession of isolated events, merely obeying the laws of sequence, but a rational continuity." Human beings have the capacity to reason and thus discover these causal relations.[46]

At the same time, to be human is to live with uncertainty and considerable skepticism about reality. In this regard, Seneca states, "I should find it difficult to say which of these people annoy me most, those who would have us know nothing or the ones who refuse even to leave us the small satisfaction of knowing that we know nothing." Thus, chance is part of the causal equation. One should "always take full note of fortune's habit of behaving just as she pleases, treating her as if she were actually going to do everything it is in her power to do."[47]

Seneca observes how "misfortune has a way of choosing some unprecedented means or other of impressing its power on those who might be said to have forgotten it." Life is fragile and we are all vulnerable to the unexpected. In a striking statement on how misfortune can lead to unanticipated outcomes, he argues:

> Nothing is durable, whether for an individual or for a society. . . . Terror strikes amid the most tranquil surroundings, and without any disturbance in the background to give rise to them, calamities spring from the least expected quarter. States which stood firm through civil war as well as wars external collapse without a hand being raised against them. How few nations have made of their prosperity a lasting thing!
> This is why we need to envisage every possibility and to strengthen the spirit to deal with the things which may conceivably come about. Rehearse them in your mind: exile, torture, war, shipwreck. Misfortune may snatch you away from your country, or your country away from you. . . .
> All the terms of our human lot should be before our eyes; we should be anticipating not merely all that commonly happens, but all that is conceiv-

ably capable of happening. . . . Fortune needs envisaging in a thoroughly comprehensive way.[48]

Aside from anticipating what could happen and preparing for it, Seneca is exhorting individuals to keep on course in the pursuit of ideals, even when confronted by setbacks.[49]

Similar sentiments pervade the writings of Marcus Aurelius, but he is more of an optimist. He notes how human beings can observe "the world of space" and "the world of time." We can expect changes over time in "everything naturally comprehended in the universe." Reason allows us to find patterns. We can "look back over the past, with its changing empires that rose and fell" and, turning to prediction, we "can foresee the future too."[50] Moreover, our rational faculty gives human beings the capacity to control our conduct. Although we are confronted with the uncertainties and the vagaries of chance, human beings retain free will. Not everything is determined for us. It is still a world in which individuals matter and what they do matters. Citing Epictetus, Marcus Aurelius asserts, true to his voluntarist approach, that "the robber of your free will does not exist."[51]

We find in Seneca and Marcus Aurelius, therefore, arguments in favor of the dignity of all individuals that reflect a cosmopolitanism alien to classical Greek thinking and even to many enthusiastic supporters of the Roman Empire who viewed all peoples beyond the borders as barbarians. It is somewhat ironic that such views were held by such worldly men who were intimately involved with the day-to-day machinations of imperial politics. Furthermore, despite their personal fates, their writings exhibit a high degree of voluntarism with respect to counteracting the vagaries of fate and fortune.

Titus Livy

Livy, the most famous of the Roman historians, was born in Padua, Italy, around 59 B.C. We know very little about him, but he made quite a mark on the literary circles of Rome. Apparently Augustus expressed an interest in his work, despite Livy's praise of Pompey, a rival of Augustus. Livy was influenced generally by Polybius, but particularly by Cicero's emphasis on writing in pure Latin and avoiding the debasement of the language that very often occurred in the hands of lesser-known writers. Furthermore, Cicero's works provided guidance on the theory and practice of historical writing, and both Cicero and Livy believed that history should serve as a guide to life. Livy's mammoth *History of Rome* consisted of 142 books, ending with the death of Drusus, brother of the emperor Tiberius, in 9 B.C. Unfortunately only thirty-five of these books survive.[52]

Livy's work is often overlooked, despite the fact that Livy's first ten books were the subject of Machiavelli's *The Discourses*. Livy also influenced both Montesquieu and Rousseau. In a comment similar to an observation Machiavelli would make on the value of reading history, Livy explained his own commitment to such study:

> In history you have a record of the infinite variety of human experience plainly set out for all to see; and in that record you can find for yourself and your country both examples and warnings; fine things to take as models, base things, rotten through and through, to avoid.[53]

At the same time, Livy admits to factual problems in his enterprise, particularly in relation to early Roman history. His account of the founding of Rome by Romulus and Remus, for example, is no more than myth duly recorded by an historian. Indeed, by his own admission, authenticating facts and differentiating these from legends or myths was difficult and, as a result, much of Livy's treatment (particularly of earlier Roman history) is problematic. Livy defends his approach by arguing he "would have spared no effort if there were any way of research arriving at the truth, but, as it is, one must stick to tradition where the antiquity of events makes certainty impossible."[54]

Anticipating Gibbon's *Decline and Fall of the Roman Empire*, Livy sees moral decay as undermining Rome's power position. One needs, he argues, to be concerned with any "general relaxation of the nation's moral fiber." He writes scornfully how "wealth has made us greedy, and self-indulgence has brought us, through every form of sensual excess, to be, if I may so put it, in love with death both individual and collective." He condemns, for example, a Bacchic cult in which "rites were held promiscuously" and "no sort of crime, no kind of immorality was left unattempted." This moral concern pervades the entire work. He deplores the prevalence of sexual promiscuity, murder, plunder, and the like. Livy also makes clear how concerned he is when "might" proves to be "stronger than right."[55] Although in other respects Machiavelli's writings parallel the views of Titus Livy, the two tend to diverge on these normative grounds.

We discuss four of the themes present in Livy's work that are of interest to students of international relations: security and war, fortune and volition, class, and republicanism. The latter topic is of particular interest because his discussion of the virtues of republican forms of government in terms of security is a major theme of Machiavelli's work.

Security and War

Livy's realist concerns are quite evident. He tells us that survival—the safety of the state—has always been the primary goal of Roman leaders. The consul, for example, is "to see to it that the state takes no harm." This may well involve efforts taken "to protect the frontier."[56] Threats to the state may emanate from enemies outside the state, as occurred in 389 B.C. when the Volscians attempted to conquer Rome.[57] Similarly, Livy describes Rome at around 349–348 B.C. as being "caught between two foreign wars at the same time, and worried too by the defection of their allies." In these circumstances, "the Senate realized that those who had not been bound by loyalty must be held down by fear." The consuls had "to exert all their powers of authority to recruit troops; for they must rely on a citizen army when their allies were leaving them."[58] This emphasis on the use of citizens as opposed to mercenaries is also the advice Machiavelli gives in *The Prince* and *The Discourses*.

What are the causes of war? To Livy, war seems to be the product of rational choice. Councils evaluate the pros and cons of going to war and reach a decision. Wars are not so much accidental as they are calculated to achieve certain objectives—a basic realist assumption. Territorial expansion may be the aim. Livy certainly celebrates the grandeur of the Roman Empire, which extended its territory while, at the same time, admitting defeated enemies as citizens. War was the means by which this empire was built. Livy asserts that "so great is the glory won by the Roman people in their wars" that they are entitled to the claim "that Mars himself was their first parent."[59]

Wars between two parties are watched closely by other parties likely to be affected by the outcome. Whether to remain neutral or to take one side or the other thus was of concern to Philip, the king of Macedon, as he observed the progress of war "between the two wealthiest peoples in the world"—Rome and Carthage.[60] In some instances, however, war between two parties may be due to relations with third parties. For example, Livy tells us that "the cause of the war" between Rome and Samnium "came from without and did not arise directly between them." The two went to war as the result of a complex set of entangling alliance commitments, circumstances similar to those prior to the outbreak of the Peloponnesian War as described by Thucydides. Although the factors leading to a decision to go to war may not be subject to control by the separate parties, it nevertheless remains, as realists argue, a deliberative process in which alternatives can be evaluated rationally by the persons involved.[61]

More than most other ancient writers, but consistent with present-day realism, Livy identifies the important economic underpinnings of military capability that contribute to the power of the state. He refers in one passage, for example, to the mobilization of economic capacity by Carthage. "The city itself, with the smiths and artisans of all trades shut up in the state workshops, rang continuously with the sound of warlike preparations." The ability to raise money to finance wars is also important. Resource limitations constrain military options. In deciding what to do about Hannibal and

Carthage, the Romans calculate that "public funds cannot support two separate armies, one in Italy, one in Africa," particularly since "no resources are left for maintaining fleets and furnishing supplies." Stocks of weapons, provisions, and money thus are essential to successful war efforts. So is the availability of manpower, a Roman advantage over Carthage. Livy observes how "the Romans had their own populace and that of Latium to supply a greater and more numerous body of young soldiers continually growing to take the place of their losses, however great." By contrast, "both the city and rural population of Carthage were utterly unwarlike—they were forced to hire mercenaries from the Africans."[62]

For Livy, military service for "the public good" takes precedence over private or personal concerns. To be effective, military units need to exhibit "the soldierly qualities of courage, discipline, and endurance." Fairness and consistency are also essential elements in maintaining military discipline. Certainly one should not act as the general Scipio was accused, perhaps unfairly, of alternately treating "his soldiers with absurd indulgence and extreme brutality." The result, if this allegation were true, was that "almost more men had been lost through mutiny than had been killed in battle."[63]

Favorable geography is obviously also important. In addition "to its possession of a considerably larger body of men of military age" than other places, the city of Oaeneum, for example, was said to be "girdled with natural defences, having on the one side a river, called Artatus, and on the other a very high mountain, a difficult ascent." Population and favorable geography "gave the inhabitants hope for successful resistance" against forces under the command of the warrior Perseus.[64]

Finally, as is also argued by present-day realists, Livy observes how forming alliances can increase one's power, reduce external threats, and enhance security. While, as noted earlier, he sees the pitfall of being drawn into war by alliance commitments, he argues that such arrangements might be required to compensate for a state's relative lack of independent economic or military capability. Seeking support from the Romans, for example, the Campians express what they see as the reciprocal security benefits to both. "Every time the Aequi and Volscians, your City's perpetual enemies, bestir themselves, we shall be on their backs, and what you have done first for our preservation, we shall always do for your empire and glory."[65] Alliances allow for coordination of strategy and pooling of resources.[66]

One occasionally gets the impression that Livy believes war is not necessarily all bad. He attributes to Hannibal, for example, the idea "that a country wasting away and mouldering in idleness would be aroused from its torpor by the clashing of arms."[67] Military values are exalted, as when the general Cato is praised for living under the same discipline as his men, "in frugal living, in endurance of sleepless nights and other hardships." Although he had the status and prerogatives of a senior commander, Livy assures us that Cato "enjoyed no privileges to distinguish him from the rest of his army."[68]

Having said that, Livy does not gloss over the horrors of war. Included in Scipio's "war prayer," for example, is a request for "the power of vengeance upon those whom we hate and our country's enemies, and give to me and to the Roman people means to inflict upon the Carthaginian state the sufferings which the Carthaginians have laboured to inflict on ours."[69] In another passage he refers to "indiscriminate slaughter," with "Roman troops butchering armed and unarmed, Carthaginians or Tarentines alike."[70] There is, however, the sense in Livy that such effects of war should be moderated. Reference is made to the Roman "anciently established custom of sparing the conquered." There is even a suggestion, consistent with Cicero, that resort to war ought to be justified—a *jus ad bellum*—as in Rome's war with Philip of Macedon, who had conspired with the Carthaginians against Rome: "Your wrongs gave us adequate justification for war."[71]

Fortune and Volition

To Livy "the most important elements in war are the numbers and courage of the soldiers, the talent of the commanders, and luck, which is a powerful influence on all the affairs of men and particularly in warfare." Alexander the Great is identified as a model commander who, in addition to his other qualities, enjoyed "good fortune" that "never failed him in a single battle."[72] In his allusion to fortune and the uncertainties of warfare, we have the essential elements of an argument developed before him by Thucydides and Polybius and later by Machiavelli and Clausewitz—the latter using such metaphors as "fog of war" and "friction" to capture the idea that unaccounted for variables might affect the military equation either positively or adversely.

That fortune is an extremely important factor pervades Livy's entire work.[73] We see it in the battle at Cannae, which the Romans lost to the Carthaginians under Hannibal. The question is raised as to whether the Roman defeat "was due to some fault and not to the anger of the gods, or to Fate, by whose law event is linked unalterably to event in human affairs." Fortunes may change. In fact, the mark "of a commander worth his salt" is "to seize his good fortune when it offers and turn to good use any unexpected stroke of luck."[74] Hannibal recognized the demand on the battlefield commander's intellect: "Many problems naturally difficult are solved by a little brainwork."[75] Caution and patience are virtues. One does not rush into battle; one should avoid precipitate action that is often associated with the impatience of youth. At the same time, when one is prepared, there is value in "taking the offensive"—"devastating your enemy's country" instead of "seeing your own ravaged." One engages in "removing the threat from one-self" and "bringing the other man into peril."[76] In sum, human beings are not powerless and can make efforts to effect desirable outcomes.

Class Analysis

Livy is a realist, but one also finds throughout his work analyses of class and interclass conflict between patricians and plebeians in Roman society—important ideas in our own time among Marxist and other globalist scholars. Livy writes of "bitter class conflict both at home and abroad."[77] Legalizing intermarriage between the nobility and the commoners, for example, was opposed in the Roman Senate because "patrician blood would thereby be contaminated" and, moreover, "hereditary rights and privileges of the *gentes,* or families, would be lost." There was concern among patricians that "the highest office of state would have to be shared with the dregs of society" or might even be "lost to the nobility and transferred to the commons." Plebeians would likely elect "men of their own class, and the most turbulent demagogues at that."[78]

To Livy, rulers who favor their own patrician class and alienate the lower classes forget that their power rests ultimately on popular support. Such leaders may be confronted with revolutionary activity against their regimes. As an example, Livy relates how at around 371 B.C. "the opportunity for a revolution seemed to have come as a result of the crushing load of debt" incurred by state authorities. In this situation "the people could hope for no relief except through placing their representatives in the highest office."[79] As Livy describes them, circumstances were particularly bad in 210 B.C.:

> It was the Roman people, it seemed, that the consuls had set about ruining and tearing to pieces. For years the people had been drained dry by taxation; they had nothing left but the land, and that was stripped bare. The enemy had burnt their houses, the state had stolen the slave-labour from their farms, either impressing the slaves as oarsmen for the fleet, or buying them cheap for military service; any silver or copper money a man might have had been taken from him either for the oarsmen's pay or for the annual tax. They could not be compelled by any force or any authority to give what they have not got."[80]

Livy also notes how at other times "the nobles were grabbing possession of public land, and there would be no room left there for the common people unless it was shared out before they seized it all." Patricians were preoccupied with "all the objects for which men's desire knows no bounds—land, money and advancement." Exploitation of the plebeians resulted in "their enslavement for debt."[81]

Class conflict such as this does not advance society and can be a catalyst for revolutionary activity. In Livy's view, divisiveness of any kind may weaken the state and expose it to the threat of foreign invasion. By contrast, Livy claims that authority in the able hands of an effective ruler—from whatever background—"was enough to make the enemy withdraw from Roman territory." Livy notes how, in history, as long as nobody who had conspicuous ability was despised, Rome's power grew. In short, to Livy it was an individual's abilities, not class origin, that should be the decisive factor.[82]

Republicanism

As evidenced by Livy's comments on class, he agrees with all of his predecessors that domestic factors affect the security of the state. The strength or power of the state depends in part upon the legitimacy and cohesiveness of the political regime. In this regard, Livy's preferred political regime, like Machiavelli's in *The Discourses,* is a representative government or republic. Livy idealizes republican Rome, "governed by annually elected officers of state and subject not to the caprice of individual men, but to the overriding authority of law."[83] He relates how in 507 B.C. the consul Valerius "called a mass meeting of the people and, before mounting the platform, ordered his lictors [officers who accompanied magistrates in public appearances], as a gesture of sympathy with popular feeling, to lower their rods." He explains that the gesture was well received because "the lowering of the *fasces*—the emblem of authority—in the people's presence was taken as an admission that the majesty of power was vested in themselves rather than in the consul."[84] To Livy "the ultimate power in the state" rests with the people rather than with an individual ruler who is merely exercising authority gained from this popular support.[85] One of the clearest statements of this view is his reference to "the people, who held supreme power over everything."[86] Patriotism, an identification with the political community, which "is founded upon respect for the family and love of the soil," contributes to cohesiveness of the state and keeps it from being "torn to pieces by petty squabbles."[87]

Finally, promulgation of laws makes possible the "creation of a unified body politic." The ruler's legitimacy is enhanced when measures are taken "to increase the dignity and impressiveness of his position." Livy argues that "Rome had originally been founded by force of arms," but that a new and "solid basis of law and religious observance" was later substituted for brute force as the foundation of the political community.[88] Changes in the international environment have their effects on domestic law: "Laws passed in peacetime are frequently cancelled by war; and peace often repeals the legislation of wartime: just as, in the handling of a ship some methods are of service in fair weather, other methods in time of storm."[89]

Aside from domestic law, the Roman idea of international law that extends beyond a particular political community appears in a number of places in Livy.[90] Treaties are binding (in international law, the principle of *pacta sunt servanda*) and Livy criticizes those who "had broken faith in respect of their treaty obligations."[91] On the other hand, circumstances at the time the treaty was signed may have changed (the international legal concept of *rebus sic stantibus*) and thus result in an alteration of the original treaty commitments—"that everybody's interest would be better served if the old treaty were brought up to date."[92] Finally, although Livy does not dwell on the notion, there is a fleeting reference to "matters of divine and human law," a distinction that would be developed later in the political theory of the Middle Ages.[93]

While Livy's observations on international law and war were read by later scholars such as Grotius, of greater interest to students of international relations is Livy's belief, following Polybius, that the nature of republican Rome—particularly its balancing and integration of different political, economic, and social forces into a unified whole—accounts for its ascendancy in such a short period of time. Not only does republicanism enhance the domestic security and stability of the state, it also aids in dealing with foreign threats and the expansion of empire. Such benefits of imperial republics to domestic and international security would also be analyzed and praised by Machiavelli. As we will see, Immanuel Kant viewed the relation between the nature of republics and international relations in a quite different manner. Unlike Livy and Machiavelli, Kant believed an international system composed of republics was the best hope for international peace, not a source of imperialist expansionism.

Plutarch

Plutarch was one of the last classical Greek historians. Born in 45 A.D. at Chaeronea, he studied philosophy in Athens and was heavily influenced by the works of Plato and the idea that knowledge is virtue. He became well known as a scholar and diplomat to Rome, where he made a number of influential friends. His *Lives of the Noble Greeks and Romans* consists of a series of paired portraits of various leaders such as Solon, Pericles, Lysander, Alexander, Caesar, Pompey, Cicero, and Cato. As a lover of tradition, he agreed with Livy that better understanding of the past would encourage contemporary leaders to emulate the more virtuous of their predecessors. Another purpose of his work was to show both Greeks and Romans that they could draw benefit from each others' traditions.[94]

More so than any other scholar surveyed in this work, Plutarch viewed momentous events in personal terms, and for this reason alone he is worthy of discussion. Unlike Thucydides, for example, he was not interested in uncovering underlying historical processes, nor did he claim, as did Polybius, that there is a natural and historical sequence in the life of a state. In contemporary parlance, the individual level of analysis was supreme in Plutarch's works, with statesmen's policies essentially a function of their personalities, not the nature of the state or international system. These latter environments provide the dramatic backdrop within which Plutarch's subjects operate.

For Plutarch, service to the state rather than the Stoic emphasis on humanity as a whole is clearly a virtue. Hence, he describes Aristides of Athens as a man who "cared nothing for personal popularity or reputation. His efforts were always aimed at securing the utmost advantage for the state that was consistent with safety and justice."[95] Similarly, Pericles is praised for his prudence that restrained the Athenian spirit of conquest, consolidated Athen's military gains, and kept Sparta in check.[96]

Whatever weaknesses an individual may exhibit privately, however, for Plutarch the critical criterion of greatness is whether or not a soldier or politician is willing and able to overcome personal vices in aid of the security of the state. While he depicts Aristides's political rival, Themistocles, as obsessed with fame, ambition, money, and a grand style of living, Plutarch's respect for patriotic men of action is nevertheless quite evident. Themistocles was able, for example, to put an "end to the fighting within Greece, to reconcile the various cities with one another and persuade them to lay aside their differences because of the war with Persia." Furthermore, Themistocles is praised for having the foresight to end the banishment of his longtime rival Aristides so the two could work together to defeat Xerxes' Persian forces at Salamis and Plataea. A similar willingness to subordinate pride to the safety of the state occurred when Pericles recalled his rival Cimon from exile.[97]

Although Plutarch reserved his deepest respect for those individuals who led a virtuous private life, when a state's interests are at stake another standard of behavior is acceptable. Hence, in foreign policy matters the much-praised Aristides "followed whatever policy his country had adopted, recognizing that this must involve a great deal of injustice on occasion." Similarly, it is perfectly understandable and acceptable that the Greek leader Cimon carried war into enemy countries, ravaged the land, and at times created new colonies.[98]

One might have the impression that given the emphasis Plutarch places on the ability of "great men of history" to influence events and outcomes, he falls on one extreme of the determinism–voluntarism spectrum. Instead, however, he recognized the limits to effective action. In the first place, a commendable leader may be up against a strong rival—witness Plutarch's (or Thucydides') discussion of how Alcibiades outmaneuvered Nicias over the Athenian decision to launch the expedition to Sicily. Secondly, although not relied upon to the extent of other authors such as Polybius and Machiavelli, Plutarch occasionally admits to the role of fate in determining outcomes. "How intricate are the workings of fortune and how unfathomable to human reason."[99] Nevertheless, of all the writers in the realist tradition discussed in this work, Plutarch emphasizes volition or free will the most.

Conclusion

This chapter examined writers associated with the philosophy of Stoicism and writers known for their analyses of the rise of the Roman Empire. The two intersect because the religious character of Stoicism made it the preferred and professed philosophy of Rome's educated elite. There appears to have been, however, an obvious disjuncture between the basic precepts of Stoicism and the actual development of the Roman Empire. The universalism of Stoicism may even have provided a convenient pretext to justify imperial control from the center. Certainly *Pax Romana* was established by conquest, with all the violence and brutality of war. Subjugated peoples were summarily incorporated into the empire, but they also were given considerable autonomy—the key to maintaining the empire over time. Rome also promoted notions of unity and the universality of citizenship, and these ideals often became a reality, at least for many of what we would call the elites in conquered territories. Notwithstanding the use of violent means that were contrary to Stoic principles, Rome as empire moved Stoic universalism from the plane of philosophical abstraction to one of political reality.

Even after the Roman Empire went into decline, Stoic ideas survived through the Middle Ages and the rise of the state system down to the present day. Stoic universalism is reflected in the argument that the concept of "political community" need not be restricted to the territorial dimensions of the small and intimate city-state preferred by Plato and Aristotle, the modern bureaucratic state, or even an empire. In rejecting the realist emphasis on the territorial state, the Stoics substituted a universalistic doctrine that transcends not only territorial divisions and the diversity or plurality of humanity, but time as well—its laws are assumed to be perpetually valid. Similar arguments would be used later, for example, by such writers as Grotius in their attempts to substantiate the claim that some degree of international society exists.

Furthermore, the Stoic tradition emphasizes a level of analysis all too often forgotten, particularly by a realist tradition that focuses on states and elite decision makers and a globalist tradition concerned with sweeping economic and social forces—the individual. By linking natural laws to the individual, the way was open for future generations of scholars and political activists to argue for the existence of universal human rights that no state should be able to abrogate. Furthermore, Stoicism's emphasis on virtue, humanity, and natural law has religious overtones. Indeed, it seems to have much in common with religions such as Christianity that substituted the laws of God for the laws of nature, a topic discussed in the following chapter.

Notes

Multiple citations within notes are listed in the order in which the quotations appear in the text.

1. Virgil, *The Aeneid,* trans. Robert Fitzgerald (New York: Random House, 1981, 1983) I, circa lines 17–40; VI, circa lines 846–67.

2. For a brief overview of the domestic and foreign policies of these emperors and the Roman Empire, see "Roman History," *Encyclopedia Britannica,* vol. 19 (Chicago: William Benton, 1973), 520–35; and "Empire," vol. 8, 344–45.

3. This discussion of Stoicism draws on William Ebenstein, *Great Political Thinkers: Plato to the Present,* 4th ed. (New York: Holt, Rinehart and Winston, 1969), 139–48.

4. "History of Ethics," *Encyclopedia Britannica,* vol. 8, 765.

5. *History of the Peloponnesian War,* trans. Rex Warner (Harmondsworth, Eng.: Penguin Books, 1954), III:82–83.

6. "Cicero," *Encyclopedia Britannica,* vol. 5 (Chicago: William Benton, 1972), 759–60.

7. Neal Wood, *Cicero's Social and Political Thought* (Berkeley: University of California Press, 1988), 2–4.

8. Cicero, *The Republic,* II:xxiii; see also I:xxvi. Cicero acknowledges the influence of Polybius, whom he refers to as an historian "unsurpassed in chronological accuracy." Ibid., X:xiv. Convenient Penguin editions include *Selected Works, Selected Political Speeches,* and *On the Good Life.* The Loeb Classical Library edition of Cicero's *De Re Publica (The Republic)* and *De Legibus (The Laws),* trans. Clinton Walker Keyes (Cambridge, Mass.: Harvard University Press, 1928, 1988) is referenced (volume XVI in the collected works of Cicero). The Loeb editions contain both the original Latin and the English translation on facing pages.

9. Cicero, *The Laws,* V, fragment.

10. *The Laws,* I:vii; I:a, II:ii. On the law of nations, see I:v, II:ii.

11. *The Republic,* I:xxxii.

12. *The Laws,* I:vi, xviii; I:vi.

13. *The Republic,* III:xxii; see also III:xi and *The Laws,* I:vii.

14. *The Laws,* I:xv; II:x; I:v; II:v, xxv.

15. II:iv.

16. Cicero, "On Duties," in *On the Good Life,* trans. Michael Grant (London: Penguin Books, 1971), 152, 169–70.

17. See the discussion in Wood, *Cicero's Social and Political Thought,* 105–19.

18. *The Republic,* I:xxv; I:ii; III:xv. See also "On Duties," 169.

19. *The Laws,* I:xvi; *The Republic,* I:i–ii; I:vi.

20. *The Laws,* II:xi. See also "On Duties," 129.

21. *The Laws,* II:v.

22. *The Republic,* II:xiv.

23. II:xiv.
24. II:iv; I:iii.
25. *The Laws*, II:xiv. See also *The Republic*, V:ii.
26. *The Republic*, III:xxiii; III:xxiv.
27. See *The Laws*, II:xiv; III:iii. *The Republic*, III:xxiv; II:xxvii. On diplomacy, see *The Laws*, II:ix; III:viii, xviii, and *The Republic*, III:xxix.
28. Introduction by Robin Campbell to Seneca, *Letters from a Stoic* (London: Penguin Books, 1969); introduction by Maxwell Staniforth to Marcus Aurelius, *Meditations* (London: Penguin Books, 1964).
29. Seneca, *Letters from a Stoic*, letter LXXXIII.
30. V, LXV. The philosopher is looking for "a rule of life in which he has brought life into line with things universal," XC. On humanity, LXV.
31. Aurelius, *Meditations*, IV:4.
32. I:14; XI:8, 18.
33. IV:27; XII:36.
34. VI:44.
35. Seneca, *Letters*, XC.
36. XC.
37. Aurelius, *Meditations*, III:5; V:1; VII:31.
38. IX:23.
39. X:15; VI:38; V:8.
40. Seneca, *Letters*, LXXXVIII.
41. XC.
42. XC.
43. Quotes from XC. See also CVIII and II.
44. XLVII.
45. LXV, XC.
46. Aurelius, *Meditations*, IV:45; V:14.
47. Seneca, *Letters*, XC, LXXVIII.
48. XCI.
49. LXXXVIII.
50. Aurelius, *Meditations*, II:12; X:7; II:3; VII:49.
51. VI:30; II:3; XI:36.
52. Penguin editions are convenient for Livy's *History of Rome*: Books I–V are contained in *The Early History of Rome*, books VI–X are in *Rome and Italy*, books XXI–XXX are in *The War with Hannibal*, and books XXXI—XLV are in *Rome and the Mediterranean*. On Livy's life, see "Livy," *Encyclopedia Britannica*, vol. 14 (Chicago: William Benton, 1973), 157–58.
53. Livy, *History of Rome*, I:1.
54. VII:6.
55. I:19; I:1; XXXIX:13; IV:9; IV:9.
56. III:4.
57. II:9.
58. IV:25.
59. XXXV:23; XXXVI:1; VII:29. Quote from I:1. See also XXVIII:28.
60. XXIII:33.
61. VII:29–32.
62. XXVI:51, 36; XXVIII:41; XLII:12; quote from XXIX:3.

63. IV:37; XXXIX:19.
64. XLIII:19.
65. VII:30.
66. For example, see XXXVI:7.
67. XXXIII:45.
68. XXXIV:19.
69. XXIX:27.
70. XXVII:16. See also XXXII:13.
71. XXXIII:12; XXXIV:23.
72. IX:17, 18.
73. For example, see XXXVII:54; VII:23, 126; III:6–7; and VIII:31.
74. XXV:6; VII:31; XXVIII:44.
75. XXV:11.
76. XXVIII:44.
77. II:60. See also I:43; III:9; IX:35–36.
78. IV:1, 2.
79. VI:35. See also IV:35–37.
80. XXVI:35.
81. VI:5; VI:35; VII:19.
82. IV:18; IV:3–4.
83. II:1.
84. II:8.
85. IV:5.
86. VIII:33.
87. II:1.
88. I:19.
89. XXXIV:6.
90. For example, see I:13–14; XXI:10.
91. XXXV:6.
92. I:52.
93. XXXIX:16.
94. Introduction by Ian Scott-Kilvert to Plutarch's *The Rise and Fall of Athens: Nine Greek Lives* (London: Penguin Books, 1960).
95. "Themistocles," in *The Rise and Fall of Athens*, p. 79.
96. "Pericles," in *The Rise and Fall of Athens*, 21. Fabius Maximus and Pericles are described as two men who through their "moderation, their uprightness, and their ability to endure the follies of their peoples and their colleagues in office, they rendered the very greatest service to their countries." in "Pericles," 2.
97. "Themistocles," 6; "Cimon," 17.
98. "Aristides," 25; "Cimon," 8.
99. "Nicias," 11, 12.

7
The Middle Ages

The decline and fall of the Roman Empire and the resulting decentralization of authority produced a high degree of pluralism in western Europe. Travel was not just a privilege of the elites, but was also at least possible for the faithful of more modest means, who were known to undertake religious pilgrimages far from home. The crusades even brought many to the Holy Land and elsewhere in the Near East. Trade grew by sea and over land, but would until later centuries remain a marginal activity in relation to the localized concentration of economic activity that is characteristic of feudalism. Armed conflicts were frequent, though in principle, if not in fact, subject to the restraints of the just war doctrine.

Still, there was in the medieval mind a sense of unity in Christendom. This idea is central to understanding Augustine, Aquinas, and other medieval writers. Even Dante and other critics who challenged the temporal authority of the church tended to see the universe as a unified whole. The Stoicism of the Roman Empire thus not only survived, but was strengthened by early Christian writers, who had quickly adopted its premises. Although, of course, never canonized, Seneca even came to be revered by many Christians *de facto* as a pre-Christian "saint." The rise of states, the emergence of market economies, and the Protestant Reformation ultimately marked the end of this medieval era. It is useful to reflect upon the Middle Ages to reiterate the point that the state and capitalist system we know today has not been the only form of international organization.

Historical Context

As we have seen, whatever unity was provided by the Roman Empire was a function of Roman law, Roman legions, and Stoic philosophy. After the final collapse of Rome in the fifth century A.D., the next thousand years came to be known by later scholars as the Middle Ages or medieval period. Its end point is generally marked by the Renaissance and the Reformation of the fifteenth century. This period should be of particular interest to stu-

The Middle Ages

Date	Historical and Literary Developments	Writers and Commentators
300	Edict of Milan (313) under Emperor Constantine legitimates Christianity throughout the empire	St. Augustine (354–430) writes City of God, Confessions, and other works
400[a]	Rome overrun in Visigoth invasion (410)	
800	Coronation of Charlemagne of Frankish-Carolingian House as Emperor of the "Romans"	
900		
1000	Beowulf, epic poem set in sixth-century Denmark and Sweden, first written down	
1100	Chanson de Roland, about Charlemagne (ninth century)	
1200	Germanic epic Nibelungenlied, set in fifth century, first written down; Hanseatic League (of German cities) formed	St. Thomas Aquinas (1225–1274) writes Summa Theologica; Dante (1265–1321) writes Divine Comedy and De Monarchia
1300	Arrest of pope by French king (1303) and subsequent movement of papacy to Avignon; "Black Death" plague (1348–1352); Decameron by Boccaccio (1313–1375); Canterbury Tales by Chaucer (1340–1400); Sir Gawain and the Green Knight about sixth-century chivalry first written down	Marsiglio of Padua (1275–1343) and William of Ockham (1290–1348) advance separation of church and state authorities
1400	Council of Constance (1414–1418): development of national churches; Malory (1400–1471) writes chivalric Le Morte d'Arthur	Vitoria (1480–1546) and Suarez (1548–1617) apply just war doctrine to emergent state system

[a]The period from 400 to 800, traditionally referred to as the Dark Ages, had a relatively low level of intellectual productivity.

125

dents of international relations as it encompasses the period immediately prior to the onset of the current state system. As we will see, the organization of the world into territorially based states claiming sovereignty was not an inevitable outcome of the Middle Ages; other possibilities existed. Furthermore, the moral philosophy of the Middle Ages also addresses a number of topics of interest to students of international relations, such as the just war doctrine.[1]

During the Middle Ages the major purveyor of the notion of the unity of mankind was the Christian church, whose teachings had been sanctioned as Rome's official state religion in 393 A.D. But as Rome's empire collapsed, Christians were understandably concerned that if an empire such as this could not even protect itself from barbarian invaders, how could it provide the necessary worldly power to help the church in its crusade to spread the teachings of Christianity?[2] Furthermore, principally because of the conversion to Christianity of the emperor Constantine, the church became an increasingly wealthy and privileged organization and therefore had much to lose from invasions and general chaos. Even later, as more and more "barbarians" came under the influence of Christianity, the church in self-defense continued to strengthen its organization and centralized authority in the papacy.[3] Despite the often corrupt and hypocritical behavior of many members of the church hierarchy, Christianity was the framework within which medieval life, private as well as public, was conducted.[4] As we will see, scholars associated with the Christian church were responsible for providing justification for the desired creation of a unified international system dominated by theocratic principles.

While the church in western Europe proclaimed the universality of its message in the sacred realm, political power in the secular realm was greatly fragmented, with a wide variety of different types of actors claiming legitimacy. Charlemagne's early ninth-century Holy Roman Empire, centered in Germany, was, as Voltaire wryly noted, not very holy, Roman, or much of an empire compared to that of the Caesars or even that of Byzantium to the east. Yet Charlemagne's successors provided a limited secular counterweight to the growing power of the church. Indeed, Christian doctrine initially allowed for two separate but essentially equal papal and imperial powers. With the collapse of the Holy Roman Empire, however, because of internal weaknesses and invasions by the Saracens, Magyars, and Norsemen, smaller political units came to the fore. Kingdoms still existed, but administratively they lacked efficient bureaucracies and permanent military forces. As a result, kings generally had little power over local barons. There developed, therefore, a contradiction between the actual pluralism and diversity of medieval institutions and the religious and philosophical desire for greater unity, whether provided by imperial or papal authorities.[5]

The power of local barons was reflected in the preeminent form of authority that had emerged earlier but had become particularly evident by the tenth century—feudalism. Feudalism can be viewed as a political, social, and economic response to the disorder and confusion resulting from the collapse of the Roman Empire. A defining characteristic of feudalism is public authority placed in private hands.[6] As a result of the chaos of late ninth-century Europe—a time in which the stability provided by Roman law and legions was fast fading from memory—public authority came to be treated as the private possession of local lords who controlled territory known as fiefs. This authority was devolved to them by often weak and distant kings. For example, courts of justice were viewed as a private possession of individual lords who conducted business as they saw fit. Similarly, a vassal's loyalty and obligation to a lord was of a personal nature; it was not owed to some distant and possibly abstract entity called "the state." Oaths of allegiance were in effect personal contracts, so that authority was private in that the right to administer inhabitants of a fiefdom resided personally with a ruler. Ownership of property by a vassal within a fiefdom was conditional on the owner accepting explicit obligations. For example, if a lord needed to defend his territory, he did not call upon all free men to bear arms in his service, but rather summoned his vassals. Conversely, a lord promised to provide the vassal protection from an often hostile and uncertain world. This (1) privatization of public authority in the hands of local nobles was a cause and consequence of (2) the predominance of local government over the claims of kings and (3) the general fragmentation of political authority throughout Europe. All three elements comprise what has been termed "feudalism."[7]

Political authority during feudal times was therefore claimed by a heterogeneous collection of institutions and individuals, including local barons, bishops, kings, and popes. Furthermore, it was also a time in which the middle-class merchants or the bourgeoisie of the towns began to become a political force and to lend their support to religious or secular leaders in return for charters allowing them to establish free "communes," and, over time, commercial leagues. For students of international politics, it is interesting to note that, depending on their status, any one of these entities could be granted or denied the right of embassy—to conduct diplomatic relations. This medieval system, which seems so alien to the modern mind, has been characterized by historians as "a patchwork of overlapping and incomplete rights of government," which were "inextricably superimposed and tangled," and in which "different juridical instances were geographically interwoven and stratified, and plural allegiances, asymmetrical suzerainties and anomalous enclaves abounded."[8]

To summarize, during the Middle Ages, besides such factors as poor communications and sparse populations, three sets of social, economic, and political institutions worked to retard the development of strong centralized governments. First, as long as feudal institutions were strong and a great deal of authority fragmented and decentralized, it was difficult for the modern state to develop.[9] Second, while feudalism worked to restrict the development of the state "from below," the universal claims of authority by the church had a similar effect "from above." Finally, the claims of the Holy Roman Empire had an impact analogous to (although lesser than) the church through its sweeping claims of authority over Europe in the secular realm. Given this situation, there was very little political space during the Middle Ages within which the modern state could develop.

Can we speak of this polyglot collection of forms of political authority during the latter half of the Middle Ages as an international or "world" political system? Definitely so, even though it does not have the elegant simplicity of an international system composed of sovereign states. If any time in history corresponded to the pluralist image, it was the Middle Ages. The distinction between internal and external political realms with rigid territorial demarcations, a centralized bureaucratic structure (the state) claiming to exercise public authority, and a claim to act independently in the world—hallmarks of the current international state system—would have seemed odd to the medieval mind.[10] Religious moral philosophy viewed the universe as a single whole and mankind as an organic, interdependent society.

But during the Middle Ages, diplomacy still existed. The papacy adopted certain Roman principles and established new ones that have become part of international law: the safe conduct of ambassadors, secrecy in diplomatic negotiations, and condemnation of treaty violations.[11] In terms of secular contributions, just as the vassalic contract was based on a personal relationship between lord and vassal, so, too, were personal relationships a key to diplomacy. Marriages were particularly important.[12] Territorial borders were fluid and relations between kingdoms were a function of dynastic connections. One did not speak of the "national interest" but rather of the interest of particular rulers or dynasties. The high Middle Ages were a much more cosmopolitan era for the elites of the time than anything we have seen since—political courtships and marriages could result in a prince of Hungary becoming heir to the throne in Naples, or an English prince legitimately claiming the throne in Castile. This web of dynastic interdependencies characterized by royal mobility was paralleled in the rising merchant classes, whose interest in commerce also made for a cosmopolitan view of the world.[13]

Nevertheless, despite the philosophical conception of Europe as an organic entity, it was a period historians have characterized as one of "feudal anarchy." It was a time when "the system of rule relied, both for order-keeping and for the enforcement of rights and the redress of wrongs, on self-activated coercion exercised by a small, privileged class of warriors and rentiers in their own interest."[14] When describing the Middle Ages of Europe as an international system, the key phrase is "system of rule." As an historian has argued: "Europeans lived in a society whose organization may seem excessively simple compared with ours, but it was organized. They shared certain mores, certain patterns of accepted behavior, certain ideals, and a store of acquired techniques."[15]

By the twelfth century, however, some headway had been made in the reconcentration of political power in the hands of kings because of changes in the nature of feudalism. Three trends were particularly important: the monetarization, systematization, and bureaucratization of feudalism. Each is worthy of brief discussion.[16]

First, the feudal relationship began to change from one based on personal service to one based on monetary payment. As vassals desired more time to develop their fiefs and pass them on to their heirs, they became less interested in spending their time engaged in personal service on behalf of the lord. Most lords acquiesced, coming to accept monetary payment by those running fiefs. This trend, however, benefited the rulers of provinces and kingdoms more than the local lords, since these greater lords (who, after all, claimed suzerainty over lesser nobles) either attempted to monopolize the payments from the fiefs or to take from the local lord most of what the latter collected. This increase in revenues greatly aided in the strengthening of kingdoms and centralized governments.

Second, feudal systems became more systematized and universalized, so that in such states as England and Normandy feudalism increasingly resembled a pyramid with distinct lines of authority. This reflected a trend in which kings made great strides toward pulling together the scattered pieces of their kingdoms and began to reinforce half-forgotten claims to suzerainty. In France, for example, the king explicitly demanded a reaffirmation of homage from the lords of the realm. Although in the twelfth century the practical effect of this policy was not particularly significant, it established a precedent for the king's legal superiority. Another example of the systematization of feudalism occurred in England and involved the development of what was called the "franchise theory of justice." This meant that when a king granted a lord the right to dispense justice, the king reserved the right to intervene in the judicial process as well as define the original terms of the grant. This became the basis upon which appeals could be made from local courts. In the process the links were further weakened between local lords and vassals as the latter increasingly looked to higher authorities for military and legal protection.

Finally, the twelfth century witnessed the bureaucratization of feudalism. This principally entailed not only the development of judicial courts, but also the establishment of administrative and financial offices. The monetarization and systematization of feudalism required educated men to oversee the expanding responsibilities and authorities of the greater lords and kings. While clerks were indispensable in running the centralized administrations, enforcement powers were granted to laymen who acted as local representatives of the king, staffed courts, and collected revenues.

These positions were unusual in that they introduced into Europe a new source of income independent from that derived from the ownership of a fief. But this also meant that officials had to remain loyal to the king lest they be removed from their positions of authority and livelihood. This increase in bureaucracy was perhaps the critical factor in the trend toward the development of the modern state.

This gradual process of the reconcentration of power was aided by larger trends evident by the twelfth century. The cessation of invasions from Europe's periphery allowed kings and nobles to devote more attention and resources to internal affairs and also helped to account for the dramatic increase in the size of the European population. A larger population helped to revive towns, increase the size of the artisan class, and encourage greater trade. With expanded economic activity, taxation reappeared and was levied against churches, towns, and nobles. This required the establishment of a salaried officialdom. Greater royal income encouraged the payment of troops as opposed to relying on the vassalic contract based on mutual obligation. Kings, therefore, began to acquire two of the key elements associated with effective rule—financial resources and coercive power.

The twelfth and thirteenth centuries were also an era in which major strides were made in education. It is impossible to underestimate the importance of the growth of literacy to the rise of the state. Up until the end of the eleventh century, Europe was basically a nonliterate or oral society in which education was restricted to a small group of clergymen. Even in the case of the clergy, writing was seen more as an art form involving manuscript illumination than a means of written communication. But as literacy expanded, the idea of written contracts gained currency, and ideals, norms of behavior, and laws could more easily be passed from one generation to another.[17] Universities were established (Paris, Padua, Bologna, Naples, Oxford, Cambridge), Roger Bacon engaged in experimental science, Dante wrote in the language of the common man, Aquinas drew inspiration from the ancient Greek writers, and Giotto raised art to a higher level. With the rise of educated bureaucrats, states formed archives that were essential to the continuity of government.[18]

This was also an era, however, in which major clashes ensued between the sacred and secular realms in three areas—learning, commerce, and politics. In terms of learning, France was the center of Western culture and scholarship in the thirteenth century. The charter of the University of Paris dated from 1200 and the institution was exempted from civil control. Members of the university were even haughty toward ecclesiastical authority and came into continual conflict with bishops and popes. The future Pope Boniface VIII aptly illustrated the tension when he wrote to scholars at the University of Paris, "You Paris Masters at your desks seem to think the world should be ruled by your reasonings. It is to us that the world is entrusted, not to you."[19] This clash between reason (or scholarship) and church authority would continue through the ages.

In the realm of commerce, the growth of capitalism led to a clash between the church's emphasis on religious man and the capitalist view of economic man. The Christian attitude toward commerce was that those engaged in business should expect only a fair return for their efforts; earning interest on the loan of money (usury) and taking in large profits were considered particularly sinful.[20] There was also a move away from the feudal notion that the ownership of property was conditional on explicit social obligations that must be carried out. Instead, there was the increasingly important, modern liberal notion that property is private and that possession and disposal of it is up to the individual owner.

Politically, the clash between the sacred and secular was epitomized by a breakdown in the balance of power between the pope and the emperor. This clash between church and empire contributed to the break-up of the unity of Christendom and hence assisted the rise of national states. In 1076 Pope Gregory VII and the German Emperor Henry IV were engaged in a power struggle. The emperor initially deposed the pope who, in turn, excommunicated and then deposed the emperor. Their struggle ended with the emperor's unconditional surrender to the pope. Clothed in penitential garb, the emperor stood barefoot in the winter cold outside the gate of one of the pope's palaces. He was forced to wait three days before being granted an audience, whereupon he pledged complete submission and was pardoned. This was, perhaps, the high point of religious power over the temporal realm.[21]

Two hundred years later, however, the situation had dramatically changed. The center of secular power had moved from the weakened empire to the emerging nation-state. This shift was evident when King Philip of France had Pope Boniface VIII arrested. Philip had levied taxes on clerical income without the pope's blessing. Boniface responded by forbidding the clergy to pay any tax to secular rulers. In 1302 Boniface went even further, declaring papal supremacy: "It is necessary to salvation that every human creature be subject to the Roman pontiff." Philip's response was to form a council to judge the pope on charges that included heresy, blasphemy, murder, sodomy, and sorcery. When the pope moved to excommunicate Philip, he was arrested in 1303 by agents of the king. The aged pope died within a month. The medieval hope of a universal church was dealt another blow when, under Philip's influence, a Frenchman was elected pope. Fearful of Italian reprisals for the treatment of Boniface, the new pope settled in Avignon. Although a fief of the kingdom of Naples and Sicily, it fell under the French sphere of influence.[22] These incidents, a consequence of the struggle between church and empire, weakened both and worked to the advantage of the rising nation-state.

This overview may leave the reader with the impression that the victory of what we now call the modern state was somehow assured. This was not the case. As late as the thirteenth century four other outcomes were still possible. First, a political federation or empire with loose centralized control could have reemerged. We have seen that empires had already been created in Europe under the Romans, and even the Holy Roman Empire provided a certain degree of unity. Indeed, it lasted (formally at least) for a thousand years from Charlemagne's coronation in 800 to the abdication of the Hapsburg emperor Francis II in 1806. By the thirteenth century, Europe culturally and economically was an even more homogeneous region than in earlier years because of the many changes we have cataloged, and hence a case could be made that it was a better candidate for unification than at any time since the halcyon days of the Roman Empire.

Second, a theocratic federation unified by the church could conceivably have emerged. While the papacy's claim to universal jurisdiction was officially in spiritual matters, the claim "was made effective, through a massive international bureaucracy, which was the chief limitation on the rudimentary sovereignty" of smaller and separate political communities, some that would eventually evolve into modern states.[23] This bureaucracy was not dismantled until after the Council of Constance (1414–1418), which marked the development of national churches aligned with the emerging national states. As we have seen, the conflict between church and empire was particularly intense from the tenth to the thirteenth centuries. The victory of secular over sacred power was by no means assured even in the thirteenth century, and religious notables held a great deal of political power for centuries to come. The papal states survived into the nineteenth century, and outside Europe (for example, the Near East) large-scale, although decentralized, priest-dominated empires persisted.

Third, an intensive trading network without a centralized political organization could have developed as a result of the spread of capitalism. Trading cities in Germany and northern Italy long resisted being swallowed by large territorial states. In Germany the Hanseatic League was to become a successful commercial federation.

Finally, there is no reason to exclude the logical possibility that feudalism could have persisted for a much longer period of time.[24] The question of why the state by 1500 had won out over these possible alternatives has preoccupied many historians, who have suggested a multiplicity of preconditions and facilitating factors. A number of these have been mentioned above. Further possible explanations will be discussed in the next chapter.

Medieval Writers

With the sacking of Rome in A.D. 410, what had seemed to be a permanent fixture of the western European system of rule and a source of stability—the Italian-based Roman Empire—was swept away. The secular support base for Christianity was now to be found in the Byzantine Empire to the east under such rulers as Constantine (324–337 A.D.) and Justinian (527–

565 A.D.). In the west, however, contemplation of the world fell basically to writers associated with religious orders, as education was only available to a handful, in particular those associated with the church. Early writers desired to help hold together the Christian community at a time when it was under attack by providing a moral compass for individuals and assuring that the gains achieved by the church during the later years of the Roman Empire were not lost.[25] As the power of the church increased over the centuries, later writers were particularly concerned with delineating what they believed to be proper relations between religious and civil powers.

The three writers selected for consideration here—Augustine, Aquinas, and Dante—have all been labeled "utopians," a term that has come to take on pejorative connotations. As a result, they tend to be dismissed as essentially irrelevant to the "real world" of present-day international politics. There are three points, however, to keep in mind. First, at the time they were writing the establishment of a religious or secular-based empire was not beyond the realm of possibility. It is only because we today view the past through the lenses of the modern state system that the views of Augustine, Aquinas, and Dante seem quaint, if not fantastical. Second, all three scholars were influenced by the Greek tradition of natural law that suggests there is a source of authority beyond those of temporal powers. In trying to bring some sort of order to a world composed of diverse actors with conflicting and overlapping claims of authority, they reflect one strain of pluralist thought that seeks to find a basis for unity in diversity. Finally, all three authors are realists in the sense that they held a sobering view of human nature, and hence understood all too well the obstacles to world peace.

Augustine and Aquinas

Augustine was born and raised in the north African realm of the Roman Empire in 354 A.D. At age sixteen, this son of a pagan father and Christian mother went to Carthage to complete his education. His interest in philosophy was stimulated by reading Cicero, and in 383 he went to Rome to teach rhetoric. Augustine moved to Milan in 386 and there converted to Christianity and foresook what he claims in the *Confessions* to have been a life of sinful debauchery. He returned to Africa and founded a religious community where he was ordained a priest, and five years later he was selected the bishop of Hippo. During his thirty-four years in the community he produced a vast outpouring of written works, the two most important being *Confessions* and *City of God*. The latter was written in part to refute Cicero's conception of providence, particularly his argument in favor of free will.

Thomas Aquinas was born in 1225 in southern Italy, attended the University of Naples, and joined the Dominicans, who sent him to Cologne for further studies. After four years there he went to Paris in 1252 where he began his career as a teacher at the Dominican college of the Jacobins. In 1259 he was appointed theological adviser and lecturer to the papal curia. It was at this time that he assiduously studied Aristotle's works. After ten years in Rome, he went back to Paris to help defend his former colleagues against political and religious attacks and then returned to Naples, where he became director of Dominican studies at the university. He died in 1274 while on his way to attend the second Council of Lyons.[26]

Augustine and Thomas Aquinas provide an interesting contrast, as their works reflect the changing position and power of the Christian church over a millenium that spanned the Middle Ages. Augustine wrote at a time when the church was in a tenuous position, and he was particularly influenced by the works of Plato. Writing in the thirteenth century, Aquinas' achievement was to provide a synthesis of theological doctrine and the writings of the Greeks (Aristotle in particular) and Romans at a time when the church was at the height of its power and in need of a universal and systematic philosophy.[27] Their work included four areas of inquiry with political import: (1) Aquinas' view of natural law, (2) the respective nature and relation between the sacred and secular realms, (3) Augustine's realism, and (4) just war doctrine.

Natural Law

Both Augustine and Aquinas believed that the ancient Greeks had discovered something important with the concept of a natural law that set limits on earthly political authority. But just as man-made law was subordinate to natural law, divine law or the laws of God ultimately should dominate. In Aquinas' *Treatise of the Laws,* we learn that "the whole community of the universe" is governed by "Divine reason." Aquinas observes that "the very Idea of the government of things in God, the Ruler of the universe, has the nature of law." This law necessarily is eternal because "the Divine Reason's conception of things is not subject to time."[28] Aquinas asserts "that no one can know the eternal law as it is in itself, except God himself."[29]

There are, therefore, severe limits to human reason that differentiate man from God. Although one cannot know the eternal law directly, as a "rational creature" an individual does have "a share of the Eternal Reason" that he or she, through the exercise of the reasoning faculty, comes to know as the "natural law." It is these "precepts of the natural law," discoverable through reason, that one applies to "the more particular determination of certain matters"—the domain of "human laws."[30] Human laws are to be in accord with the natural law. Beyond natural law, there also is revealed "law given by God." This divine law fills an important gap in human understanding of what one "ought to do" or what one "ought to avoid." In any event, "all laws, insofar as they partake of right reason, are derived from the eternal law."[31] What if certain human laws are not in accordance with natural and eternal law? For Aquinas, laws that are not just are not laws at all. Indeed, if a human law "differs from the law of nature, it is no longer a law but a corruption of law."[32]

Beyond the civil law of a given political unit, there is a "law of nations" that is also derived from natural law. Reflecting both Aristotelian and Stoic influences, Aquinas argued that a law of nations exists because it is in conformity with man's nature as a social animal who engages in commerce. "To the law of nations belong those things, which are derived from the law of nature as conclusions from premises, just buyings and sellings, and the like, without which men cannot live together, which is a point of the law of nature, since man is by nature a social animal, as is proved in the *Politics*" of Aristotle.[33]

To say that international law is derived from general principles of the natural law is not to deny customary bases. Concerning human law in general, Aquinas notes how customs can have the force of law because "by repeated external actions the inward movement of the will, and concepts of reason are most effectually declared." In short, "when a thing is done again and again, it seems to proceed from a deliberate judgment of reason."[34] Of course, to have legal effect, customary practice must be in accordance not just with natural law, but also with the divine law as revealed to human beings.

Sacred and Secular Realms

This hierarchical conception of divine, natural, and human law had two implications for the church's preferred organization of the medieval world. First, the unity of the physical and metaphysical worlds is reinforced by conceiving of these realms in terms of parallel and mutually reinforcing hierarchies that should reflect divine and natural laws. In the medieval view, the metaphysical reflects the same structure as the more familiar physical world. The heavens have a hierarchy of saints who can intercede on behalf of the faithful in supplications to the Lord of lords. Similarly, as we have noted, in the physical world a vassal might seek the favor of his lord to intercede for him to a higher authority. Even a writer such as Dante, whose work was condemned by the church, adopted this perspective.[35]

Unfortunately, the world is beset by human imperfection or sin, as reflected in Augustine's "city of man" (figuratively, Babylon); yet, there are also the seeds of a perfect world, the "city of God" (figuratively, Jerusalem). The two "cities" or communities are not empirically distinct or separable, because individuals representing both are interspersed. They are "outwardly mingled together, yet separated in heart."[36] Human imperfection stems from the error of Adam that has been perpetuated in the city of man—commitment to self-oriented, earthly values.

The second politically explosive implication of the hierarchical conception of law, however, was the relation between the sacred and secular realms. On the one hand, Augustine was primarily concerned with individual faith and salvation. He did not view the world as a struggle between church and state, but rather between two opposing ways of life—the love of self versus the love of God. Nowhere does one find Augustine calling for a theocracy. Aquinas, however, quite clearly came down on the side of the church, arguing that secular kingdoms are ultimately subject to the church, as the latter is concerned with the most important end of all—the salvation of souls.[37]

Augustine's Realism

The preceding observations on human imperfection speak to what can be termed the Augustinian tradition of political realism and his view that the cause of war is to be found at the individual level of analysis. While the classical Greeks placed a great deal of emphasis on the ability of the mind to control human passions, impulses, and lusts, Augustine was not so sanguine. He did not simply argue that the "rule of the flesh" dominates "the rule of the spirit." As he states, "the corruption of the body, which weighs down the soul, is not the cause of the first sin, but its punishment. And it was not the corruptible flesh that made the soul sinful; it was the sinful soul that made the flesh corruptible.[38] Given this pessimism, it is not so easy, as the Stoics would have one believe, for an individual to obtain happiness through right conduct. Similarly, given the corrupted nature of human beings, Augustine would probably be more "realistic" about the slim possibility of achieving Plato's ideal republic than would Plato himself.

Moving from the level of human nature to the state-societal level, Augustine's realism is also evident. Aside from realistic assessments and descriptions of the problem of individuals living together in communities, he was fully aware of how secular authorities and state power could benefit the church and its missions. Despite Augustine's criticisms of the decadence and depravity of the Romans (Part I of *City of God*), he recognized the fact that the empire served as a vehicle for the spread of Christianity. Hence, for example, his praise of Constantine and his expectation that Christian rulers should "put their power at the service of God's majesty, to extend his worship far and wide."[39] Conversely, good Christians make better citizens, which is to the benefit of the state. As with other authors we have surveyed, the unity of the state is an important source of domestic stability and international security. On this point there is even a suggestion of what Rousseau later would call the "general will." The "interests" of a state as republic or commonwealth "are common to all," given that the state amounts to "a multitude of men bound together by some bond of accord."[40]

Finally, at the level of the international system (what he terms the "third level of human society," following the household and city), Augustine is also quite aware of the obstacles to a sense of world community. He states "the world, being like a confluence of waters, is obviously more full of danger than the other communities by reason of its greater size." Cooperation is difficult as the "diversity of languages separates man from man." Even the attempt of the Roman Empire to create unity was at a high cost. "Consider the scale of those wars, with all that slaughter of human beings, all the human blood that was shed." And although those wars eventually ended, the "misery of those evils is not yet ended." Not only is there "no lack of enemies among foreign nations," but "the very extent of the Empire has given rise to wars of a worse kind, namely, social and civil wars."[41] Such pessimism is rooted in Augustine's conception of human beings, whose "self-love" is the source of evil. His realism is the recognition of the power of egotism at the individual and collective level, and he hopes to attain the most achievable form of peace and justice given the circumstances.

Optimism and voluntarist inclinations, however, are also evident in Augustine's work. Despite his view of human imperfection, it should be noted that Augustine holds out hope for individuals being able to enter the City of God because human behavior is not fixed or predetermined—"enmity to God arises not from nature but from choice, in violation of a nature essentially good."[42] According to Reinhold Niebuhr, for Augustine:

> Good and evil are not determined by some fixed structure of human existence. Man, according to the biblical view, may use his freedom to make himself falsely the center of existence; but this does not change the fact that love rather than self-love is the law of his existence in the sense that man can only be healthy and his communities at peace if man is drawn out of himself and saved from the self-defeating consequences of self-love.[43]

Human behavior is hence not permanently fixed, individuals can make choices, and the role of the church is to help guide people to the City of God. This city is not Plato's territorially defined and restrictive city-state, or Cicero's empire, but is a spiritual bond that aspires to include the entire human race. As Augustine states, the City of God or Heavenly City "is on pilgrimage in this world," calling out "citizens from all nations and so collects a society of aliens, speaking all languages. She takes no account of any difference in customs, laws, and institutions."[44] All of these differences will continue to exist; what is important is for more and more individuals to enter the spiritual Heavenly City, for in so doing peace on earth will be enhanced.

Justice and War

Neither Augustine nor Aquinas, however, expected war to be abolished anytime soon. Recognizing this, both scholars felt compelled to address the issue of just war. Augustine modified the Roman doctrine of Cicero by infusing it with a Christian spirit. He took into account criticisms of the Roman doctrine by Tertullian and other early Christian writers who essentially argued against Christian participation in war. Augustine disagreed, stating that such participation in war was acceptable or just under certain circumstances and noting that Jesus accepted soldiers as performing a legitimate function; he did not tell them "to cast away their arms." Reconciling Christianity and the state, Augustine opposed "those who say that the doctrine of Christ is incompatible with the State's well-being." More to the point, it is entirely possible "to please God while engaged in active military service."[45]

Augustine gives due credit to Cicero for having discussed the question of justice in war, an account from which Augustine draws heavily. The objectives of war must be just. "A state should engage in war for the safety which preserves the state permanently in existence."[46] Moreover, just wars are waged for legitimate purposes or objectives, not by individuals as such, but by legitimate authorities. "A great deal depends on the causes for which men undertake wars, and on the authority they have for doing so."[47]

Although Augustine departs from the absolute pacifism of early Christians, he does not offer a bellicose doctrine in its place. Instead, he advocates a doctrine of war avoidance and restraint in war. Indeed, he argues that properly it is "with the desire for peace that wars are waged" and "that peace is the end sought for by war."[48] In general, one refrains "from the passion of revenge" and seeks instead "when one has suffered wrong, to pardon rather than punish the offender."[49] War is thus not the first resort, but even the good may need to engage in war "for it is the wrong-doing of the opposing party which compels the wise man to wage just wars."[50]

At the same time, because "war is waged in order that peace may be obtained," one must "even in waging war, cherish the spirit of peacemaker." He adds that "mercy is due to the vanquished or the captive."[51] The means one uses in war thus are important if wars are to be just. "The real evils in war are love of violence, revengeful cruelty, fierce and implacable enmity, wild resistance, and the lust of power."[52] By contrast, the use of force in just wars is restrained such that "after the resisting nations have been conquered, provision may be more easily made for enjoying in peace the mutual bond of piety and justice."[53]

The practical effect of Augustine's writings on just war was to provide the doctrinal basis for the church in its struggle to contain or end violent feuds that were pervasive in the centuries following the collapse of the Roman Empire.[54] Perhaps of even more importance were the writings of Aquinas on just war doctrine. Aquinas used a very precise, ordered form of logical exposition in his works—the so-called scholastic method—in which he took a proposition and in reaching his own conclusion considered both the set of objections that can be raised against the proposition and the set of replies to these objections.

Citing Augustine's biblical reference to Jesus having accepted soldiering as a legitimate function, Aquinas in his *Summa Theologica* rejected the proposition that "it is always sinful to wage war." At the same time, consistent with Augustine, Aquinas specified three conditions for a war to be considered just:

> First, the *authority of the sovereign* by whose command the war is to be waged. . . . And as the care of the common weal is committed to those who are in authority, it is their business to watch over the common weal of the city, kingdom or province subject to them. And just as it is lawful for them to have recourse to the material sword in defending that common weal against internal disturbances, . . . so too, it is their business to have recourse to the sword of war in defending the common weal against external enemies. . . .
>
> Secondly, a *just cause* is required, namely that those who are attacked should be attacked because they deserve it on account of some fault. . . .
>
> Thirdly, it is necessary that the belligerents should have a *right intention,* so that they intend the advancement of good, or the avoidance of evil.[55]

The second stipulation was the critical prerequisite for going to war and, when combined with the other two, represented the essence of the Thomist doctrine. As all three prerequisites are, according to Aquinas, norms of moral theology, the issue of just war falls within the jurisdiction of the church. Although Aquinas' views were not all that different from those of Augustine, it was his elaboration of the problem that became the basis for the Christian doctrine on war.[56]

It should be noted that throughout the Middle Ages writers argued for the existence of a universal moral community based on a Christian brotherhood among *individuals*—the modern territorial state associated with the idea of "national interest" did not exist. Hence Augustine, for example, was essentially concerned with bloody and destructive feuds between individual princes. It was not until the sixteenth century that such religious scholars as the Spanish Dominican Francisco de Vitoria (1480–1546) broke with the idea of universal empire, viewed the world in terms of independent states, and interpreted just war doctrine as part of *jus gentium,* which concerned "what natural reason has established among all *nations*" as opposed to among *individuals*. [emphasis added] This line of thinking was later followed by the Spanish Jesuit Francisco Suarez (1548–1617).[57]

Dante

In the work of Dante Alighieri of Florence (1265–1321) we find an interesting amalgam of medieval and modern views. *The Divine Comedy* reflects one of the clearest expressions of the medieval world view. There is an essential unity of the physical and metaphysical worlds, depicted as concentric circles, all parts of a larger whole. Dante does differentiate between temporal and spiritual realms, but he also sees heaven, earth, and hell as interconnected places with what amounts to passageways between these places—a unified world view.

On the other hand, Dante's works also express a number of ideas that would later come to be associated with the fifteenth century Renaissance view of politics—the separation of philosophy from theology and church from empire. In the case of both Augustine and Aquinas, philosophy was part of, but necessarily subordinate to, the revealed wisdom of God contained within religion. Similarly, while both claimed to accept the notion of parallel secular and sacred kingdoms, they argued for the preferred ranking of the latter over the former.

As with Machiavelli two hundred years later, Dante's active participation in Florentine politics illustrated his voluntarist inclination that "all that concerns polity is subject to our power."[58] He came under attack for criticizing the Pope for summoning a foreign army to help repress Florence's prorepublic, antichurch party to which Dante belonged. Dante's opponents won, however, and in 1302 presented trumped-up charges of graft against him. Ordered to pay a fine and banished for two years, he refused to pay and the banishment was declared for life with orders given to burn him alive should he ever again set foot on the territory of the republic. Dante claimed he was now a citizen of Italy if not the wider world, and joined those "to whom the world is [their] native country, just as the sea is to the fish." In the twenty years of exile until his death at age fifty-six, he never returned to Florence. As with other banned intellectuals who followed him, Dante put his time to good use by producing such works as *The Divine Comedy* and *De Monarchia*.[59]

More so than either Augustine or Aquinas, Dante directly addressed topics of interest to students of international relations. In *De Monarchia* he laid out his solution to the problems of war, unrest, and the anarchic structure of the late Middle Ages—a world government run by a monarch. In the process he hoped "to set forth truths unattempted by others. . . . Amongst other unexplored and important truths the knowledge of the temporal monarchy is most important and least explored."[60] He stated that universal peace is the most important blessing that can be bestowed upon humanity. In order to achieve it, the world needed to be organized properly. Taking his cue from Aristotle, Dante makes, in effect, a levels of analysis argument, noting that in the case of the individual household, village, city, and kingdom, each unit must be rightly ordered to achieve one particular end. In the case of the kingdom, the ultimate goal is "tranquillity" or peace, and in order to achieve it "there must be one king to rule and govern, else not only do they in the kingdom fail to reach the goal, but the kingdom itself lapses into ruin. . . . Thus it appears that for the well-being of the world there must be a monarchy or empire."[61]

One aspect of his argument for world government has a distinctly modern ring—his call for the peaceful settlement of disputes where "between any two princes, one of whom is in no way subject to the other, contention may arise." What is needed is some power with "wider jurisdiction who, within the compass of his right, has princedom over both. . . . And he will be monarch or emperor." Dante then approvingly quotes Aristotle: "Things love not to be ill-disposed; but a multiplicity of princedoms is ill; therefore, one prince."[62] Note that this ultimate power to keep principalities in line should be in the hands of a secular ruler with the church playing no role. This in part reflects Dante's admiration of the Roman Empire and the peace it enforced for so many years.

For Dante, the power of the monarch to intervene was to be derived directly from God, not via a religious intermediary such as the pope. Each, in effect, was directly subordinate to God. Dante was quite explicit about this. "The authority of the Empire by no means depends on the church."[63] This was truly a revolutionary idea at the time, as it called for the strict separation of the church from the world state and a refusal to subordinate secular political life to that of religion. Church and universal empire were to be coordinate powers, each autonomous and supreme in their respective realms. The empire was to be guided by reason and philosophy, the church by faith and theology. Just as the empire was not to be subordinate to the church, so, too, should philosophy not be subordinate to theology, a distinctly nonmedieval view. Not surprisingly, *De Monarchia* was placed on the church's list of banned books and it was not removed until the twentieth century.

Conclusion

All too often any work that does not view politics through realist lenses is labeled idealist. The inappropriateness of this tendency to lump together what are essentially disparate views is evident when one compares the writings of the Stoics to the works of Augustine and Aquinas. While the Stoic emphasis on the brotherhood of humanity would seem to parallel if not anticipate Augustine's community of the City of God, there are basic differences. Despite the professed Stoic emphasis on humanity as a whole, it is primarily an individualistic philosophy emphasizing an ability to calmly accept adversity. Despite its professions of a belief in universal brotherhood, it does not tell us what practical steps can be taken to transform society and mankind to create a wider sense of humanity—it is a philosophy of acceptance of the world, not transformation of it. For Augustine and Aquinas, however, acceptance of the status quo is wrong. This is not to suggest that they are extreme voluntarists—far from it. Augustine, for example, in re-futing complete free will strikes a balance between God's foreknowledge of man's acts and the latter's free will.[64] The point is that the two religious scholars realize the road to the City of God will not be an easy one.

This realization is directly a result of their more realistic view of human nature. It is not easy for individuals to triumph over "self-love" and the corruption of the soul—Augustine's own life is witness to how difficult this is. As with Kant, Augustine and Aquinas are realists to the extent that they take seriously the difficulty of achieving a peaceful world community given the nature of human beings (Augustine and Aquinas) or the nature of non-republican forms of government (Kant). The two religious scholars are plu-ralists to the extent that they recognize nonstate forms of international au-thority that transcend borders (the church) and universal norms (divine law).

As for Dante, like Augustine and Aquinas, he also desired to see a uni-versal community and an end to the anarchy of the Middle Ages. But for the two religious philosophers, this universal community was viewed strictly in terms of faith and the church. Dante's argument represents the beginning of a trend that would increasingly come to dominate the world—the polit-ical triumph of the secular over the sacred. Writers such as Marsiglio of Padua (1275–1343) and William of Ockham (about 1290–1348), extend-ing the ideas of Dante concerning separate religious and temporal realms, called for a much stricter separation of the state from ecclesiastical author-ity. By the Renaissance, the widespread reemergence of Greek Classical thought was to provide further support for philosophy over theology as the means by which to interpret and bring order to the world. This seculariza-tion of political thought was particularly apparent in commentaries on what would come to be known as the modern state.

Notes

Multiple citations within notes are listed in the order in which the quota-tions appear in the text.

1. More broadly, one historian has argued that "no longer regarded as a phil-osophical detour between Aristotle and Machiavelli, the political thought of the Middle Ages speaks to a steadily widening circle of inquirers," particularly those who "reject the view that the State should be all-inclusive and all-absorbing." E.F. Jacob, "Political Thought," in *The Legacy of the Middle Ages*, ed. C.G. Crump and E.F. Jacob (Oxford: Oxford University Press, 1926), 505.

2. William Ebenstein, *Great Political Thinkers*, 4th ed. (New York: Holt, Rinehart, and Winston, 1969), 172.

3. "Middle Ages," *Encyclopedia Britannica*, vol. 15 (Chicago: William Ben-ton, 1973), 404.

4. "It [the church] governed birth, marriage, and death, sex, and eating, made the rules for law and medicine, gave philosophy and scholarship their subject matter." Barbara W. Tuchman, *A Distant Mirror: The Calamitous 14th Century* (New York: Alfred A. Knopf, 1978), 32.

5. Ebenstein, *Great Political Thinkers*, 212.

6. Marc Bloch, *Feudalism*, trans. L. Manyon (Chicago: University of Chicago Press), ch. 29; J.R. Strayer, "Feudalism in Western Europe," in *Lordship and Community*, ed. Frederic L. Cheyette (New York: Holt, Rinehart, and Winston, 1968), 14.

7. Joseph R. Strayer and D.C. Munro, *The Middle Ages, 395–1500*, 5th ed. (New York: Appleton-Century-Crofts, 1970), 114–16.

8. John Gerard Ruggie, "Continuity and Transformation in the World Polity," in *Neorealism and Its Critics*, ed. Robert O. Keohane (New York: Columbia University Press, 1986), 142, citing, respectively, J.R. Strayer and D.C. Munro, *The Middle Ages* 4th ed. (New York: Appleton-Century-Crofts, 1959), 115; Perry Anderson, *Lineages of the Absolutist State* (London: New Left Books, 1974), 37–38.

9. As one author argues: "A perfectly feudal condition of society would be not merely a weak state, but the negation of the state altogether. Such a condition was never completely realized at any time or anywhere; but it is obvious that the tendency of feudalism to disperse among different classes those powers which in modern times we regard as normally concentrated in the state, or at any rate as under the state's ultimate control, had to pass away before states in our sense could come into existence." J.L. Brierly, *The Law of Nations: An Introduction to the International Law of Peace*, 6th ed. (New York, Oxford: Oxford University Press, 1963), 3.

10. Ruggie, "Continuity and Transformation," 142–43.

11. W. Ulman, *The Growth of Papal Government in the Middle Ages* (1952), 450, as cited by Martin Wight, "De Systematibus Civitatum," *Systems of States* (Leicester, Eng.: Leicester University Press, 1977), 28–29.

12. "Marriages were the fabric of international as well as internoble relations, the primary source of territory, sovereignty, and alliance and the major business of medieval diplomacy." Tuchman, *A Distant Mirror*, 47. As we will see, however, the term "sovereignty" has distinctly modern connotations that render it an inappropriate term to use to describe medieval political units.

13. On the other hand, the life of the commoner was marked by extreme insularity and parochialism. See, for example, Frances Gies and Joseph Gies, *Life in a Medieval Village* (New York: Harper and Row, 1990). On relations between the few and the many, see the comparative study by Reinhard Bendix, *Kings or People: Power and the Mandate to Rule* (Berkeley: University of California Press, 1978).

14. Gianfranco Poggi, *The Development of the Modern State: A Sociological Introduction* (Stanford, Calif.: Stanford University Press, 1978), p. 31.

15. Frederic L. Cheyette, "The Invention of the State," in *Essays on Medieval Civilization*, ed. Bede Karl Lackner and Kenneth Roy Philip (Austin, London: University of Texas Press, 1978), 149.

16. The following three trends are derived from Joseph R. Strayer, *Medieval Statecraft and the Perspectives of History* (Princeton, N.J.: Princeton University Press, 1971), 80–89.

17. One historian goes so far as to argue, "The invention of the state is the

story of how this small minority of literate men slowly imposed upon the nonliterate their special ways of thinking about politics and law." Cheyette, "The Invention of the State," 150.

18. Marc Bloch, *Feudal Society,* vol. 2 (Chicago: University of Chicago Press, 1964), 421–22; Tuchman, *A Distant Mirror,* 9.

19. Tuchman, *A Distant Mirror,* 22.

20. For a discussion of the church's view of capitalism and the conflict between Philip and Boniface, see Tuchman, *A Distant Mirror,* 37–39 and 25–26, respectively.

21. Ebenstein, *Great Political Thinkers,* 263.

22. Tuchman, *A Distant Mirror,* 25–26. As one scholar has summarized the Middle Ages, "The medieval theory of legitimate power depended upon both emperor and pope; their mutual dependence was galling to both, but for centuries inescapable. There was constant friction, with advantage now to one side, now to the other. At last, in the thirteenth century, the conflict became irreconcilable. The Pope was victorious, but lost moral authority shortly afterwards. The Pope and the Holy Roman Emperor both survived, the Pope to the present day, the Emperor to the time of Napoleon. But the elaborate medieval theory that had been built up concerning their respective powers ceased to be effective during the fifteenth century. The unity of Christendom, which it maintained, was destroyed by the power of the French, Spanish, and English monarchies in the secular sphere, and by the Reformation in the sphere of religion." Bertrand Russell, *The History of Western Philosophy* (New York: Simon and Schuster, 1945), 392–93.

23. Wight, "De Systematibus Civitatum," 28.

24. Charles Tilly, "Reflections on the History of European State-Making," in *The Formation of National States in Western Europe,* ed. Charles Tilly (Princeton, N.J.: Princeton University Press, 1975), 26–27.

25. "The rise of the Christian church, as a distinct institution entitled to govern the spiritual concerns of mankind in independence of the state, may not unreasonably be described as the most revolutionary event in the history of western Europe, in respect both to politics and political philosophy." Prior to this time, the state or empire was considered to be dominant in these matters. George H. Sabine, *A History of Political Theory,* rev. ed. (New York: Holt, 1950), 180.

26. Biographical information is from John O'Meara's "Introduction" to St. Augustine, *City of God* (London: Penguin Books, 1984); "Aquinas," *Encyclopedia Britannica,* vol. 2 (Chicago: William Benton, 1973), 162.

27. Ebenstein, *Great Political Thinkers,* 215.

28. St. Thomas Aquinas, "Treatise on Law," in *Summa Theologica,* Part I of 2nd Part: XCI:1. A good source for Aquinas's magnum opus, the *Summa Theologica,* is in Robert Maynard Hutchins, ed., *Great Books of the Western World,* vols. 19, 20 (Chicago: Encyclopaedia Britannica, 1952, 1986).

29. Aquinas, "Treatise," XCIII:2.

30. XCI:2–3.

31. XCI:4; XCIII:3.

32. XCV:2.

33. XCV:4.

34. XCVII:3.

35. Over the centuries—particularly during times of social and political chaos and in the modern age, which is often marked by individual anomie and alienation—

writers have tended to exhibit a certain nostalgia for the supposed unity of the Middle Ages, ignoring the more repressive aspects of the period. An example of this line of thinking that attacks the modern conceptual paradigm of Cartesian ways of thought is in Fritjof Capra's, *The Turning Point: Science, Society, and the Rising Culture* (New York: Simon and Schuster, 1983).

As reality obviously diverged from this vision of unity in Christendom, two scholars of contemporary international relations have concluded that the idea "that Latinized Europe constituted a special community" was "the dominant medieval myth." (Yale H. Ferguson and Richard W. Mansbach, *The Elusive Quest: Theory and International Politics*. Columbia: University of South Carolina Press, 1988, 50–52.) Nevertheless, to dismiss this vision as mere myth is potentially to overlook its very real implications or consequences for medieval society and politics. One scholar of the Middle Ages observes that the notion of "heaven, earth and mankind" as being one continuum is "one of the oldest and most persistent ideas in human history." Acknowledging in reference to the supposed unity of the Holy Roman Empire that "imperial theory" was "always more satisfactory than the reality," he nevertheless identifies the consequences of this mode of thought—the "constant effort to rationalize and humanize the system through the sacralization of its institutions," to rely on the "sacred mode" as "the only theoretical basis for human action," and to hold that "order" was "absolutely dependent upon hierarchy." Stephen Tonsor, "Order and Degree: The Medieval Quest for Individuality Within the Bounds of Community," *The Intercollegiate Review* (Fall 1988):29–38.

36. Henry Paolucci, ed., *The Political Writings of St. Augustine* (Washington, D.C.: Regnery Gateway, 1962, 1990), 317. St. Augustine's *The Confessions, The City of God,* and *On Christian Doctrine* are contained in Hutchins, ed., *Great Books of the Western World,* vol. 18. Paolucci presents a particularly excellent compilation of Augustinian political writings. Subsequent quotations from *City of God* are from the 1984 Penguin edition.

37. Ebenstein, *Great Political Thinkers,* 173, 220. Hence, for Aquinas the two key areas whereby the church could intervene in secular affairs were (1) situations where the state exceeded its jurisdiction, such as in matters of justice, whereby man-made law should be subordinated to natural law as derived from divine law; (2) violations of faith such as heresy. Charles N.R. McCoy, "St. Thomas Aquinas," in *History of Political Philosophy,* ed. Leo Strauss and Joseph Cropsey (Chicago: Rand McNally, 1963), 206–7.

38. St. Augustine, *City of God,* XIV:3.

39. V:24. On Constantine, see V:25.

40. Paolucci, *The Political Writings of St. Augustine,* 174.

41. *City of God,* XIX:7. "If I were to describe, with an eloquence worthy of the subject, the many and multifarious disasters, the dour and dire necessities, I could not possibly be adequate to the theme, and there would be no end to this protracted discussion." XIX:7.

42. Ibid., XII:3.

43. Reinhold Niebuhr, "Augustine's Political Realism," in Niebuhr, *Christian Realism and Political Problems* (New York: Charles Scribner's Sons, 1953), 130.

44. *City of God,* XIX:17.

45. Paolucci, *The Political Writings of St. Augustine,* 180.

46. Ibid., 163.

47. Ibid., 165.

48. *City of God,* XIX:11–12.

49. Paolucci, *The Political Writings of St. Augustine,* 173.

50. *City of God,* XIX:7.

51. Paolucci, *The Political Writings of St. Augustine,* 182–83.

52. Ibid., 164.

53. Ibid., 179.

54. Arthur Nussbaum, *A Concise History of the Law of Nations* (New York: Macmillan, 1947), 40–41.

55. St. Thomas Aquinas, "Treatise on Faith, Hope and Charity" in *Summa Theologica,* part II of the 2nd part, question 40 ("Of War"), which can be found in Hutchins, *Great Books,* vol. 20, 577–81. Emphasis added.

56. Nussbaum, *A Concise History,* 42.

57. For an elaboration of Vitoria's and Suarez's views on just war, see Nussbaum, *A Concise History,* 58–72.

58. Dante Alighieri, "De Monarchia," *The Portable Dante,* ed. Paolo Milano (New York: Penguin Books, 1977, 1988), 640.

59. Milano, "Editor's Introduction," *The Portable Dante,* xiii–xiv.

60. Dante, "De Monarchia," 639.

61. Ibid., 643–44.

62. Ibid., 644–45.

63. Ibid., 648.

64. St. Augustine, *City of God,* V:9.

8

The Rise of the State System

The rise of states and a European state system to replace the sense of unity in medieval Christendom is the subject of this chapter. Observers of these matters included such luminaries as Machiavelli, Hobbes, Bodin, and Grotius. Their writings began conceptually with the new international order, drew on the writings of those who preceded them, and then developed in a contemporary context ideas associated with power and the balance of power, sovereignty and sovereign authority, and international law. These concepts were closely tied to the development of the state and system of states and contributed to our understanding of the transformation and legitimation of this newly emerging international order.

Historical Context

The movement from feudalism to the modern state system should be of particular interest to scholars of international relations, because it represents the most recent Western historical example of a systems transformation. As noted in the previous chapter, however, the important point to keep in mind is that the development of this European state system was not preordained. During the latter part of the thirteenth century, for example, representative assemblies were created throughout Europe that enhanced the power of the middle classes at the expense of kings bent on the centralization of power—Castile and Leon in 1250, Catalonia in 1285, the summons of Rhenish towns to the German Diet in 1255, the addition of lower classes into the parliament in 1265 that would eventually become England's House of Commons, and the first appearance of the Third Estate in France in 1302. While a critical function of these parliaments was to appropriate revenue the kings hoped would enhance their centralization of power, in some cases these institutions instead became rivals to the power of kings.[1]

The fourteenth century, however, was a particularly difficult time because of the Black Death, which swept through Europe from 1348 to 1352.[2] It was also a time of popular insurrections and the first concrete evidence

The Rise of States and the Westphalia International System

Date	Historical Developments	Writers and Commentators
1200	Rise of parliaments	
1300		
1400	Black Death plague (1348–1352); Hundred Years' War (1338–1453): England and France; Renaissance and Reformation begin	Machiavelli (1469–1527), More (1478–1535), Vitoria (1480–1546), Luther
1500		(1483–1546), Calvin (1509–1564), Bodin (1530–1596), Botero (1540–
1600	Age of Discovery and Colonialism in Americas	1617), Suarez (1548–1617), Gentili (1552–1608), Grotius (1583–1645), Hobbes (1588–1679), Spinoza (1632–
1700	Thirty Years' War (1618–1648); English civil war (1640s); Reign of King Louis XIV (1638–1715), the high point of French monarchical power	1677), Pufendorf (1632–1694), Vattel (1714–1767)
1800	French Revolution (1789)	

of the rise of national consciousness. By the following century, Henry V could count on the passionate support of the English in wars against France, just as Joan of Arc appealed to the patriotism of the French. The fifteenth century was also a time of decay in parliamentary institutions. Over time, the power of the king and his councils increased—for example, Louis XI in France, Edward IV and Henry VII in England, Ferdinand in Aragon, and Isabella in Castile. As one author noted, "Parliaments, cortes, estates-general were the bridge over which the medieval monarchs passed to the control of the centralized, popularly supported, governments of their respective countries."[3] England was the primary exception.

During the sixteenth century there was much conflict and resistance to monarchical state-building on the part of ordinary people coerced into surrendering crops, labor, money, and sometimes land to the emerging states. In England, for example, rebellions were put down in 1497, 1536, 1547, 1549, and 1553. Lesser nobles and other authorities, often members of local assemblies, not surprisingly also resisted. The religious wars in France in the sixteenth century were in part a function of a contest between royal prerogatives and regional liberties. A common thread running through all types of resistance to the emerging state was the issue of taxes. Increased taxation provided monarchs with revenues that supported larger armies which, in turn, were then used to defend and expand frontiers and overcome internal resistance to the centralizing states.[4]

Two immensely important developments during the one hundred years commencing with the mid-fifteenth century were the Renaissance and the Reformation. Taken together, they have been viewed by historians as the twin cradles of modernity.[5] The Renaissance, generally associated with western Europe's cultural rebirth, contained ethical and humanistic overtones and tended to glorify the individual. The Reformation, closely associated with the German religious leader Martin Luther (1483–1546) and his personal struggle for a right relationship with God, was particularly important in undercutting papal authority and the hope for the unity of Christendom. This process was further aided by Luther's belief, shared by the French-born Geneva Protestant, John Calvin (1509–1564), that state or secular authority should be separate from religious authority. With the growth of religious pluralism, national monarchies grew in strength as religious differences among the ruling houses exacerbated political problems.

Conflict over religion and the power of the emperor of the Holy Roman Empire touched off civil war in Bohemia in 1618 and eventually expanded throughout Europe into what has come to be known as the Thirty Years' War. The Thirty Years' War was really three wars. First, the imperial civil war that ended with the Peace of Prague in 1635; second, the western war that pitted Spain against the Netherlands and France; and finally, the Baltic war that was fought mainly in Germany and involved at various times Denmark and Sweden against the emperor and his allies. Although religion was an important factor, the underlying cause of war was arguably the shifting balance of power among the major states, which theoretically harkens back to Thucydides' discussion of the origins of the Peloponnesian War.[6]

There were a number of important results from the Thirty Years' War. First, the Peace of Prague in 1635 settled the religious problem in the empire and made it unlikely that religion would be the primary cause of war. As a result, secular leaders of Catholic countries could ignore the papacy's call for a militant counterreformation policy. Second, with the growing power of a number of German princes, it became more appropriate to speak of the dominions of the Hapsburgs as opposed to the Holy Roman Empire. The Hapsburgs became increasingly interested in their lands to the east as their weaknesses elsewhere within the official boundaries of the empire were now evident. The chance, therefore, of a secularly based empire and a united Europe was now as distant as the pope's hope for the unity of Christendom under papal guidance. Finally, a new balance of power emerged that witnessed the rise of Brandenburg-Prussia, Sweden, and France as the most powerful states in Europe.[7] To a certain extent, the character and organization of these states resulted from their involvement in military struggles.[8]

All three consequences have one thing in common—the emergence of the territorial state as the primary political unit in Europe by 1660. Even fifty years earlier, in 1610, "older institutional patterns like the empire, papacy, estates and free cities were still alive and active rivals."[9] But the peace agreement at Westphalia in 1648 helped to solidify the trend of increasing the power of the modern state at the expense of the other forms of political units. With the realignment of territorial borders, the notion of "sovereignty" of the state (to be discussed later at some length) came to the fore. This was reflected by the fact that the Peace of Westphalia initiated a new diplomatic practice whereby at the end of a war ambassadors would gather to negotiate a peace settlement based on the sovereign equality of both victor and vanquished.[10]

The rise of the state was not only seen in the political, diplomatic, and military spheres, but in the economic realm as well. Indeed, economic developments were critical in contributing to the ultimate victory of the state system over other contenders. For example, the seventeenth century was the heyday of large trading companies. But while in earlier years these companies were associated with families, now the companies were chartered by monarchs in the name of the state—for example, the East India Company (1600), the Dutch East India Company (1602), the Hamburg Company (1611). As these state-backed firms increased in power, private city-based firms and trading associations declined. By 1629, for example, only the cities of Lubeck, Hamburg, and Bremen (members of the earlier Baltic commercial association, or Hanseastic League) maintained their importance. Similarly, leaders of the large territorial states such as England and France worked to free themselves from their dependence on the foreign Florentine and German banking houses. In part this was because such family firms were unable to provide the amount of capital monarchs required in order to carry out their wars. Commercial and industrial firms also came to prefer more secure domestic capital sources and their need led to the rise of national banks.[11]

The development of state trading companies and banks were part of the dominant economic doctrine of the seventeenth century—mercantilism. Mercantilism preached that the state should play a major role in the economy by seeking to accumulate domestic capital or treasure by running continual trade surpluses in relation to other states. This practice was not in pursuit of some lofty moral aim or simply for the benefit of private entrepreneurs; the ultimate objective was to provide resources that could be used for war or conquest. As the French statesman and financier Jean-Baptiste Colbert stated, "Trade is the source of public finance, and public finance is the vital nerve of war."[12] In the name of regulating and protecting commerce, authoritarian state bureaucracies emerged that contrasted dramatically with the primary economic units of the late Middle Ages, the autonomous and self-regulating guilds. These national bureaucracies viewed competition in zero-sum terms—whatever one state gained came at the expense of another.[13]

In retrospect, all of these developments may seem to have led inexorably to the rise of a system of autonomous, belligerent states. This was certainly the view, as we will see, of such realists as Niccolo Machiavelli and Thomas Hobbes. But there were also developments working to counteract or at least mitigate this trend. They included developments of a transnational character that writers in the pluralist tradition would point to—the impetus to commerce resulting from the discovery of America and new routes to the Indies; a common intellectual background resulting from the flowering of the Renaissance; sympathy of coreligionists in different states that transcended national borders; and a common revulsion at armed conflicts because of the horrifying cost of religious wars. As one author argues, such "causes co-operated to make it certain that the separate state could never be accepted as the final and perfect form of human association, and that in the modern world as in the medieval world it would be necessary to recognize the existence of a wider unity."[14] This was recognized in the development of international law and the concept of external sovereignty (the claimed right of every state to be independent or autonomous in its international relations). As we will see, such writers as Grotius abandoned the medieval ideal of a world-state and accepted the existence of the modern, secular, sovereign state. But they denied the absolute separateness of these states and the extreme version of international anarchy as propounded by Hobbes. However limited it might be, the idea of community or international society could be applied, they argued, to the modern state system.

The historical developments we have summarized briefly cannot be understood completely unless one grasps how political thought about the state influenced these developments and vice versa. Not only did theorizing about the state provide justification for many of these developments, but it also entailed critiquing and attacking other possible forms of rule that, as we have noted, still provided alternatives by which international political life could have been organized.

Machiavelli

The importance of Niccolo Machiavelli (1469–1527) to political theory is well known. He is considered to be the first truly modern political theorist because of his emphasis on what is as opposed to what should be. This supposedly empirical, nonutopian orientation is captured quite nicely in his reference to much of the classical Greek and medieval philosophizing: "Many have dreamed up republics and principalities which have never in truth been known to exist; the gulf between how one should live and how one does live is so wide that a man who neglects what is actually done for what should be done learns the way to self-destruction rather than self-preservation."[15] The impact of Machiavelli's writings were, in the words of one historian, like "a sword which was thrust into the flank of the body politic of Western humanity, causing it to shriek and rear up."[16] The purpose of politics was not to make men virtuous, nor was the purpose of the state to pursue some ethical, religious, or metaphysical end, as asserted by many ancient Greek and medieval writers. Rather, politics was the means to pursue and enhance the internal and external security of the state. Despite being characterized as the first modern political theorist and the most important thinker in the realist tradition since Thucydides (whose work Machiavelli knew through his reading of Polybius, if not directly from Thucydides' ancient Greek text), Machiavelli is also a transitional figure between the medieval and modern world due to his obvious affection for the Italian city-state form of government and his admiration of the ancient Roman republic. In order to understand his contribution to the legitimation of the modern state, it is necessary to discuss the context within which he was writing.

Machiavelli was born in Florence into an old Florentine family. We know little of his youth, but in 1498 he was appointed to an administrative post at a time when Florence was a republic. He was engaged in diplomatic missions and also had the opportunity to observe domestic politics at close hand. In 1512 the Medici family was restored to power, the republic ended, and Machiavelli lost his government position and was imprisoned. Upon his release he attempted to reenter the political arena and, just as with Thucydides, began writing and analyzing the world around him. Political events during the last thirty years of Machiavelli's life had a tremendous influence on his work and view of politics. He witnessed the devastation of Italy by invasions of the French, Spanish, and Germans. Governments collapsed, civil chaos spread, and small city-states were devoured by more powerful forces. Despite his republican credentials, he came to look back upon the reign of Lorenzo de Medici as a golden age of political stability. His writing, therefore, revolved around the question of how civil order and security could be restored throughout Italy. More generally, he addressed the issue, as did Thomas Hobbes over a century later, of how to bring the state into existence and secure its independence.

To answer these questions he turned to history. The humanist tradition of his age had glorified the classical past, and so it was not surprising that Machiavelli turned to Roman history. To understand the dismal condition of sixteenth-century Italy, he was interested in learning what about republican Rome had allowed it to succeed for as long as it did. His in-depth analysis is to be found in *The Discourses on the First Ten Books of Titus Livy*, although the influence of Polybius, Plutarch, and Tacitus is also apparent.[17]

Republics and Security

Machiavelli begins by examining the development of Rome's constitution. Following the Aristotelian tradition, he contrasts principality, aristocracy, and democracy with the corresponding degenerate forms of tyranny, oligarchy, and anarchy. The three ideal forms are praiseworthy, but they are difficult to maintain and tend to slip into the degenerative forms. In adopting Polybius's cyclical theory of governmental change, he notes that as a result of domestic turmoil, the transition from one form of government to another may result in the state falling prey to a neighboring power. To avoid such dangers and the defects of each form of government, prudent legislators should choose a form of government that combines the best aspects of principality, aristocracy, and democracy.[18]

As with Aristotle, Polybius, Cicero, and Livy, Machiavelli argues that a mixed form of republican government is the most stable. The historical example he gives (probably based on Plutarch) is that of Lycurgus of Sparta who "assigned to the kings, to the aristocracy, and to the populace each its own function, and thus introduced a form of government which lasted for more than eight hundred years."[19] Although not a democrat, Machiavelli believed that the importance of a free citizenry stems from its ability to restrain the abuse of power by the governing class. Furthermore, as we will see, the ability of rulers to mobilize popular support makes republics better at defending a state's security than any other form of government.

According to Machiavelli, the key virtue of a republic that aids stability is its flexibility. In a discourse with a title that would be appropriate for a contemporary study of comparative foreign policy, "The Need of Adaptation to Environment," Machiavelli argues:

> A republic has a fuller life and enjoys good fortune for a longer time than a principality, since it is better able to adapt itself to diverse circumstances owing to the diversity found among its citizens than a prince can do. For a man who is accustomed to act in one particular way, never changes. . . . Hence, when times change and no longer suit his ways, he is inevitably ruined.[20]

A further advantage of republican flexibility is that in times of crisis, dictatorial powers can be temporarily granted to authorities. According to Machiavelli, during a crisis the slow working of republican institutions poses a potential threat to the security of the state because it takes time to reconcile diverse views. Such powers, however, must be granted by the institutions of the republic, not unilaterally seized by a dictator.[21]

Machiavelli, therefore, assumed that it is possible for even dictators to work for the common good. He goes so far as to make it a general rule that a state—republic or kingdom—is "well-ordered at the outset" or able to be "radically transformed" only if it is done by one person. He claims that in organizing a kingdom or constituting a republic, "it is a sound maxim that reprehensible actions may be justified by the effects, and that when the effect is good . . . it always justifies the action."[22] This comment would seem to reflect the cynical, superrealist Machiavelli condemned by commentators throughout history. But one important point needs to be noted. While princes may be superior in creating kingdoms or republics, the populace is "superior in sustaining what has been instituted."[23] In other words, just as dictatorial powers may be required at certain times, so too the maintenance of the state requires an active and engaged citizenry. Whether kingdom or republic, it is also essential that it be regulated by good laws, not the whim of the prince or the public.

Machiavelli's general preference for republics is also seen in his discussion of confederations. While temporary dictatorial powers may be required during certain crises, at other times the fact that republics are slower to act is beneficial if the issue is whether or not to break a treaty or dissolve a confederation. In an argument with which Kant probably would have agreed, Machiavelli claims "republics abide by their agreements far better than do princes."[24] The latter tend to break treaties for even small advantages, while republics tend to take a longer-term view of their security interests.

As noted, Machiavelli's emphasis on the virtues of domestic political stability (the state-societal level of analysis) seems to echo the importance given to political unity by Aristotle, Polybius, Cicero, Livy, and other writers we have discussed. But his view of mixed government has a dynamism earlier theories lacked in that he argues discord among the elements of a republic can actually strengthen a state. There are certain advantages at certain times to conflict among classes. For Machiavelli, the republican institutions of the Roman constitution and even liberty itself arose from such conflict. As he states near the beginning of *The Discourses,* "the quarrels between nobles and the plebs . . . were the primary cause of Rome's retaining her freedom." Furthermore, he generalizes that "in every republic there are two different dispositions, that of the populace and that of the upper class and that legislation favorable to liberty is brought about by the clash between them."[25] Public tumult not only serves as a catharsis, but it also makes the citizenry see that it is an effective element of the political system.

Here, therefore, we have perhaps the most important theme in *The Discourses* that is of relevance to international relations theory. According to Machiavelli, without the "affection of peoples for self-government . . . cities have never increased either in dominion or wealth." It is not "the well-being of individuals that makes cities great, but the well-being of the community."[26] Conversely, if tyranny replaces a republic, at a minimum the state ceases to grow in power and wealth, if it does not actually decline. What Machiavelli presents, in effect, is a theory of republican imperialism, using Rome as a case study. The dynamism of early Rome—exemplified by the creative tension between the people and the aristocracy—is critical in accounting for Rome's territorial expansion and glory.

What other factors were important? Machiavelli argued that aside from a good constitution, the political stability, power, and independence of the

Roman state derived from its leadership, religion, a citizen army, and arms. These themes were also taken up in *The Prince*. Machiavelli argued that the early Roman leaders in particular were successful because they had the talent to combine intelligence and will, thought and action. This ability to implement one's political ideas is essentially what Machiavelli meant by the term *virtù*, sometimes translated as "prowess" or "prudence." In a kingdom, if one weak prince follows another, the kingdom probably will not survive. But in early Rome, where power was vested in elected consuls, succession of competent and virtuous rulers was assured.[27] Machiavelli therefore exhibited what we have termed a voluntarist strand of thought in believing that individual leaders could make a difference in the realm of politics. This is also reflected in the fact that his most famous work, *The Prince*, was a practical handbook of politics dedicated to the ruler of Florence.

Secondly, Machiavelli also believed religion was a critical factor binding people together during the golden age of the republic. As he states in *The Discourses*, "All things considered, therefore, I conclude that the religion introduced by Numa [Romulus's successor] was among the primary causes of Rome's success, for this entailed good institutions; good institutions led to good fortune; and from good fortune arose the happy results of undertakings."[28] Religion helps to unify the people, so that a ruler does not have to rely on the self-defeating policy of coercion of his own citizens. Furthermore, pagan religions with their bloody sacrifices and rituals helped to incite warriors to be bold and fearless in war, while Christianity "has glorified humble and contemplative men, rather than men of action."[29] As the pagan religion of Rome decayed, so did the sense of community and the empire itself. It was such arguments, of course, that Augustine had attempted to rebut in the *City of God*.

It should be noted, however, that Machiavelli believed religion should be a means to reinforce the secular order and be a force for unity, not to dominate the secular realm or encourage disunity. In the case of Italy at the time he was writing, Machiavelli believed the church of Rome actually did more harm than good. Due to the "bad example set by the Court of Rome, Italy has lost all devotion and all religion." Worse yet, the church "has kept, and keeps, Italy divided." On the one hand, "neither its power nor its virtue has been sufficiently great for it to be able to usurp power in Italy and become its leader," nor "has it been so weak that it could not, when afraid of losing its dominion over things temporal, call upon one of the powers to defend it against an Italian state that had become too powerful. . . . The church, then, has neither been able to occupy the whole of Italy, nor has it allowed anyone else to occupy it."[30] It would be incorrect, therefore, to say that Machiavellli was antireligious or even categorically antichurch. What he objected to were those religious authorities whose selfish or misguided policies resulted in undermining the possibilities of attaining Italian unity.[31]

Third, Machiavelli argued that one reason the ancient Roman republic was robust and strong was that it relied on a patriotic citizen army. The willingness of citizens to die for the republic was a sign of the essential unity and strength of the republic. Mercenary armies, typical of the Italian city-states of his day, could not be trusted. While rulers were afraid to arm poorer citizens, Machiavelli argued that it was even more dangerous to trust the fate of government to an army of mercenaries who were "disunited, thirsty for power, undisciplined, and disloyal."[32] Similarly, for a state to place its trust in the troops of an ally is equally misguided.[33]

Finally, Machiavelli argues that it is necessary for a state to be well armed in order to deter and defend itself from outside threats. As he postulates, "Among private persons, faith is kept by laws, writings, and pacts; among rulers it is kept only by arms."[34] While good laws aid domestic stability, well-armed states expand the range of foreign policy choices for leaders.

Republics and Political Decay

Despite these virtues, however, the Roman polity and society eventually decayed. Why? Here Machiavelli introduces his view of human nature and his cyclical view of institutions. He accepted the part of the Christian tradition that views human beings as essentially fallen beings, sinful and corrupt, if not evil, "wretched creatures who would not keep their word to you."[35] There is a slight possibility of moral improvement, but this can only be achieved by a combination of the aforementioned good constitution, good leadership, religion, citizen army, and arms. But because of the basic evil of human beings, whatever institutions may be created and no matter how effective they may be at the outset, they are destined eventually to decay. This cyclical view of human institutions reflects the classical heritage, particularly the works of Polybius, which also led Machiavelli to argue that *fortuna*, or fortune, plays a major role in determining how long constructive political institutions will last. We see here a degree of determinism in his work; but his counsel that the prince needs to be bold in dealing with *fortuna* is also evidence of a voluntarist approach of exercising human will to control as much as one can.[36]

For Machiavelli, the social and political good is defined by the interests of the community or the "common good." This means that, in terms of the individual, one is pursuing the good if one acts for the interests of the community as a whole. This emphasis on serving the general interests of the community has a long tradition in Christian thought. But whereas Augustine and Thomas Aquinas emphasized a higher divine law, Machiavelli departed from this Christian tradition by restricting his argument to the level of a secular community. It will be recalled that Christian thought, as exemplified by Augustine, professed the doctrine of two kingdoms, with the secular kingdom (City of Man) inferior to the City of God. Machiavelli rejected this idea, making earthly power and secular politics the centerpiece of his political thought.

Because of the cyclical nature of human institutions, he argued, there will be good times as well as bad times for a political community. During these bad times it is necessary for a leader to act in accordance with the prevailing morality. While Machiavelli's preference was for leaders to be able to act as did those leaders of the early Roman republic, he lived during a time in which public order was lacking and war threatened the very existence of many Italian city-states. Hence, a leader "should not deviate from what is good, if that is possible, but he should know how to do evil, if that is necessary."[37] In other words, the prince should focus on what is realistic and possible, not simply on what is desirable. Even during this difficult time, effective leadership could contribute greatly to public order and the maintenance of a city-state's independence or even the unification of Italy.

This notion of using as one's standards the prevailing morality of an age has given "Machiavellism" negative connotations. It is sometimes forgotten, however, that in the last chapter of *The Prince* Machiavelli appeals to the national sentiment of all Italians in the hope that someone such as a Medici could unite Italy, end the civil chaos, and protect Italy from foreign invasions. By emphasizing a strong leader who could use nationalism as a means to strengthen the bonds of a political community, Machiavelli contributed to the literature that justified the centralization of power in the modern state. On the other hand, his ideal community was the small Roman republic and he exhibited a sentimental attachment to the small Italian city-state. He realized, however, that the city-state system on the Italian peninsula was increasingly becoming a political anachronism during a time when decisive political power on the European stage was being wielded by France, Spain, and England, which were taking on the attributes of the modern state. In order to defend itself, Italy needed to be united.[38]

Realism

Machiavelli's contribution to the realist image of international politics can be summarized as follows. First, the primary concern of the leader should be the security and independence of the state. His definition of the state is found in the first line of *The Prince*. "All the states, all the dominions under whose authority men have lived in the past and live now, have been and are either republics or principalities." The three component parts, therefore, are *dominion* (territory), the right or *authority* to command, and *people* located in the territory who obey and view the commands (laws, orders, decrees) as rightful.[39] In terms of security, the prince "must not flinch from being blamed for vices which are necessary for safeguarding the state."[40] This requires him to be alert to two dangers: "internal subversion from his subjects; and external aggression by foreign powers. Against the latter, his defence lies in being well armed" and, despite Machiavelli's reservations, having good allies. Internal turmoil can be avoided if the prince "keeps the people satisfied."[41] As for independence, "princes should do their utmost to escape being at the mercy of others."[42]

Secondly, Machiavelli believed that a leader could rationally plan and institute policies that could enhance the security and independence of the state if he were blessed with *virtú*. This is the voluntarist strand found throughout *The Prince*. As we have noted, the other, more determinist part of the political equation, is *fortuna* or fortune. As he states, "So as not to rule out free will, I believe that it is probably true that fortune is the arbiter of half the things we do, leaving the other half or so controlled by ourselves." These two concepts are constantly paired throughout his works.[43]

Finally, Machiavelli has a great deal to say about the conduct of relations among states. Much of his advice is located in his *Art of War* and in book two of *The Discourses*.[44] He examines such topics as three methods of expansion (leagues, alliances, hegemonies), basic causes of war (provoked and unintended), the relative advantages and disadvantages of offensive and defensive strategies, and the dangers of following a policy of neutrality.[45] As with other realists, Machiavelli believed that a permanent or perpetual peace was a dangerous illusion. Any leader who operated under such assumptions risked something worse than war—his country's loss of liberty, if not existence. He did not favor war for war's sake, but rather spoke of "necessary" wars designed to keep that which is worse than war at bay. In making his argument, Machiavelli used the language of just war doctrine. Toward the end of *The Prince* he approvingly quotes Livy: "Because a necessary war is a just war and where there is hope only in arms, those arms are holy."[46] Arms can act as a deterrent, but they will also play a critical role in terms of defense.

Machiavelli was one of the foremost contributors to the realist image of international politics, and in the process he became one of the most important observers and analysts of the emerging modern state. But Machiavelli's realism, as that of Thucydides, is not simply that of cynical power politics; such a depiction of his views borders on caricature. If one goes beyond *The Prince* and examines his other works, it is apparent that Machiavelli seriously wrestled with moral and ethical concerns. Furthermore, his recognition of the need for leaders to cope continually and creatively with political change and flux belies the stereotype of Machiavelli as provider of little more than political platitudes devoid of historical context and nuance.

Thomas More

Thomas More (1478–1535) is an author whose name is usually not associated with the literature on international relations. Writing at the same time as Machiavelli, he is generally viewed as an interesting contrast to the Italian. While Machiavelli is renowned for his political realism, More is typically associated with the unreal, communistic society he depicts in the second section of his *Utopia* (1516). Such a dichotomy is overdrawn.

More and Machiavelli are strikingly similar in one important aspect. Both agree on the need for kings of increasingly powerful modern national states to receive able advice from learned and experienced individuals in order to govern effectively and justly. Machiavelli, of course, initially served the republic of Florence and later hoped to return to public service. More, two years after he finished *Utopia*, was appointed privy councillor to Henry VIII and eventually rose to the important position of Lord Chancellor.

It is evident in book one of *Utopia* that More is quite aware of the problems in providing advice to princes. The central character, Raphael, has just returned to Europe after living for five years in the distant land of Utopia. Far from being merely a professional sailor, Raphael is a man of rare qualities, "more like Ulysses, or even Plato,"[47] according to More's friend, Peter Gilles, who appears as himself in the book. Gilles tells Raphael, "I can't think why you don't enter the service of some king or other. I'm sure any king would jump at the chance of employing you. With your knowledge and experience, you'd be just the man to supply not only entertainment, but also instructive precedents and useful advice."[48] More, also playing himself, asks Raphael to bring himself "even at the cost of some personal inconvenience, to apply" his talents and energies to public affairs. "If you can't completely eradicate wrong ideas, or deal with inveterate vices as effectively as you could wish, that's no reason for turning your back on public life altogether."[49]

Raphael, however, is skeptical and believes his unconventional views and straight talking would be unappreciated by kings and cause jealousies among the royal advisers. In a theme also of concern to Machiavelli, Raphael claims that royal advisers follow the maxim, "We'll never get human behavior in line with Christian ethics, so let's adapt Christian ethics to human behavior."[50] Raphael cannot accept this cynical approach. He argues, "I can't see what good they've done. They've merely enabled people to sin with a clear conscience."[51] The More character, however, argues that an adviser "must go to work indirectly. You must handle everything as tactfully as you can."[52] It is undoubtedly in this dialogue between the characters of Raphael and More that the author explores his own ambivalence toward public service, addresses the pitfalls and problems of providing advice to a prince, and raises the issue of the relation between politics and morality.

Other interesting similarities are to be found in the works of More and Machiavelli. Both utilize contemporary events (such as the French subjugation of Italy) to illustrate major points and evince an appreciation for classical works. Even more important, they both recognized the essential fact that the national state was emerging as the dominant political force in Europe. They both recognized that state power was increasingly being used arbitrarily, unchecked by the natural and divine laws propounded by bibli-

Swedish possessions

Spanish possessions

Hohenzollern possessions

Habsburg possessions

Boundary of the Empire

Norway
(Danish)

Scotland
Edinburgh

Ireland
Dublin

Denmark

Bremen

England

Amsterdam

London

Dutch Republic

Spanish Netherlands

Paris

German States of the Empire

Bavaria

Franche comté

Switz.

Savoy

Milan

Piedmont

Venice

France

Avignon
(papal)

Parma Modena

Genoa

Portugal
(claiming independence)

Lisbon

Madrid

Barcelona

Spain

Corsica
(to Genoa)

Tuscany

Rome

Naples

Sardinia

MAP III. Europe

Finland

Russia

Sweden

Stockholm

Baltic

Moscow

Courland

Copenhagen

Prussia

Poland

Brandenburg

Warsaw

Silesia

Habsburg Empire

Vienna

Hungary

Azov

Budapest

Crimea

Ottoman Empire

Black Sea

Papal States

Constantinople

Naples

Sicily

in 1660

cal teachings. They both also saw as their ideal a smaller social, economic, and political unit. In Machiavelli's case, it was the early Roman republic. More, a critic of the enclosure movement that was destroying pastoral communities in England through the erection of fences, was concerned that the growing power of the state was at the expense of the pluralism of medieval life, and he was favorably disposed toward the city-state called for by Plato and Aristotle.[53] More, of course, was sent to his death because he refused to accede to the absolutist claims to power by Henry VIII. As for Machiavelli, though shunned by the rulers of Florence, his reluctant acceptance of the need for a strong national Italian state in order to repel foreign aggressors helped lay the intellectual groundwork for later justifications of the modern state system.

Botero and Reason of State

The development of a legitimating theory of statecraft that "restrained dynastic exuberance and defined political interest in practical terms" came to be known as *raison d'état,* or reason of state.[54] The historian Friedrich Meinecke viewed the concept in the following manner: "Raison d'état is the fundamental principle of national conduct, the State's first Law of Motion. It tells the statesman what he must do to preserve the health and strength of the State. . . . For each State at each particular moment there exists one ideal course of action, one ideal *raison d'état.* The statesman in power tries hard to discern this course, and so too does the historian surveying the past in retrospect."[55] Here we have all of the essential elements of the realist image of international politics: the state as the key actor, with statesmen rationally calculating the best course of action for the state as a whole in order to preserve and strengthen the security of the state.

An Italian following in the footsteps of Machiavelli popularized the notion of reason of state.[56] Giovanni Botero's (1540–1617) *Della Ragion di Stato* (1589) was apparently must reading for those of that day and age with political interests. There is a certain irony, however, concerning this work. Botero, a counter-Reformation Jesuit, was trying to find a way to aid the papacy in pursuit of its goals. Botero felt that this required the church to seek secular support, just as it had following the collapse of the Roman Empire. His hope, therefore, was to mobilize the resources of the state in pursuit of these papal goals. Reason of state, however, could also be used to justify more secular pursuits, and over time the power of the state was justified in terms of its being a rational tool for the achievement of expressly political, as opposed to political-religious or moral, ends. Instead of being simply one political actor among various types of political units claiming autonomy, the centralized state deserved to be bestowed with supreme power because it had unique duties to carry out, such as defense of the realm. Under Cardinal Richelieu in France what could be termed the cult of state reached its climax. To this day the term is capitalized in French as *Etat*, as if to wrap the state in a cloak of mystery.[57]

Not surprisingly, there were also writers at the time who vigorously opposed such justification for increased state power. They endeavored to make the case for the maintenance of the powers of the representative estates. The medieval order, as we have noted, consisted of several estates such as the king, nobility, and clergy. The king, in other words, was one estate among several, and unity was encouraged by the adoption of a common Christian faith. In medieval times, estates could carry on negotiations with foreign princes or even other foreign estates. But the Thirty Years' War proved to be the turning point, decisively leading to the victory of the king's state over the estates. The estate form of organization was not an efficient means to conduct war, and in fact proved a hindrance to a king who needed to marshall resources quickly to prosecute a war effectively. The degree of the king's power certainly varied from state to state—less in England because of Parliament's assertion of supremacy after 1640, more in France as evidenced by the Estates General not meeting between 1614 and 1789.[58] The writer in the seventeenth century who is most closely associated with *raison d'état* thinking and the elevation of the secular state to the status of the supreme and all-powerful political entity is the Englishman Thomas Hobbes.

Hobbes

Along with Thucydides and Machiavelli, Thomas Hobbes (1588–1679) is renowned for his brilliant contributions to political theory and to the realist perspective on international relations. Aside from translating Thucydides' work into English, he attempted to do no less than place political philosophy on a scientific and secular basis and, in the process, he became one of the foremost theorists on the state and the nature of power. The son of a clergyman, at age four Hobbes could read and write, at six he learned Greek and Latin, and at fourteen he entered Oxford, where he found the university to be an insufficient challenge to his talents. At twenty he became a companion and tutor to the eldest son of Lord Cavendish, one of the more prominent aristocratic families of the day. Hobbes' association with the Cavendish family lasted throughout his life, and through the family he was able to meet some of the great men of his day, such as Bacon, Descartes, and Galileo. He also spent some twenty years on the continent, most of the time in Paris, which exposed him to a diverse array of philosophical and scientific developments.[59]

Given his association with the Cavendish family and his royalist leanings, Hobbes fled to Paris in 1640 when Parliament asserted its authority and beheaded King Charles I during the English Civil War. From 1646 to 1648 he served as mathematics tutor to Charles II, son of the executed monarch. In 1651 he returned to England and pledged his allegiance to the commonwealth. He remained in England until his death in 1679.

Hobbes' most famous work, *Leviathan,* was published just before his return to England. As with Thucydides, who experienced the Peloponnesian wars, and Machiavelli, who witnessed the Italian wars, Hobbes also wrote against the backdrop of conflict, the English Civil War. It is an important work for a number of reasons, among them the fact that it is the first modern work on political theory to be published in English. As with most political philosophers, Hobbes is principally concerned with issues associated with domestic rule, such as the relationship between the ruler and the citizens, and *Leviathan* is overwhelmingly devoted to this topic. But his impact on realist thinking about international relations has also been pervasive because of his discussion of two topics in particular—the "state of nature" and natural law.[60] Although there is some dispute on the subject, scholars of international relations have come to see his arresting image of the state of nature as analogous to the anarchic international system—a world without central authority.

Hobbes' view of natural law breaks rank with the writers who preceded him in that his particular conception did not emphasize restraints placed upon rulers, but rather how natural laws require absolute power to reside in the ruler. Taken together, the result is a view of international relations that sees sovereignty chiefly in terms of its internal aspects, with much less attention paid to the sovereignty of a state in relation to other sovereign states. Thus, like Machiavelli, Hobbes believed that security and order in the state are of the highest value. Furthermore, Hobbes leaves little hope either for international cooperation among states or for the mitigation of the effects of the international system's anarchic structure.

State of Nature

Hobbes did not claim that the state of nature he describes—a time prior to the creation of civil society—actually existed. Rather, the state of nature is his attempt to imagine what the world would be like without governmental authority or, for that matter, society without any governmental structure. As with other political theorists, his critical starting point is the question of human nature; how one answers this question dramatically affects one's prescriptions concerning the most appropriate type of political system. In the state of nature, men are ruled by their passions and are by nature roughly equal, so that even though some may be physically stronger than others, "the weakest has strength enough to kill the strongest, either by secret machination, or by confederacy with others."[61] Out of this basic equality comes the hope of attaining desired ends, and, as two men cannot enjoy the same thing equally, conflict results. "[D]uring the time men live without a common power to keep them all in awe, they are in that condition which is called war; and such a war, as is of every man, against every man."[62] Hobbes is not suggesting that in such a state of nature there is constant fighting; rather, war represents a constant "disposition" or "inclination," just as threatening weather may promise the possibility of rain.[63]

This condition has devastating consequences, because in a state of nature such uncertainty over one's security means no industry, no culture, no trading, no cumulative knowledge, no arts, no letters, no society, and, worst of all, "continual fear, and danger of violent death; and the life of man, solitary, poor, nasty, brutish, and short."[64] In such a situation there is no such thing as right or wrong because "where there is no common power, there is no law: where no law, no injustice. Force, and fraud, are in war the two cardinal virtues."[65] In other words, it is only where a civil society has been created with a supreme authority to regulate disputes and enforce contracts that we can speak of such things as justice.

Hobbes' description of the state of nature has been viewed as analogous to the international system. Just as in the state of nature where man stands alone, so, too, in the international system, do states strive to maintain their independence. Just as individuals in the state of nature have a predisposition toward war, so, too, is the international system marked by constant tension and the possibility of conflict. The single most important passage in which the comparison is made is:

> But though there had never been any time, wherein particular men were in a condition of war one against another; yet in all times, kings, and persons of sovereign authority, because of their independency, are in continual jealousies, and in the state and posture of gladiators; having their weapons pointing, and their eyes fixed on one another; that is, their forts, garrisons, and guns upon the frontiers of their kingdoms; and continual spies upon their neighbors; which is a posture of war.[66]

Both the state of nature and the international system therefore reflect a condition in which there is "no common power" to enforce order. In other words, it is a condition of anarchy, which means, as we have seen in the discussion of Thucydides, a system whose structure encourages suspicion and distrust. It should be noted, however, that for Hobbes such suspicion and distrust are due not just to the fact that no common power exists; rather, such attitudes and behavior reflect human nature unconstrained by any common power.

Natural Law

Is there any hope of escaping such a condition? What about natural laws, which earlier writers claimed should encourage greater civility in relations among men and secular authorities by providing common and restricting standards of behavior? Hobbes believed in natural laws, but conceived of them in a new way. He broke ranks with writers in the earlier tradition who argued that civil or man-made law is subordinate to higher natural or divine laws. Hobbes rejected this view, in part because he saw its revolutionary implications that would allow citizens to use natural law as a justification for the overthrow of a monarch, his preferred form of government, and in part because the crux of his analysis did not rely upon religious justification.[67]

For Hobbes, the key unit of analysis is the individual, and laws of nature are really rules of prudence designed to aid and guide individuals in their struggle for survival; they are not based on religious dictates. An individual's most basic right is that of self-preservation, resulting in the right of each person to do anything "in preserving his life against his enemies."[68] But given the fact that anyone can kill anyone in the state of nature, the most basic passion is fear of death. This leads to the first law of nature, which inclines individuals to seek peace so as to avoid being constantly afraid of death. When combined with reason, this leads one to "lay down this right to all things; and be contented with so much liberty against other men, as he would allow other men against himself."[69] This second law of nature leads individuals to seek "convenient articles of peace, upon which men may be drawn to agreement" as a way to escape the state of nature.[70]

Hobbes' other laws of nature, such as justice, cannot reach their full fruition outside an organized commonwealth that has transcended the state of nature.[71] Therefore their implementation requires a covenant, agreement, or "convenient articles of peace" among individuals. But what assurance is there that individuals will fulfill their obligations? Hobbes argues that this requires the creation of what he termed a "Leviathan," or supreme sovereign power. This Leviathan is not party to the covenant, but is charged with making sure each party fulfills all aspects of the agreement. The third law of nature, for example, defines justice in terms of individuals fulfilling their covenants. This is prudent because if each person does so, chances of escaping a violent death are enhanced. But, as Hobbes argues, "Therefore before the names of just, and unjust can have place, there must be some coercive power, to compel men equally to the performance of their covenants, by the terror of some punishment, greater than the benefit they expect by the breach of their covenant."[72]

Hobbes offers a unitary conception of the state, whether republic or monarchy, when he asserts that all power may be conferred "upon one man, or upon one assembly of men, that may reduce all their wills, by plurality of voices, unto one will," but his preference for monarchy is evident. This Leviathan "is called Sovereign, and said to have sovereign power; and every one besides, his subject." Factions are "unjust" as they are "contrary to the peace and safety of the people, and a taking of the sword out of the hand of the sovereign."[73] Hobbes, therefore, turns the traditional conception of natural law on its head; laws of nature do not result in restraints placed upon the ruler, but rather they devolve absolute power upon the ruler so that individuals who are party to a covenant can enjoy the benefits, particularly security, accruing from escaping from the state of nature. As Hobbes states: "Covenants, without the sword, are but words."[74]

We have thus come a long way from the medieval vision of community and in the process see a major justification offered for centralizing power in the modern state. Aside from his image of the state of nature and his unusual conception of laws of nature, what else did Hobbes have to say about relations among commonwealths? Hobbes states that the Leviathan is charged with providing citizens not only "peace at home," but also "mutual aid against their enemies abroad."[75] As with individuals in the state of nature, so, too, do commonwealths have the right to do anything to enhance their security. "So in states, and commonwealths not dependent on one another, every commonwealth . . . has an absolute liberty, to do what it shall judge . . . most conducing to their benefit. But withal, they live in the condition of a perpetual war, and upon the confines of battle, with their frontiers armed, and cannons planted against their neighbours round about."[76]

Are there any circumstances under which commonwealths might band together? Hobbes states that this is possible. "Therefore leagues between commonwealths, over whom there is no human power established, to keep them all in awe, are not only lawful, but also profitable for the time they last."[77] The overall tenor of his analysis, however, would suggest that he did not have a great deal of faith in the durability of such alliances. Nor does one even find Hobbes suggesting that ethical or moral considerations should play a role in conducting relations among kingdoms. International law is never mentioned. Finally, Hobbes does not suggest that the essential anarchy of interstate relations can be overcome through the creation of a worldwide Leviathan to provide peace and security. As a result, Hobbes seems to be suggesting that the state of nature for individuals is worse than the conditions faced by states; the former see the logic in needing to transcend anarchy, the latter do not. For while Hobbes claims, as noted above, that kings "are in continual jealousies" and in "a posture of war," he continues "there does not follow from it [posture of war] that misery, which accompanies the Liberty of particular men" in the state of nature.[78]

We see in Hobbes' work, therefore, the basic elements of the realist image, although presented in their most extreme form. The state is the supreme political organization. Unity is enforced by the Leviathan, who should not allow factions and who is also charged with dealing with the world beyond the kingdom's borders. While it is rational for the individual to escape the state of nature, it is also rational for individual Leviathans to guard against one another by, as previously quoted, "having their weapons pointing, and their eyes fixed on one another."

Sovereignty

Aside from reason of state, another critical concept that helped to legitimize the idea of an international system of states is that of sovereignty. The term is applicable both domestically and internationally.

The notion of sovereignty as the basis of authority has been termed the "constitutional" justification of absolute political power. The term appears in European history at a time when the issue of where supreme power should ultimately reside in the political community was in dispute. As argued by F.H. Hinsley, the concept of internal sovereignty was "an enforced compromise between those who claimed it lay with the ruler and those who claimed that it lay with the ruled. It is the justification of absolute authority that can arise and exist only when a final power is considered necessary in a body politic, and only when the body politic and its government are considered necessary to each other."[79]

These conditions were not met until the rise of the territorially based state, in which one could differentiate between the ruler and the ruled, state and society, and there was a felt need to establish an appropriate relation between the two. The ancient Greeks did not need to develop the idea of sovereignty because the concept of *polis* did not distinguish between the community and the state.[80] Conversely, while the Greek city-states were essentially "communities without distinctive state forms," empires such as those of Macedonia were essentially "states in search of communities" that "thought of themselves as lords of many communities and varied peoples, as kings of kings, as rulers of a whole continent if not of all the world. On the other hand, the impact of their forms of government upon their communities under their rule was negligible."[81] The Romans and their Byzantine successors developed the idea of internal sovereignty with final authority resting with the emperor. The impetus was a desire to overcome social and political chaos, and in the case of Rome the end result was despotic rule. With the decay of empire and the decentralization and fragmentation of power, however, the Roman idea of sovereignty faded into the background.

As we have seen, in medieval European communities there were many overlapping authorities claimed by a number of different actors or institutions. Although the notion of a final authority wielded by pope or emperor was not universally recognized, the pervasive influence of the medieval idea that Europe comprised a single community united as Christendom was one reason the idea of the internal sovereignty of states did not take hold until the sixteenth century. This idea of universal community, however powerful ritually, in reality was an inadequate basis for rule by a single sacred or secular authority who claimed dominion over all of Europe. At the regional level, single rulership needed to be united with a true sense of community for the idea of internal sovereignty to take root, with social disorder providing the needed impetus to move away from the excessive plurality of political authority in medieval Europe. These circumstances encouraged the concentration of power in the new regional, territorially based states. The critical formulation of this doctrine of internal sovereignty was the Frenchman Jean Bodin's *Six Books on the State,* published in 1576.[82]

Bodin

It is not surprising that the concept of sovereignty came to the fore in France. The development of judicial, administrative, and legislative institutions occurred in a country where the sentiment of nationalism was evident in the thirteenth century struggle between King Philip IV and Pope Boniface VIII. Jean Bodin (1530–1596) was born into the middle class, studied law in Toulouse, and lived at a time when France's progress toward unity was being threatened by Catholic–Protestant conflict. As so often happens, fanaticism on both sides made reconciliation difficult. Bodin was associated with the *Politiques,* a group dedicated to halting fanaticism. Although Catholic, the *Politiques* placed the state and nation above the Catholic church and recognized the political virtues of religious tolerance.[83]

In *Six Books on the State,* Bodin attempted to find a basis upon which harmony could be restored in the French political community. He agreed with Machiavelli and Hobbes that some centralized authority wielding preponderant power was needed to achieve this goal. Bodin, however, rejected Machiavelli's argument that the solution entailed freeing the prince from all religious limitations and restraints based on custom. Bodin argued that the body politic should be viewed as comprising ruler and ruled (similar to Machiavelli's definition of the state in the first line of *The Prince*), but he declared the ruler must respect moral and legal rules. The desire of the political community to escape chaos was not enough—the power had to be "sovereign."[84]

Bodin defined sovereignty as "the absolute and perpetual power of the state, that is, the greatest power to command." Bodin made an important distinction between government and state. A particular government exercises sovereign functions for a period of time. Sovereignty itself, however, is unlimited and perpetual. Governments headed by diverse individuals come and go, just as different types of governments may come and go. But sovereignty continues as long as the state exists. The absolute aspect of sovereignty refers to the assertion that there is no legal authority above the state. As Bodin claims, "Only he is absolutely sovereign who, after God, acknowledges no one greater than himself." The reference to God reflects the fact that Bodin still held the medieval sentiment that the sovereign king should not violate the divine laws of God and nature, an outlook that includes the idea that a king must keep whatever agreements he has made with his subjects.[85]

Although his primary focus was on internal sovereignty, Bodin also deserves credit for beginning a discussion on the implications of external sovereignty. Two obvious external threats to the sovereignty of the state were empire and the claims of the universal church. Bodin argued against their interference in the ecclesiastical and secular affairs of the state. As for relations with other states, Bodin viewed sovereignty as referring to the equal legal status of states. Political power, of course, varied, and some states were politically and militarily dependent on others. But no state was *legally* subject to the authority of any other state.[86]

To summarize, the concept of internal sovereignty refers to final and absolute authority within the state and society, while the concept of sovereignty as applied to relations among states involves the principle that no supreme authority exists over and above a collection of states.[87] While internal sovereignty means that one supreme authority exists in the domestic realm, the external concept of sovereignty rejects the idea of one final, absolute international authority. Each state is equally sovereign, with no other state having the right to tell it what to do internationally or how to handle its domestic affairs. While internal sovereignty works to aid domestic unity, sovereignty in its external manifestations reinforces state autonomy and the anarchic, decentralized structure of the international system. Medieval and universalistic claims of the papacy and empire were thus undermined.

External Sovereignty

If it took hundreds of years for the idea of internal sovereignty to take root, the external application of sovereignty involved an even longer and more tortuous process. Roman law was not of much help because it reflected Rome's rapid transformation from tribal city and republic to empire with no stops along the way. The sovereignty of the emperor in Rome was viewed in terms of its internal manifestations within the empire, not in terms of international or interempire relations.[88] Until the time of Bodin, kings might claim that they were *de jure* independent of the pope or emperor in terms of their right to govern their own communities as they saw fit, without external interference. But this did not imply that they saw themselves and the kingdoms they governed as isolated from these universal authorities or even from other states. The reason for this goes back to the idea that, despite differences, these states and their leaders were still part of a single community, united as Christendom.

It took perhaps another century after Bodin before the idea of applying sovereignty to interstate relations was worked out satisfactorily. The problem of developing an international version of sovereignty was similar to the earlier problem of developing the concept of internal sovereignty. It will be recalled that widespread acceptance of internal sovereignty required a balance between a ruler's desire to be superior to any man-made laws and his willingness to be subjected to ethical premises and political limits demanded by the ruled. In the case of the international application of the concept of sovereignty, it could not be applied "until the notion of the sovereign power of the individual state had been reconciled in some way with the ethical premises and the practical needs of an international community of states."[89] By the end of the seventeenth century, there were four basic schools of thought on international relations, all but one failing to recognize the need for such a reconciliation.

First, there were conservative writers who were part of a pluralist unity-despite-diversity school of thought. These individuals continued to cling to the medieval notion of the European international system as a single society in which divine and natural law, in the tradition of Aquinas and More, imposed common rights and duties on all states. The best known of these scholars was Francisco de Vitoria (1480–1546), a Dominican professor of theology, who utilized theological and natural law reasoning in his discussions of just war. Clerical writers naturally continued to argue for the power of the pope over the emperor and kings, or at least that the emperor should maintain power over local rulers in the name of the unity of Christendom. More secular-minded writers had other reasons to support the idea of a unified European order—fear of the growing anarchism of interstate relations and distrust of Machiavellism and *raison d'état* theories that appeared to encourage this anarchism.[90]

Second, legal positivists such as Francisco Suarez (1548–1617) and Alberico Gentili (1552–1608) emphasized the autonomy of the state and argued that international laws could and should exist. These laws, however, were extremely pragmatic in that they could only deal with codifying the diplomatic practices of sovereign states. The extent to which a community of sovereign states existed was the extent to which states were tied together by a mutually agreed upon body of laws.

Thirdly, so-called naturalists such as Samuel Pufendorf (1632–1694) argued that an international political society could not be created through the introduction of positivist international law. If there were to be any restraints on relations among states, they would derive from laws of nature that predated the historical state. Pufendorf was optimistic that through experience and reason these laws of nature could be known and established as legally binding principles, but he had no illusions concerning the likelihood of a universal society. At best, a society of sovereign states could be established.[91] Other naturalists exhibited even greater pessimism. The most extreme position was held by Benedict Spinoza (1632–1677), who essentially argued that might makes right and "the big fishes devour the little fishes by natural right." Thomas Hobbes, the most famous of the writers labeled as naturalists, argued that the international state of nature was really a state of war; as noted, neither international law nor ethical restraints are mentioned in those few passages of his works that deal with international politics.[92]

The final school of thought, which we could term the Bodin-Grotian perspective, saw the need to reconcile the internal sovereignty of the autonomous state with the notion of an international community. In the process, these writers paved the way for the modern conception of external sovereignty.

Grotius

The most important writer of this latter group was the Dutch legal theorist Hugo Grotius (1583–1645), who is credited with being the father of international law. On the one hand, Grotius is a realist in that he accepted the state as the key political unit and the fact that competition and war are inescapable aspects of the international system. On the other hand, he has contributed to the pluralist image of international politics by arguing that there is a basis upon which one can view the state system as a community that exhibits something less than a "war of all against all." As a Dutchman and Protestant, however, he rejected the direct or indirect authority of empire and church.

Grotius combined two strands of thought by believing that man-made and natural laws can both contribute to a tempering of conflict among states. On the one hand, he conceived of *jus gentium* (as did the positivists) as man-made laws resulting from human volition. On the other hand, he followed the moral theology tradition of Aquinas and Vitoria by also emphasizing laws derived from the laws of nature.[93] According to natural law, men in the state of nature were equal and free, with no superior. States, by the same natural law, are also free and equal. But just as individuals cannot live in isolation, as they are not sufficient unto themselves and must associate with one another in order to survive, so, too, must states. This conception requires augmenting the basic laws of nature through the creation of laws of nations based on custom, consent, or contract.[94] Hence, Grotius has no single term for international law, but discusses *jus naturae et gentium*—the law of nature and of nations or peoples. He contributed greatly to the emancipation of international law from theology, however, by stating that the laws of nations would still "have a degree of validity even if we should concede that which cannot be conceded without utmost wickedness, there is no God, or that the affairs of men are of no concern to Him."[95]

This tentative yet obvious desire to liberate natural law from theology reflects the fact that, although Grotius was apparently a dedicated Protestant, he was extremely tolerant compared to earlier Catholic and Protestant writers, who viewed those of differing religions as heretics. Perhaps because he was writing during the bitter religious wars of the first part of the seventeenth century, he realized that the growing corpus of international law had to be truly secular; otherwise, it would never be acceptable to both Catholics and Protestants.[96]

In his most famous work, *The Law of War and Peace* (1625), Grotius discusses all types of laws, including laws among nations. His discussion of just war doctrine approvingly quotes such writers as Augustine, Aquinas, Cicero, Livy, and Thucydides. Grotius argues that there are three justifiable reasons for going to war: "defence, recovery of property, and punishment."[97] But before war begins, the state that is accused of causing injury has the right to submit the matter to arbitration. The realist in Grotius recognized that in most cases this course is unlikely, hence the upholding of laws of nations must be undertaken by the aggrieved party through the use of force. In other words, war is a means to enforce a state's legal rights, analogous to judicial remedies in a domestic polity. Aside from the fact that war should not be undertaken "except for the enforcement of rights; when once undertaken, it should be carried on only within the bounds of law and good faith."[98]

It is in the third book that he deals with these "rules of warfare." Grotius discusses such topics as the treatment of civilians, prisoners of war, pillaging, and the duty of the victor toward those who offer unconditional surrender. The key idea running through his discussion of the laws of war is "moderation."[99]

The Law of War and Peace was an immediate success. The Latin original was published in almost fifty editions, and the book was translated into Dutch, English, French, German, Swedish, and Spanish. In Heidelberg a chair for the Law of Nature and Nations was established, dedicated to the study and elaboration of Grotius' work. Other European universities followed suit.[100]

In sum, Grotius dramatically differs from Hobbes in that he believed that states are subject to laws of nations and that the observance of these laws is in the self-interest of states. Given the fact that he was writing during the Thirty Years' War, Grotius believed "such a work is all the more necessary because in our day, as in former times, there is no lack of men who view this branch of law with contempt as having no meaning outside of an empty name."[101] Grotius' work gained even greater importance after the Peace of Westphalia in 1648. As we have noted, the war and its settlement completed the process of the transformation of an international system based on the tenuous unity provided by the papacy and the Holy Roman Empire to a system of sovereign states. In order to regulate relations among these new entities, a system of law was required. Grotius provided the intellectual foundation for this evolving interstate system.[102] He also served as an inspiration for later writers such as Emmerich de Vattel (1714–1767), who argued that a recognition of moral obligations among states could coexist with balance of power policies designed to assure the stability and independence of states.[103] Similarly, what Hedley Bull has termed the "Grotian conception of international society" has directly influenced much of the literature on regional integration and international regimes.[104]

Conclusion

All of the authors discussed in this chapter grappled with the emerging international order in western Europe that followed the breakup of the notion of unity in the Middle Ages provided by Christendom and empire. Machiavelli, perhaps the preeminent scholar in the realist tradition, drew upon the classical works of Greek and Roman scholars in his attempt to understand why Rome became such a world power in such a short period of time and hoped to find lessons and guidelines for rulers of emerging national states. For him, the key was to be found at the state-societal level of analysis— Rome's republican institutions. The dynamic nature of the republic allowed leaders to make the most of the opportunities provided by fate. In the course of his analysis, moral justifications for the state were discarded. Practical concerns as to how a leader can get power and keep it came to the fore and paved the way for such writers as Giovanni Botero, whose reason of state arguments were used to justify the further expansion of state power. If Machiavelli could still evince a certain nostalgia for the glory of the Roman Empire, Thomas More exhibited a similar sentimental attachment to the small medieval community and city-state. Nevertheless, More was a realist to the extent that he recognized the increasing importance of the modern national state and the need for statesmen to be provided with sound advice on how to use their extraordinary power.

Thomas Hobbes placed political philosophy on a more scientific basis, while using such traditional ideas as the state of nature and natural law. Such concepts were used to justify a powerful centralized state able to end domestic anarchy. In the process of making this argument, however, he elevated the concept of anarchy to the level of the international system and noted the war-like posture of states in a world without a superordinate authority to enforce covenants. His concept of the all-powerful Leviathan also contributed to the realist idea of the unitary and rational actor dedicated to maintaining the security and independence of the state.

The realist emphasis on the state as the principal actor in the international system, unified and calculating how best to preserve its physical integrity, was given a further boost by the concept of sovereignty, which reinforced state autonomy and undermined the universal claims of papacy and empire. What Bodin did for internal sovereignty, other scholars did for external sovereignty, so that the implications for relations among states were gradually worked out. Various schools of thought held different views on the nature of the rights and duties among states, but it was Grotius who realized that it was necessary to develop some basis upon which states could relate to one another in an anarchic realm. In the process, he argued that, to a certain extent, an international community existed, thus contributing to both the realist and pluralist images of international politics. For all of those writers who came after Grotius, the interstate system was a given of political life. Arising out of particular historical circumstances, political leaders and scholars asserted the sovereign state should claim the loyalty of its citizens, not some larger idea of humanity in general. Humanity was to be divided politically and territorially, the political community circumscribed, with the state and sovereignty henceforth to be treated as givens. Political thought therefore turned to analyzing the nature of this state system or ways to transform or transcend it.

Notes

Multiple citations within notes are listed in the order in which the quotations appear in the text.

1. "The whole system of estates—parliament, cortes—whatever its denomination, was in origin a monarchical device to attain ends of interest primarily to the ruler; but after the institution had taken shape, after use had given it security of position, and after the power of numbers, organization, and money had disclosed itself, these assemblages regularly used their powers to serve their own ends and in some countries to become rivals of the king in the government of the state." Edward P. Cheyney, *The Dawn of a New Era, 1250–1453* (New York: Harper and Row, 1936, 1962), 331.

2. This period is the subject of Barbara Tuchman's *A Distant Mirror: The Calamitous 14th Century* (New York: Alfred A. Knopf, 1978).

3. Cheyney, *The Dawn of a New Era,* 332.

4. Charles Tilly, "Reflections on the History of European State-Making," in *The Formation of National States in Western Europe,* ed. Charles Tilly (Princeton, N.J.: Princeton University Press, 1975), 22–23.

5. Lewis W. Spitz, *The Protestant Reformation, 1517–1559* (New York: Harper and Row, 1985), 5.

6. Myron P. Gutmann, "The Origins of the Thirty Years' War," in *The Origin and Prevention of Major Wars,* ed. Robert I. Rotberg and Theodore K. Rabb (Cambridge: Cambridge University Press, 1989), 181. See also Geoffrey Parker, *The Thirty Years' War* (London: Routledge Chapman and Hall, 1985).

7. Gutmann, "The Origins," 195.

8. This impact of war is an important theme in the works of Otto Hintze. See, for example, *The Historical Essays of Otto Hintze,* ed. Felix Gilbert (New York: Oxford University Press, 1975).

9. Carl J. Friedrich, *The Age of the Baroque, 1610–1660* (New York: Harper and Row, 1952), xiii. "It is proverbially easy in retrospect to be wiser about events than were the contemporaries. For example, it now seems perfectly clear that

nothing but the establishment of the modern state system could have been expected in 1610. Yet at the time, many thoughtful men were very uncertain. The activists of the Counter Reformation were, in fact, determined to re-establish the lost unity of Christendom, if necessary by force."

10. Friedrich, *The Age of the Baroque,* 193. For an overview of the specific political and territorial provisions of the treaty, see page 192.

11. Ibid., 6–8.

12. Ibid., 12.

13. As one writer at the time stated, "The increase of any estate must be upon the foreigner, for whatsoever is somewhere gotten is somewhere lost." As quoted by Friedrich, *The Age of the Baroque,* 13. It is also of interest to note that during the seventeenth century attempts were made to collect basic data on national life. The name given to this new science was "statistics," because the facts gathered were of concern to the rulers of the emerging states. Ibid., 3.

14. J.L. Brierly, *The Law of Nations: An Introduction to the International Law of Peace,* 6th ed. (New York, London: Oxford University Press, 1963), 6–7.

15. Niccolo Machiavelli, *The Prince,* trans. George Bull (London: Penguin Books, 1981), XV.

16. Frederich Meinecke, *Machiavellism: The Doctrine of Raison d'Etat and Its Place in History* (New York: Praeger, 1965), 49.

17. Niccolo Machiavelli, *The Discourses,* trans. Leslie J. Walker (London: Penguin Books, 1970, 1983). The first complete edition of Tacitus' works was published in Rome in 1515. Later, a committee of Venetian scholars blamed Tacitus for his influence on Machiavelli, "who would destroy public virtues." Tacitus, *The Annals of Imperial Rome,* trans. and introduction by Michael Grant (London: Penguin Books, 1956, 1971), 23.

18. Machiavelli, *The Discourses,* I:2.

19. I:2.

20. III:9.

21. I:34.

22. I:9.

23. I:58.

24. I:59.

25. I:4.

26. II:2.

27. I:20.

28. I:2.

29. II:2.

30. I:12.

31. "Niccolo cannot be found to speak irreverently of God. The same cannot be said for his writings about the church and churchmen. Though divinity and morality are typically established in a church, church and religion are not the same." Sebastian de Grazia, *Machiavelli in Hell* (Princeton, N.J.: Princeton University Press, 1989), 87.

32. Machiavelli, *The Prince,* XII.

33. II:20.

34. "Words to Speak on Providing Money, Given a Bit of Proem and Excuse," (1503), as cited by de Grazia, *Machiavelli in Hell,* 110.

35. *The Prince*, XVIII.

36. For Machiavelli's interpretation of Livy's view on fortune, see *The Discourses*, II:29.

37. *The Prince*, XVIII.

38. For Machiavelli's analysis of why France was well organized and governed, see *The Prince*, XIX.

39. *The Prince*, I. At other times Machiavelli restricts the term "state" to the command sector or distinguishes state from country. The latter is viewed as an object of love or devotion. As Machiavelli has one Florentine citizen rebuke another in his *Florentine Histories*, "This game that you play will deprive our country of its liberty, deprive you of the state and your substance, deprive me and others of [our] country." Cited by de Grazia, *Machiavelli in Hell*, 160. For an extended discussion of Machiavelli's views on the state, see de Grazia, 158–64.

40. *The Prince*, XV.

41. XIX. It is quite clear that Machiavelli saw the importance of a leader keeping the support of his subjects. As he states, for example: "It is necessary for a prince to have the friendship of the people; otherwise he has no remedy in times of adversity." IX.

42. XXI.

43. For examples of the relative importance of *fortuna* and *virtú* in the coming to power of two rulers, Francesco Sforza and Cesare Borgia, see *The Prince*, VII. In the case of the rise of Rome, see *The Discourses*, II:1.

44. Niccolo Machiavelli, *Art of War*, trans. Ellis Farneworth (New York: De Capo Press, 1990).

45. It is of interest to compare Machiavelli's analysis of neutrality with Thucydides' discussion of Athenian policy toward Mytilene and Melos. See Machiavelli, *The Discourses*, II:23; Thucydides, *History of the Peloponnesian War* (Harmondsworth, Eng.: Penguin Books, 1954), III:36–50; V:84–116.

46. *The Prince*, XXVI. See also de Grazia, *Machiavelli in Hell*, 172–73.

47. Thomas More, *Utopia*, trans. Paul Turner (London: Penguin Books, 1965), 38.

48. Ibid., 41.

49. Ibid., 42, 63.

50. Ibid., 64.

51. Ibid., 65.

52. Ibid., 64.

53. Such a preference was also evident in the writings of Erasmus, who always signed his works "Erasmus of Rotterdam" and preferred to live in the small semi-independent communes of Switzerland and the Netherlands. Myron P. Gilmore, *The World of Humanism, 1453–1517* (New York: Harper and Row, 1952, 1962), 138.

54. Gordon A. Craig and Alexander L. George, "The Emergence of the Great Powers," in *Force and Statecraft: Diplomatic Problems of Our Time*, ed. Gordon A. Craig and Alexander L. George (New York, Oxford: Oxford University Press, 1983), 5.

55. Meinecke, *Machiavellism*, 1.

56. "[The] emphasis on success of operations leads Machiavelli to a kind of emphasis on expediency, a purely pragmatic rationality in connection with politics. It is this rationality which the term 'reason of state' is meant to designate. 'Reason

of state' is a pragmatic rationality that is not concerned with whether the goals being sought are intrinsically reasonable or not. Its concern is purely with the question of how to conduct operations that lead to a successful conclusion." Carl J. Friedrich, *An Introduction to Political Theory* (New York: Harper and Row, 1967), 139.

57. Friedrich, *The Age of the Baroque*, 15–17. For another brief overview of Botero, see Meinecke, *Machiavellism*, 66–70.

58. Friedrich, *The Age of the Baroque*, 16–17.

59. William Ebenstein, *Great Political Thinkers: Plato to the Present*, 4th ed. (New York: Holt, Rinehart and Winston, 1951, 1969), 363.

60. It should be noted that Hobbes never actually uses the term "state of nature" in *Leviathan*. Instead he refers to a condition "out of civil states" or one of "no common power." He uses the term "state of nature" in his *De Cive (The Citizen)*. See Thomas Hobbes, *Man and Citizen*, ed. Bernard Gert (Gloucester, Mass.: Peter Smith, 1978), 114, 116.

61. Thomas Hobbes, *Leviathan* (Harmondsworth, England: Penguin Books, 1968), I:13.

62. *Leviathan*, I:13. Or as he later states, "That the condition of mere nature, that is to say, of absolute liberty, such as is theirs, that neither are sovereigns, nor subjects, is anarchy, and the condition of war." II:31.

63. I:13.

64. I:13.

65. I:13.

66. I:13.

67. It should be noted that Hobbes had a masterful command of religious texts such as the Bible. Indeed, about half of *Leviathan* is concerned with the topic "Of a Christian Commonwealth." What he essentially did, however, was to show how divine law is actually in line with his view of natural law, upon which his secular analysis of power and government rests. What are these divine laws "grounded in nature"? The same laws of nature he had discussed earlier (page 399). As Hobbes states in *The Citizen*, "The same law which is *natural* and *moral*, is also wont to be called *divine*, nor undeservedly" (page 153). To what extent he was simply attempting to mollify religious authorities of the day is subject to debate.

68. *Leviathan*, I:14.

69. I:14.

70. I:13.

71. "Therefore notwithstanding the laws of nature (which every one hath then kept, when he has the will to keep them, *when he can do it safely*) if there be no power erected, or not great enough for our security; every man will, and may lawfully rely on his own strength and art, for caution against all other men." *Leviathan*, II:17. Emphasis added.

72. I:15.

73. II:17, 22.

74. II:17.

75. II:17.

76. II:21. He later notes: "For all men that are not subjects, are either enemies, or else they have ceased from being so by some precedent covenants. But against enemies, whom the commonwealth judgeth capable to do them hurt, it is lawful by the original right of nature to make war." (II:28) And as he states in *The*

Citizen, "For the state of commonwealths considered in themselves, is natural, that is to say, hostile. Neither if they cease from fighting, is it therefore to be called peace; but rather a breathing time, in which one enemy observing the motion and countenance of the other, values his security not according to the pacts, but the forces and counsels of his adversary" (pages 260–61).

77. *Leviathan,* II:21.

78. I:13. This suggests that one should be wary of making facile comparisons or analogies between Hobbes' depiction of the state of nature and international relations.

79. F.H. Hinsley, "The Concept of Sovereignty and the Relations Between States," *Journal of International Affairs,* 21, no. 2 (1967): 243–44.

80. "The *polis,* while it had become a highly organized community, was still essentially a community where the outlook of its members had not yet freed itself from kinship and tribal limits, and where the structure of government had not yet sufficiently separated itself from the ways and institutions of the tribal society to produce the forms and procedures of the state." F.H. Hinsley, *Sovereignty* (London: C.A. Watts, 1966), 28.

81. Ibid., 30–31.

82. Ibid., 120–25.

83. Ebenstein, *Great Political Thinkers,* 349–50.

84. Hinsley, *Sovereignty,* 121–22.

85. Ebenstein, *Great Political Thinkers,* 350–51. Hobbes took the concept one step further by arguing the social contract among individuals that established the Leviathan resulted in the sovereignty of the state that was unlimited and not bound by religious or customary law. Hinsley, *Sovereignty,* 143–44.

86. For a discussion, see Alan James, *Sovereign Statehood: The Basis of International Society* (London: Allen and Unwin, 1986).

87. Hinsley, *Sovereignty,* 158.

88. Ibid., 36–37.

89. Ibid., 186.

90. Hinsley, "The Concept of Sovereignty," 246.

91. For a discussion of Pufendorf's views, see Andrew Linklater, *Men and Citizens in the Theory of International Relations* (New York: St. Martin's Press, 1982), 62–79.

92. Linklater, *Men and Citizens,* 246; Friedrich, *The Age of the Baroque,* 29. See the comments on Hobbes, Pufendorf, and Spinoza in Arthur Nussbaum, *A Concise History of the Laws of Nations* (New York: Macmillan, 1947), 112–18.

93. Nussbaum, *A Concise History,* 104.

94. James Brown Scott, "Introduction," to Hugo Grotius, *The Law of War and Peace* (New York: Bobbs-Merrill, 1925), xxx–xxxi.

95. Grotius, "Prolegomena," 13.

96. Nussbaum, *A Concise History,* 104–5.

97. Grotius, *The Law of War and Peace,* 171.

98. Grotius, "Prolegomena," 18.

99. See, for example, the headings to chapters 12 through 16 in book three, pages 745–82.

100. Nussbaum, *A Concise History,* 110.

101. Grotius, "Prolegomena," 9.

102. Oskar Piest, "Editor's Introduction" to Grotius, *Prolegomena to the Law of War and Peace* (Indianapolis: Bobbs-Merrill, 1957), xiv. As James Bryce has stated, "When by the peace of Westphalia a crowd of petty principalities were recognized as practically independent states, the need of a body of rules to regulate their relations and intercourses became pressing. Such a code (if one may call it by that name) Grotius and his successors compiled out of the principles which they found in the Roman law, then the private law of Germanic countries, thus laying the foundation whereupon the system of international jurisprudence has been built up during the last three centuries." James Bryce, *The Holy Roman Empire* (5th ed., 1904), 436 (no further citation) as cited by Piest, xiv–xv.

103. For an analysis of Vattel's work, see Linklater, *Men and Citizens*, 80–96.

104. Hedley Bull, "The Grotian Conception of International Society," in *Diplomatic Investigations: Essays in the Theory of International Politics*, ed. Herbert Butterfield and Martin Wight (Cambridge, Mass.: Harvard University Press, 1966), 51–73. Hedley Bull, *The Anarchical Society: A Study of Order in World Politics* (New York: Columbia University Press, 1977), ch. 4. A. Claire Cutler, "The 'Grotian Tradition' in International Relations," *Review of International Studies*, 17, no. 1 (January 1991): 41–65. See Stephen D. Krasner, ed., "International Regimes," special issue of *International Organization*, 36, no. 2 (Spring 1982): 192–94. See also Evan Luard, *International Society* (Basingstoke, Eng.: Macmillan, 1990).

9

Eighteenth- and Nineteenth-Century Thinking on International Relations

The formal emergence of the sovereign state and system of sovereign states in the 1648 Peace of Westphalia was reflected in the fifteenth-, sixteenth-, and seventeenth-century scholarly writings that preceded, accompanied, or soon followed this event. Steeped as they were in the corpus of Greco-Roman and medieval thought, these early modern writers established an important intellectual foundation that would be built upon in the eighteenth, nineteenth, and early twentieth centuries. With the notable exception of Grotius, however, sixteenth- and seventeenth-century writers tended to focus primarily on the domestic aspects of the state and did not look very far beyond its borders. Thus, Machiavelli was concerned largely with politics among city-states on the Italian peninsula, although he recognized the importance of such great powers of the day as Spain and France. Similarly, Hobbes and Bodin focused primarily on the domestic aspects of sovereignty. By contrast, Grotius and those writers on international law who followed him looked outside the confines of the state or the politics of a region to the world as a whole. They went well beyond realism and contributed intellectually to the advancement of a pluralist conception of world order.

While speculation continued on the relation between human nature and conflict, the state-societal and international levels of analysis became increasingly important foci of attention. Whether or to what degree structure (or lack of it) in the international environment affects the nature and behavior of states is a question addressed by Montesquieu, Rousseau, and Kant. Or is it the nature of the domestic regime or society that matters more? These questions, as well as those on economic aspects of international politics addressed by Adam Smith, Karl Marx, and nineteenth-century liberals, are the central issues of this chapter. Despite differing interests, arguments, and conclusions, these writers share one characteristic: their works were influenced, to varying degrees, by the basic assumptions and principles of the seventeenth- and eighteenth- century Enlightenment.

181

Eighteenth- and Nineteenth-Century Thought

Date	Historical Developments	Writers and Commentators
1600		Descartes (1596–1650)
	Colonialism in Americas, Austrians defeat Ottomans outside Vienna (1683); William and Mary: "Glorious Revolution" in England (1688)	
1700		Montesquieu (1689–1755) Hume (1711–1776), Rousseau
	Treaty of Utrecht (1713) curbs French power for 75 years; publication of *The Federalist Papers* (1787–1788); French Revolution (1789) followed by	(1712–1778), Smith (1723–1790), Kant (1724–1804), Hegel (1770–1831), Ricardo (1772–1823)
1800	Napoleonic period of European conquest; Defeat of Napoleon and Congress of Vienna (1815); Latin American independence movements; repeal of Corn Laws advances free trade liberalism in England; 1848 revolutions sweep Europe; Crimean War curbs Russian power in southeastern Europe (1854–1856); Prussia defeats France in 1870–1871 war; Germany unites; Western imperialism in Africa, Middle East, Asia, and Pacific	Cobden (1804–1865) Marx (1818–1883) Hobson (1858–1940), Weber (1864–1920), Lenin (1870–1924)
1900	World War I (1914–1918)	

Historical Context

The European state system in the years following 1648 was marked by multiple rivalries and shifting alliances. The Turkish challenge to Austrian power was arrested by the defeat in 1683 of the Ottoman invaders just outside Vienna. English preoccupation with the domestic turmoil of the civil war and the Cromwell period finally ended with the ascendance to the throne in 1688 of William and Mary. French ambitions on the continent were blocked militarily in a series of battles conducted by the British in association with the House of Savoy in northern Italy. The Treaty of Utrecht (1713) was part of a settlement that effectively curbed the French for the seventy-five years prior to the revolution of 1789.

The French Revolution itself was a watershed, not just for France, but for all of Europe. Competing ideas and emerging ideologies would cast a long shadow over the nineteenth and twentieth centuries to our own time. In contrast to such liberal and democratic ideas as *liberté, egalité, fraternité* was authoritarianism—whether Jacobin or Bonapartist—models that would find many emulators over the next two centuries. The Napoleonic period not only upset the Westphalia system by replacing it for a short time by an empire with France at its center, but also witnessed the spread of French language and culture, French-style central administration of state affairs, and the idea of universal national military service by citizen-soldiers (the *levée en masse*). All of these elements would remain in Europe long after Napoleon's final defeat and the subsequent restoration of the "Westphalia system" of sovereign, independent states that was completed at the Congress of Vienna in 1815.

Attention in Vienna was paid to restoring a balance among the Great Powers and providing a conflict-management system—the Concert of Europe. Thus, France was restored as a major power in what was seen as an overall balance on the continent and in Europe as a whole. Small wars were fought from time to time, but Europe remained free of general war until 1914. The periodic conferences of the "concert" approach to managing conflict within an overall European balance proved reasonably successful in the immediate decades after the 1815 settlement, but broke down as an effective instrument in the last half of the century. The breakdown of the concert was clearly marked by the Crimean War (1854–1856), in which Britain joined France and Turkey in a dispute against Russia that effectively curbed the latter's role in southeastern Europe. French defeat in 1870 in the Franco-Prussian War and the subsequent unification of Germany marked the beginnings of Great Power rivalry outside of any European concert, a development that ultimately reached its conclusion in World War I.

The focus in this volume on European history and thought stems from the fact that contemporary international relations theory and practice are drawn primarily from this European experience. In the eighteenth and nineteenth centuries we see the expansion of both the European system of sovereign states and European notions of a capitalist market economy to include the entire globe. Colonialism, which began in the late fifteenth century, reached global scope in the eighteenth and nineteenth centuries. While some European states established colonies in Africa early, much of the rest of Africa and Asia was not colonized until the imperial era of the nineteenth century. Although most American states established independence from Europe early in the nineteenth century, large-scale decolonization in Africa and Asia did not occur until the twentieth century in the aftermath of two world wars.

The important point, however, is not the precise date when specific states came into existence. Rather, it is that all did so in accordance with a European pattern formally established at Westphalia. Ideas originating in Europe thus came to define international relations for the world as a whole. Moreover, the Europeans (and the Americans, who were a product of these European ideas) left behind realist, pluralist, and globalist concepts of world politics and economics.

The Enlightenment

Despite the diversity of thought of such writers as Montesquieu, Rousseau, Kant, Hegel, Smith, and Marx, they had one characteristic in common: all were influenced, to greater or lesser extents, by the basic assumptions and principles of the seventeenth- and eighteenth-century Enlightenment. Despite a common starting point, however, their interests, analyses, and prescriptions varied widely.

The basic assumptions of the Enlightenment are perhaps best revealed in the works of the French rationalists of the eighteenth century who published the first volume of the *Encyclopédie* in 1751. Such individuals—Diderot, d'Alembert, Helvetius, d'Holbach, and later Condorcet—were influenced by the scientific method of the past century that used mathematical reasoning as a means to establish truth by a method independent of God's revelation. These writers contributed to the development of a systematic philosophy based on the classical Greek assumption that individuals are rational, reasoning beings, and the assertion of René Descartes (1596–1650) that "the mastery and possession of nature" is possible.[1] They argued that through the application of reason it is possible to overcome superstition, prejudice, and tradition and to understand the laws that govern nature as well as—more importantly—human society. These laws were understood to be universal, particularly the law of reason, and hence applicable to all of humanity. This overpowering belief in the importance of acquiring knowledge and the development of a science of politics akin to what was occurring in the natural sciences resonates today in the social sciences, including much of the work on international relations. In this regard, the Enlightenment was to a great extent concerned with the issue of the appropriate methods required to understand human behavior.

But there was another important element of Enlightenment thought that moved one from the realm of analysis to the realm of action: Rational individuals could exercise reason to create eventually an environment reflecting the revealed laws of nature. For example, through reason the nature of justice could be discerned, and in turn the just society could be created. Enlightenment thinkers had great faith in the progress of humanity, and a result was their political argument, following the Stoics, that all people are linked by nature in universal brotherhood. Some writers took the next step and argued that what divided humanity was the increasingly powerful sovereign state. As a result, writers who embraced unreservedly the values of the Enlightenment often called for world citizenship, with such diverse notables as Voltaire, Samuel Johnson, and Goethe deploring patriotic prejudice.[2]

The political implications, particularly in France, were revolutionary. Rejecting the idea of original sin and the assumption of innate aggressiveness, these writers argued that the failings attributed to human nature were not inborn, but rather the result of a corrupt environment. If environment caused humanity to be less than reason and nature intended, a program of societal restructuring became a moral imperative; the perfectibility of humanity was possible. The embrace of this extreme form of voluntarism was exhibited during the French Revolution. Not only was it the duty of the revolutionaries to liberate the people of France from the *ancien régime* and the weight of the past, but they also believed it was their duty to engage in wars of liberation abroad. The excesses of the French Revolution not only destroyed the monarchy, but also shocked the serene confidence in the perfectibility of man. The skepticism of David Hume (1711–1776), his thorough critique of human reason, and his claim that morality should be in accordance with passions contributed to the disintegration of this voluntarist movement.[3] Our concern, however, is less with the historical political influence of the Enlightenment and more with its methodological implications as reflected in the authors under consideration.

In this chapter, as elsewhere in this volume, we have not attempted an exhaustive survey and summary of every writer whose commentaries have had a bearing on the development of international relations theory. In our eighteenth- and nineteenth-century focus here, we necessarily have had to be very selective. We relate in this section the progression of thought on the state and system of states offered by Montesquieu, Rousseau, Kant, Hegel, Weber, and the authors of the *Federalist Papers* because of the profound effect their thought has had, directly or indirectly, on many present-day international relations theorists. Given the importance of international political economy as a central part of international relations, we have selected the contributions of two classical political economists (Smith and Marx), the work of nineteenth-century liberals, and the analyses of imperialism by Hobson and Lenin as the subject of the latter part of this chapter.

Montesquieu

Charles Louis de Secondat, Baron de la Brède et de Montesquieu (1689–1755) was born to an old aristocratic French family, as his full name and titles suggest. After studying law at the university of Bordeaux, he moved to Paris, but after the death of his father returned home to administer the family estate. His financial security afforded him the opportunity to pursue his intellectual interests, which included further study of Roman law. But it was the publication of his satirical analysis of contemporary France, *The Persian Letters*, that brought him fame. Foreign travel, particularly his experiences in England, further stimulated his interest in politics and constitutions. As a serious student of ancient Greek and Roman writings, Montesquieu was familiar with the mixed constitutions as they appeared in Plato's *The Laws* (book 3) and Aristotle's *Politics* (books 4 and 5). Like

Machiavelli, he placed great emphasis on statecraft and rejected the view of the Greek classics that the primary function of political theorizing was to encourage virtue. He was also more in tune with Machiavelli about the effect of both necessity and choice in the formation of laws, and hence he diverged from the Enlightenment's supreme confidence in voluntarism and the ability to transform societies. Indeed, in his *Spirit of the Laws* (1748), he describes how historical, geographical, and climatic circumstances created diverse human cultures and a diverse "general spirit" of each nation. Montesquieu believes that all nations live more by passion and prejudice, and less by reason.[4]

Nevertheless, he argues that such diversity is intelligible only in the light of general causes. Montesquieu reflects Enlightenment thinking by defining laws in his famous opening formulation as being "necessary relations arising out of the nature of things," and this necessity is by definition universal.[5] Following the Stoics, he claims these laws "govern" the actions of all things, and provide the standard by which human law is to be judged. In contrast to Aquinas, nature, not God, is the ultimate source of law. His view of natural law expressed a hope of establishing a science of human affairs, parallel to Cartesian and Newtonian physics.[6] Does this mean that only one particular form of government or set of laws is in accord with nature? No. "Law in general is human reason, inasmuch as it governs all the inhabitants of the earth; the political and civil laws of each nation ought to be only the particular cases in which this human reason is applied."[7] Compared to the utopian French rationalists, this acceptance of diversity in part reflects Montesquieu's belief in the limits to purposive human action.

Polybius no doubt was responsible for Montesquieu's advocacy of a separation of powers that would balance governmental powers among competing departments or branches—an idea adopted by American federalists concerned with avoiding too strong a central government. For Montesquieu, such an arrangement most effectively promoted liberty. While, like the ancients, he believed a stable polity was in and of itself a worthwhile goal, he ranked liberty as the top priority. One can read in the *Federalist Papers* of Alexander Hamilton, James Madison, and John Jay a similar concern for liberty.

On the relation between regime type for a given political system and the way that country projects itself in its foreign affairs, Montesquieu's republican preference is clear. He states that "the spirit of monarchy is war and enlargement of dominion." By contrast, "peace and moderation is the spirit of a republic."[8] This sentiment aligns him with such thinkers as Kant, as opposed to Machiavelli, who not only argued that republics are best able to defend themselves, but also best at expansionism. What all three men had in common, however, was a belief that the domestic character of a state and its society does influence its behavior internationally.

There are intellectual links among Montesquieu, Rousseau, and Kant in their writings on politics in general and international relations in particular. Montesquieu influenced Rousseau, and we know that Kant incorporated insights drawn from his reading of Rousseau. In formulating their own positions, all three rejected a Hobbesian (or Machiavellian) negative view of human nature. There is in Montesquieu a profound critique of Hobbes. One can find it in his early work, *The Persian Letters,* as well as in his *Spirit of the Laws.* To Montesquieu it is not human nature that is defective. The problem arises when human beings enter civil society from their natural state. Moreover, the problem is compounded by the formation of separate nations and the relations that occur among them. Montesquieu's argument therefore links together three levels of analysis—the nature of the individual, society, and the international system.

Rousseau's argument on the formation of society upon departure from a state of nature has a familiar sound when one already has read Montesquieu. The state of nature is not, as Hobbes would have it, a state of war. Indeed, Montesquieu tells us that "as soon as mankind enter into a state of society, they lose the sense of their weakness, the equality ceases, and then commences the state of war."[9] The state of war thus occurs after the formation of society, not before. For Montesquieu (and for Rousseau, who would follow this line of reasoning), war is an artifact of society, not characteristic of human nature as such.

How is such societal strife to be overcome? Part of the answer is to be found in what Rousseau would later term the "general will." Montesquieu observes that "the particular force of individuals cannot be united without a conjunction of all their wills." It is "the conjunction of those wills" that Montesquieu calls "the civil state."[10] Also laying a foundation upon which Rousseau would build in *Emile,* Montesquieu places emphasis on the Enlightenment concern with "education," by which individuals are prepared for "civil life."[11]

Montesquieu recognizes divine and natural law, but focuses on the different categories or "orders of laws" that apply to moral, religious, domestic, and international domains of human beings and their societies. Montesquieu refers to the law of nations as "the civil law of the universe, in which sense every nation is a citizen."[12] From a juridical perspective, then, states are like persons and, as such, are understood as unitary actors. Rousseau's later development of the idea of general will for a society clearly would be consistent with this unitary notion of the state as a singular actor representing the multitude of individuals comprising it. Indeed, in realist thought one of the clearest expressions of Rousseau's general will is the notion that the foreign policies of states are unitary and are formulated in the service of the national interest.

In a world of many nations "each particular society begins to feel its strength" and, as a result, there "arises a state of war between different nations." To regulate their conduct, Montesquieu writes, nations "have laws relative to their natural intercourse, which is what we call the law of nations."[13] He observes that the law of nations holds "that different nations ought in time of peace to do one another all the good they can, and in time of war as little harm as possible, without prejudicing their real interests." And a central interest for all nations is their "preservation." Indeed, Montesquieu tells us that "the safety of the people is the supreme law."[14]

States thus have a right to go to war in their own defense. Montesquieu comments that "among societies the right of national defense carries along with it sometimes the necessity of attacking" as "when one nation sees that a longer peace will enable another to destroy it, and that to attack that nation instantly is the only way to prevent its own destruction." Moreover, Montesquieu allows for a "right of conquest," but he argues that it rests upon this same preservationist principle.[15]

In sum, Montesquieu's work reflects an appreciation for republican or mixed forms of government, a tradition of thought dating back to ancient Greece. As with Kant, but contrary to Machiavelli, Montesquieu believed "peace and moderation is the spirit of the republic." His realism is evident in his acceptance of the diversity of states and a view of international law that conceives of states as unitary actors pursuing their respective national interests. Statecraft is important, requiring leaders to make reasoned choices while operating under constraints. War is to be expected, and hence states develop laws and norms to regulate their relations to the extent possible. His realism downplays the idea that individual leaders are able to control foreign policy outcomes or collectively work to transform the international system into a different type of order.

Rousseau

Jean-Jacques Rousseau (1712–1778), whose work reflected influences as diverse as Montesquieu, Locke, and Plato, provided an extraordinary intellectual legacy subject to numerous interpretations (and misinterpretations). The problem in understanding Rousseau stems from the complexity of his thought, compounded by changes made to his manuscripts by editors who did so without his approval. Born in Switzerland as the son of a watchmaker, his *Confessions* describes a difficult early life filled with varied experiences, including being the ward and then lover of a Mme. de Warens. Various trips to Paris to seek his fame and fortune in the arts met with little success. His interest in social-political matters was stimulated by his association with Denis Diderot, editor of the *Encyclopédie*. At Diderot's encouragement, Rousseau competed in an essay contest on the relation between morality and the sciences and the arts. After he won, fame immediately followed. Two of his works, *Emile* and *On the Social Contract,* offended authorities, and the subsequent issuing of an order for his arrest caused him to flee France. Eventually he went to England under the encouragement of David Hume, but the two quarreled, and Rousseau returned to France where he lived out his days.[16]

The influence of Enlightenment thinking on Rousseau, as with other social contract theorists such as John Locke, is best expressed in his argument that individuals escape the state of nature by way of a mutually beneficial agreement or social contract; creation of society is an act of volition or will. One finds Rousseau's concept of the state of nature (a formulation that departed from the natural law concept so central to Locke's presentation of human rights) most clearly stated in his *Discourse on the Origin of Inequality*. The state of nature to Rousseau was an egocentric world in which "man's first sentiment was that of his own existence; his first concern was that of his preservation." In this primitive state individuals might collaborate "but only insofar as present and imperceptible interests could require it." They were concerned only with the short run "since foresight meant nothing to them, and far from concerning themselves about a distant future, they did not even give a thought to the next day."[17]

In a passage particularly noteworthy for international relations theorists, Rousseau states:

> Were it a matter of catching a deer, everyone was quite aware that he must faithfully keep to his post in order to achieve this purpose; but if a hare happened to pass within reach of one of them, no doubt he would have pursued it without giving it a second thought, and that, having obtained his prey, he cared very little about causing his companions to miss theirs.[18]

For many current theorists, the importance of this passage stems from its presentation of a scenario that exhibits the same sorts of dilemmas and dynamics resulting from the anarchical structure of the international system. Are states like these primitive hunters, serving their individual, short-run, self interests? Or do they recognize the advantages of fulfilling mutual commitments? In short, will states be willing to forgo short-term gratification for themselves and act for common interests that serve longer-term advantages for all—an enlightened self interest?[19] As should be apparent by now, the authors under consideration in this work overwhelmingly explain conflict and lack of cooperation among states in terms of human nature and the nature of states or societies. In Rousseau, we see a rare emphasis on how the decentralized structure of a system—the state of nature, and, by analogy, the international system—also contributes to suspicion, distrust, and conflict. In other words, the difficulty of cooperation among egocentric actors (states or individuals) stems as much from the self-help nature of the system itself as it does from the nature of the actors themselves.

To Rousseau, therefore, the structure and values of the social setting (to include the international environment) have a great deal to do with the behavior of individuals (and states) within it. Echoing Montesquieu, Rousseau tells us when individuals left the relatively happier state of nature, "emerging society gave way to the most horrible state of war since the human race, vilified and desolate, was no longer able to retrace its steps or give up the unfortunate acquisitions it had made."[20] Rousseau laments:

> The first person who, having enclosed a plot of land, took it into his head to say *this is mine* and found people simple enough to believe him, was the true founder of civil society. What crimes, wars, murders, what miseries and horrors would the human race have been spared, had someone pulled up the stakes or filled in the ditch and cried out to his fellow men: "Do not listen to this imposter. You are lost if you forget that the fruits of the earth belong to all and the earth to no one."[21]

Thus, property and the divisions that stem from the resulting inequality are, to Rousseau, at the root of human conflict, whether among individuals or states. Rousseau observes how "more murders were committed in a single day of combat and more horrors in the capture of a single city than were committed in the state of nature during entire centuries over the entire face of the earth."[22] These are the "effects one glimpses of the division of mankind into different societies." The anarchy of the state system is responsible for "the national wars, battles, murders, and reprisals." The numerous "bodies politic" exist in a condition "more deadly" than previously had existed "among the private individuals of whom they were composed."[23]

At the state-societal level of analysis, Rousseau argues that in these bodies politic governance is to be in accordance with the general will as if the political community were a single person or unit. The present-day realist view of the state as a unitary rational actor is certainly consistent with this Rousseauan view of a political unit guided or driven by a singular general will. "So long as several men together consider themselves to be a single body, they have but a single will, which is concerned with their common preservation and the general well-being."[24] It is "only the general will" that can "direct the forces of the state according to the purpose for which it was instituted, which is the common good."[25] Sovereignty cannot be divided into parts; it "is indivisible for the same reason that it is inalienable. For either the will is general, or it is not. It is the will of either the people as a whole or only a part."[26] Moreover, articulation of policy is with one voice: "Each of us places his person and all his power in common under the supreme direction of the general will; and as one we receive each member as an indivisible part of the whole."[27]

Rousseau departs from Montesquieu in questioning whether war for conquest could be a right.[28] Moreover, he is a strong advocate of *jus in bello:* "War does not grant a right that is unnecessary to its purpose."[29] More specifically, the prince who wages war is under real constraints:

> Since the purpose of war is the destruction of the enemy state, one has the right to kill the defenders of that state so long as they bear arms. But as

soon as they lay down their arms and surrender, they cease to be enemies or instruments of the enemy. They return to being simply men; and one no longer has a right to their lives.[30]

Rousseau has had diverse influence on other writers. Many have seen in Rousseau's general will a well-spring of democratic thought; however, others have seen the general will as justification for authoritarian rule—the more effective way to serve the common or societal interest. Rousseau's ideas on property and its relation to inequality were picked up by Marx and Engels. They answer Rousseau's famous claim that "man is born free, and everywhere he is in chains"[31] with an equally famous assertion in *The Communist Manifesto* that, by committing themselves to revolution, workers have "nothing to lose but their chains." Finally, Rousseau also contributed to the ideology of nationalism by noting the important role of political indoctrination in creating a national identity:

It is the task of education to give to each human being a national form, and so direct his opinions and tastes that he should be a patriot by inclination, by passion, by necessity. On first opening his eyes a child must see his country, and until he dies, must see nothing else.[32]

Much has been made of differences in interpretation of Rousseau's view of international relations by two present-day realists, Kenneth Waltz and Stanley Hoffmann. They agree on a number of points, such as the fact that for Rousseau "the international milieu" is one "in which the absence of any common superior over states is seen as the 'permissive' cause of war."[33] As Waltz would have it, "Rousseau's answer is really that war occurs because there is nothing to prevent it. Among states as among men there is no automatic adjustment of interests. In the absence of a supreme authority, there is the constant possibility that conflicts will be settled by force."[34] Hoffmann comments, however, that "the solution to the problem of war and peace in Rousseau's mind, is really" not at the international, but at the state level. "Establish ideal states all over the world, and peace will follow."[35]

Where the two differ substantially is on the degree to which they see Rousseau emphasizing federation (or confederation) of states as a solution to the security problem posed by the international anarchy of sovereign independent states. In dispute are passages drawn from two of Rousseau's lesser-known essays, *State of War* and his summary and critique of the Abbé de St. Pierre's *Perpetual Peace*. Waltz believes a federation is Rousseau's prescription to remedy the problem of international anarchy if it were, in fact, desirable to alter that condition. In Hoffmann's view, however, Rousseau put relatively more emphasis on improving states and their citizens than on making changes in the structure of the international environment. Hoffmann observes that Rousseau's preference was for smaller communi-

MAP Ⅳ. *Europe*

St Petersburg

Stockholm

Baltic

Sweden

Courland

Copenhagen

Russia

Russia

Moscow

.Moscow

Hohenzollern possessions

Habsburg possessions

Boundary of the Empire

Warsaw
Poland

Silesia

Galicia

Habsburg

Empire

Vienna

Budapest

Hungary

Azov

Crimea

Black Sea

Kutchuk Kainardji

Ottoman

(TO VENICE)

Venice

Papal States

Constantinople

Naples

Empire

Sicily

1789

ties, which are more conducive to effective realization of the general will than would be possible in a large federation. For advocacy of the latter, Hoffmann gives more credit to Kant.[36]

A close reading of Rousseau's critique of St. Pierre's proposal for a confederacy as a means to establish peace makes clear that Rousseau is not so hostile to the logic of St. Pierre's argument as he is to its impracticality, the very real obstacles Rousseau thinks will preclude putting such a mechanism into effect. While Rousseau is concerned to avoid "universal monarchy" or too strong a central authority, he does not express this as his reason for opposing St. Pierre's scheme, which to Rousseau is as well intentioned as it is naive. The problem with St. Pierre's vision is not so much that it would fail to eliminate war or, in doing so, threaten the general will of the smaller communities or states within the federation. The problem for Rousseau is what he considers the utopian character of St. Pierre's vision.

Kant

The East Prussian scholar Immanuel Kant (1724–1804) attended the University of Königsberg. After serving as a tutor to several aristocratic families, he became an instructor at the university, where he lectured on such diverse topics as physics, logic, and the natural sciences. In 1781 he published perhaps his most famous work, *Critique of Pure Reason,* and during the last twenty years of his life he wrote a number of remarkable books and papers. He did not ignore politics, and shared Rousseau's interest in the problem of war and peace in international relations. An optimist, Kant believed the ultimate perfection of individuals and their countries was to be slow but steady; humanity was not condemned to an endless repetition of wars and civil strife. Because of his support of the American Revolution against England and his belief in the validity of the values of the French Revolution, it took courage to publish his *Idea for a Universal History* (1784) and *Perpetual Peace* (1795) during the reign of Frederick William III. While influenced by Hume and Rousseau, the Stoic roots of Kant's thought on world politics are also clear in this work—his universalism, his concept of world citizenship, and his advocacy of a federation of (or compact among) states as a means to peace. Kant's vision is of a pluralist world order in which human beings can live freely and without war. The achievement of such a vision would allow individuals to fulfill their duty to fellow citizens and the state as well as to humanity as a whole.[37]

Kant, however, was no wooly-minded idealist, and he rejected the idea that the transformation of world politics was either imminent or easy to achieve. For him, the sovereign state was a reality, and any plan to deal with international anarchy had to take states into account. Even if it were possible, for example, to eliminate states and create an empire, this would not solve the problem of war, as the inevitable result would be the rise of war-ring groups and the ultimate dissolution of the empire. Similarly, the idea of trying to overcome anarchy by creating a federation of states with a com-bined military force was also not realistic. Such a force, if effective, would eventually put states out of business—something government leaders would not allow. As one scholar has noted, Kant parted company with such pre-decessors as Grotius, Pufendorf, and Vattel in that he believed none of them paid "the Stoic-Christian ideal of the unity of mankind the supreme com-pliment of taking its political consequences seriously."[38] His task, therefore, was to come up with a proposal that balanced aspiration with practicality.

Familiar as he was with Rousseau's thought, and holding to liberal prin-ciples, Kant proposed "a federation of states which has for its sole purpose the maintenance of peace" because it "is the only juridical condition com-patible with the freedom of the several states."[39] This "league of nations" still leaves the separate sovereignties of league members intact: "This league does not tend to any dominion over the power of the state but only to the maintenance and security of the freedom of the state itself and of other states in league with it."[40] International law "presupposes the separate existence of many independent but neighboring states."[41] A "federative union" is preferred by Kant because in his view it "is rationally preferable to the amalgamation of states under one superior power" or "univer-sal monarchy."[42]

How did Kant arrive at this conclusion? As with a number of writers, an important starting point is his view of human nature. He shares with Rousseau a vision of man in the state of nature as subsisting "in anarchic freedom by hunting, fishing, and shepherding."[43] On one important point, however, Kant agrees with Hobbes (and thus differs from Rousseau) when he notes that "the natural state is one of war" or "at least an unceasing threat of war." Peace thus must be established as a result of human action.[44] Similarly, just as Hobbes characterizes kingdoms as being in a "posture of war," Kant asserts, "Peoples, as states, like individuals, may be judged to injure one another merely by their coexistence in the state of nature (i.e., while independent of external laws)."[45] The negative effect of anarchy is further increased, as Kant notes, by "the perverseness of human nature which is nakedly revealed in the uncontrolled relations between nations."[46]

Still, there is hope. Adversity and discord among human beings will lead them to learn ways in which to avoid future wars. It is part of nature's design. "Nature brings it to pass through selfish inclinations" of human beings who come into conflict with one another that they employ "reason as a means for its own end, the sovereignty of law, and, as concerns the state, for promoting and securing internal and external peace."[47] Further-more, this process of moving toward peace is aided by a development em-phasized, in particular, by nineteenth-century liberal theorists—economic imperatives. As Kant argues, "the spirit of commerce, which is incompatible with war, sooner or later gains the upper hand in every state." Given the fact that money is a critical source of state power, "states see themselves forced, without any moral urge, to promote honorable peace."[48]

Kant takes a strong position against realist maxims of conduct that lead statesmen to sow discord at home and abroad and to be bold and unapologetic in pursuing state interests aggressively. Such practice, he argues, amounts to "an immoral doctrine of prudence" or expediency.[49] Again, he has faith that ultimately the good in world politics will displace the evil, "though only through a slow progress." Kant notes in this regard that "moral evil" has the quality of "being opposed to and destructive of its own purposes."[50]

Morality and politics to Kant are thus inextricably linked. "True politics can never take a step without rendering homage to morality." If "politics say, 'Be ye wise as serpents,'" then "morality adds, as a limiting condition, 'and guileless as doves.'"[51] As a practical matter, then, there is a continuing tension between power and principle in politics—a theme the twentieth-century writer E.H. Carr would raise in his discussion of international politics between the two world wars.[52] However descriptive of international politics this tension may be (or have been in Carr's or Kant's time), Kant's position is that with the progress of humanity over time, expediency ultimately must give way to moral principle. "Nature inexorably wills that the right should finally triumph."[53]

Hannah Arendt comments how Kant was deeply concerned toward the end of his life with the "problem of how to organize a people into a state, how to constitute the state, how to found a commonwealth, and all the legal problems connected with these questions."[54] To Kant there is in human discord the necessary element in nature's design by which progress is possible. War itself carries the seeds of later progress toward peace, as human beings gradually come to realize how awful it is.[55] Arendt summarizes Kant's view: "It is by virtue of this idea of mankind, present in every single man, that men are human, and they can be called civilized or humane to the extent that this idea becomes the principle not only of their judgments but of their actions." From a Kantian perspective, Arendt observes how "one is a member of a world community by the sheer fact of being human; this is one's 'cosmopolitan existence.'"[56]

How, then, is progress toward peace to be made? Echoing Montesquieu, Kant prefers constitutional arrangements that check or balance competing interests. A federation of such republics inclined toward peace and under the law of nations can be extended gradually to include additional members, a line of argument later associated with Woodrow Wilson.[57] Harmonization comes from structuring the domestic and international environments within which we live. Though the transformation of the human condition will not be achieved in a short time, to Kant it remained "our duty to work toward this end."[58]

The influence of Hugo Grotius on theories of regional integration and international regimes was noted earlier. Similarly, Kant's emphasis on the ability of leaders to learn and to realize that it is rational and in their individual and collective self-interest to cooperate, his obvious belief in the possibility of change, and his recognition of the need to link aspiration and reality are also characteristic of much of this literature.[59]

The Federalist Papers

The writers of *The Federalist Papers*—Alexander Hamilton, James Madison, and John Jay—were faced with the practical problem of helping to sway the American public to support the idea of replacing the current confederation of states with a republican form of government that entailed greater power at the national level. As part of this effort to get the states to ratify the proposed constitution, a series of articles appeared in New York newspapers in 1787–1788 under the pseudonym "Publius." *The Federalist Papers* make interesting reading in that they reflect a point consistently made throughout this book—the tendency of the writers under consideration to be thoroughly conversant with the works of their predecessors. In *The Federalist Papers*, for example, there is a heavy reliance on Montesquieu, obvious familiarity with other earlier works on republicanism, and references to Plato, Polybius, Plutarch, and Grotius. Similarly, the use of such phrases and terms as state of nature, human nature, love of power, perpetual peace, anarchy, passions, justice, interests, virtue, reason, and self-love evinces an impressive grasp of the concerns of political theory through the ages.

The Federalist Papers should be of interest to students of international relations for at least two reasons. First, it is often suggested that realism was essentially introduced into the realms of U.S. foreign policy and academics by European-born scholars following World War II. In fact, the writers of *The Federalist Papers* exhibit a thoroughly realist perspective when discussing relations among states or factions. Secondly, Madison's important discussion on factions has influenced the work on interest group theory by American political scientists, which in turn has found its way into the international relations literature dealing with bureaucratic politics and the domestic sources of foreign policy.

An early theme discussed by the authors in *The Federalist Papers* is the nature of relations among the states if each claimed sovereignty and went their separate way, or even if they remained associated only in the loosest form of confederacy. The argument made by both Jay and Hamilton is that the result would be similar to relations among any states—conflict. According to Jay, "like other bordering states, they would always be either involved in disputes and war, or live in the constant apprehension of them." In an argument that sounds remarkably similar to that of present-day power transition theorists, he argues that even if the states were initially of equal strength, this condition would soon change. Various circumstances would work to "increase power in one part and to impede its progress in another" so that the "relative equality in strength and consideration would be destroyed." Jay then advances a hypothesis that could have been written by Thucydides when he argues that if any state "should rise on the scale of political importance much above the degree of her neighbors, that moment would those neighbors behold her with envy and with fear."[60]

Hamilton takes up this theme in the next paper, arguing that "to look for a continuation of harmony between a number of independent, unconnected sovereignties situated in the same neighborhood would be to disregard the uniform course of human events, and to set at defiance the accumulated experience of ages." Compared to Jay, however, he presents a wide array of possible causes of conflict among states that range up and down the levels of analysis, to include the observations that "safety from external danger is the most powerful director of national conduct," "men are ambitious, vindictive, and rapacious," there is a "love of power" and a "desire of pre-eminence and dominion" as well as "equality and safety."[61]

Hamilton then examines the state-societal level of analysis and refers to "visionary or designing men" who advocate a "perpetual peace" among states and claim that republics are pacific and that "the spirit of commerce" dampens the possibilities of war. He raises an historical and empirical question that is still a research concern today: "Have republics in practice been less addicted to war than monarchies?" He observes that there have been almost as many popular wars as royal wars, and in many cases these are "contrary to the real interests of the state." As for commerce, he argues that commercial motives, joining the desire for territory or dominion, have indeed contributed to the onset of wars. By the way of example, he cites the experiences of Sparta, Athens, Rome, and Carthage.[62]

Perhaps the most famous tracts are *Federalist* 10 and 51 by Madison. In the first, he outlines the problems of factions and the danger they present to the unity of the state—a traditional republican concern. Passions, divergent interests, and the unequal distribution of property have divided humanity and made it difficult to cooperate for the common good. One of the virtues of a republic, however, is that representative government tends to "refine and enlarge the public views by passing them through the medium of a chosen body of citizens, whose wisdom may best discern the true interest of their country."[63] But in a brilliant line of reasoning, Madison goes on to argue in *Federalist* 51 that, far from requiring a Leviathan to overcome domestic divisions, factions can actually be turned into a virtue. This is because in a republic "the society itself will be broken into so many parts, interests and classes of citizens, that the rights of individuals, or of the minority, will be in little danger."[64] This "multiplicity," or what we could term plurality, of interests keeps a permanent majority from forming and encourages the creation of various coalitions depending on the issue at hand. This is similar to some versions of balance of power theory that predict that it is natural for states to band together to prevent being dominated by a larger state or coalition of states. It is also a contribution to the pluralist image of domestic and international politics that emphasizes the variety of actors or groups that make up a state and the competition among them.[65] Finally, it should also be noted that this argument concerning the virtues of republican forms of government is quite different from the argument made by Machiavelli. While for Machiavelli conflict among classes may ultimately serve to enhance the external power and prowess of the republic, for Madison the salutary effects of checks and balances is designed to keep *too much* power from being concentrated in any one domestic institution or group. Foreign policy considerations are secondary.

Hegel

The thought of Georg W.F. Hegel (1770–1831) on international relations is often overlooked, perhaps because of the complexity of his world view, an aversion to his authoritarian orientation in relation to state power or, later, its association with Marxism (notwithstanding his emphasis on the role of ideas in changing history, in contrast to Marx's materialism). This neglect is unfortunate. Indeed, certain of his writings have had a direct bearing on the development of methodology and realist thought. For Hegel, history is not the random occurrence of unconnected events. In fact, the historical process is one in which humanity has continued to make spiritual and moral progress. This is in part due to the ability of individuals to reflect upon their circumstances and increase self-knowledge. Hence, for Hegel, reason and history are inseparable, and the historical process is essentially a rational, dialectical process that unfolds the "Ideal of Reason," which is most closely realized in the historical development of the state. Hence, the function of philosophy is not to dream up some ideal state or to discern supposedly transhistorical natural laws, but rather to deal with the reality of the state in a particular historical epoch.[66]

Hegel's adoption of an historical perspective contributed greatly to the rise of a tradition of political theory that became increasingly important in the nineteenth-century—historicism. Historicism was highly critical of the individualistic and universalistic components of so-called rationalist thought associated with the Stoics and the Enlightenment. Historicists rejected the "uniformity of human nature and the supposed timelessness of moral principles."[67] First and foremost, historicists argued that moral beliefs and values varied from culture to culture and throughout history. Hence, for example, the natural law teachings of the Stoics simply reflected a response to the historical dissolution of the Greek city-state.[68] As there was no universal, suprahistorical and transcendental set of values or natural laws, procedures to criticize beliefs and actions varied from society to society. In other words, reason was relative to culture, and so one should not utilize some universal standard of behavior to judge a state. Furthermore, historicists were also critical of social contract approaches to the origins of the state and the emphasis on the individual; they argued that values held by an individual are socially produced, and not a reflection of universal laws of nature. Hence, the fundamental fact of humanity was cultural diversity, resulting in the division of the world into states.[69] As one of the foremost exponents of the historicist perspective, Heinrich von Treitschke, stated: "The idea of one universal empire is odious—the ideal of a state co-extensive with humanity is no ideal at all."[70] A state had an absolute right to sovereignty, disputes among states were inevitable, and moral ties among individuals of various states as well as perpetual peace were illusory.

Such themes are to be found in Hegel's writings, particularly his preoccupation, if not obsession, with the state, his acceptance of the sovereignty of individual states, and, consequently, the international anarchy that exists among states. As Hegel asserts in *The Philosophy of History,* "The State is the Divine Idea as it exists on Earth," the "embodiment of rational freedom, realizing and recognizing itself in an objective form."[71] Furthermore, "the nation state is mind in its substantive rationality and immediate actuality and is therefore the absolute power on earth. It follows that every state is sovereign and autonomous against its neighbors."[72] As duty is to one's own state, Hegel rejects the long tradition of political thought that asserts a community of nations should, could, or does exist. In contrast to Rousseau and especially Kant, therefore, Hegel does not seek perpetual peace or anything approaching it. To him, war has a salutary effect on societies by keeping them from the decline associated with long-term peace. More important, history's progression is the result of wars. War is not entirely an accident in an anarchic system—a view also found in Rousseau and the work of present-day neo-realists.[73]

Weber

Another German, Max Weber (1864–1920), is a prime example of a theorist and social scientist who is generally not associated with the international relations discipline, but whose impact—however indirect—on realists and pluralists has been profound. His influence is particularly pronounced in four areas: the sociology of knowledge, his conception of the state, the study of bureaucracies, and the dilemmas of political leadership.

Weber is part of the scientific tradition—dating back at least to Aristotle—that assumes there are regularities to human behavior. Hence, through deductive and inductive reasoning, it is possible to generate hypotheses and subject them to empirical testing. This faith in the scientific method as a means to comprehend a complex reality was not unusual at the turn of the century. Indeed, the expansion of knowledge in the natural sciences during the previous one hundred years buttressed confidence—dating back to the seventeenth century—that similar advances could be made in understanding human behavior and, as a result, the functioning of societies. In contrast to a number of noted academics of the nineteenth and early twentieth centuries, however, Weber rejected essentially one-cause explanations in his attempts to explain the development and functioning of societies. Marx's insights on economic factors, for example, were noted by Weber, but balanced with a careful weighing of cultural, political, and military considerations. Understanding required interpretation.

The realist in Weber is best revealed in his belief that the modern state represents the ultimate form of sovereign political authority. This is because the modern state "has been successful in seeking to monopolize the legitimate use of physical force."[74] Like Hegel, Weber was a German nationalist, although of liberal persuasion and hence suspicious of state power interfering with the autonomy of the individual. Personal preferences aside, Weber's emphasis on the state was in part a result of his life-long study of why empires and decentralized feudal authorities ceased to exist in the modern world. For Weber, the critical factor was what he called the process of "rationalization." Weber stated, for example, that far from Marx's characterization of capitalism as "anarchy of production," capitalism was actually the very embodiment of rationality in terms of the productive use of resources. Similarly, Weber equates the rise of bureaucratic administration—within the public as well private spheres—with rationality. Indeed, the principle of rationalization is the key component of Weber's view of history, although he sees the process as interrupted by the occasional emergence of charismatic movements that abhor routine.[75]

As noted, the process of rationalization is exemplified by the manner in which the modern state managed to "monopolize the legitimate use of physical force." While during ancient times, the early medieval period, and feudalism the individuals who composed the armies were essentially self-equipped, the modern military state provides the equipment and provisions. As a result, "War in our time is a war of machines. . . . Only the bureaucratic army structure allowed for the development of professional standing armies which are necessary for the constant pacification of large states of the plains, as well as for warfare against far-distant enemies."[76]

The realist in Weber is also quite evident in his observations on international relations. For him, "all political structures [that is, states] use force," but "the attitude of political structures towards the outside may be more 'isolationist' or more 'expansive.' "[77] Switzerland, he notes, tends toward isolationism and its independence is protected by a balance of power among the larger states. Furthermore, contrary to Marxist-inspired theories of imperialism, economic factors at best "codetermine the extent and manner of political expansion."[78] The norm, however, tends to be for political leaders of states to be driven by a "desire for power-oriented prestige," which "means in practice the glory of power over other communities."[79] As Weber argues:

> Every political structure naturally prefers to have weak rather than strong neighbors. Furthermore, as every big political community is a potential aspirant to prestige and a potential threat to all its neighbors, the big political community, simply because it is big and strong, is latently and constantly endangered.[80]

For Weber, therefore, political threats to peace often result in war because of the desire for prestige on the part of "those having vested interests in the political structure."[81]

Weber's attitude toward the historical process of "rationalization" is ambivalent. While bureaucratic machines may be more efficient, the liberal in Weber obviously feels for "the individual bureaucrat [who] cannot squirm out of the apparatus in which he is harnessed. In contrast to the honorific or avocational 'notable,' the professional bureaucrat is chained to his activity by his entire material and ideal existence."[82] Furthermore, Weber is fully aware that, however efficient and effective bureaucratic organizations may generally be in the fulfillment of their assigned tasks, they also have limitations. In a footnote he comments, "Here we cannot discuss in detail how the bureaucratic apparatus may, and actually does, produce definite obstacles to the discharge of business."[83] The functioning of bureaucracies in general, and the possible dysfunctions they spawn, has been the focus of attention on the part of the public administration discipline, which is heavily indebted to the works of Weber.[84] In turn, the international relations literature that examines the role of bureaucracies in foreign policy decision making and crisis situations is also beholden to Weber's legacy.[85]

Finally, it should be noted that Weber has an affinity with Machiavelli in terms of sympathy and respect for the dilemmas and problems faced by the professional politician.[86] Just as Machiavelli refused to find comfort in the universal laws of nature, so too did Weber question the Enlightenment's faith in the power of reason to overcome the political problems of governing. For Weber, states pursue conflicting values, and hence the statesman's primary duty is to promote national values.[87] Just as Machiavelli argued that political leaders had to deal with the unexpected as reflected in the concept of *fortuna,* so too did Weber realize how political actions resulted in unintended consequences. "The final result of political action often, no, even regularly, stands in completely inadequate and often paradoxical relation to its original meaning."[88] The dilemmas faced by a politician are best expressed in Weber's famous speech at Munich University in 1918, "Politics as a Vocation," in which he addresses the issue of the relation between ethics and politics. He argues that ethical conduct for those engaged in politics can be guided by two very different maxims: an ethic of ultimate ends (as an individual driven for religious or other purposes), or an ethic of responsibility (as when political leaders must anticipate the consequences of their decisions and actions). To follow the ethic of ultimate ends—which Weber associated with writers of the Enlightenment and nineteenth-century liberals—is to assume that the goal being pursued is of such importance that how one achieves the goal or the concomitant costs are of secondary importance; it is the view of the impassioned prophet. Hence, a true believer in revolution may undertake actions that precipitate a harsh government reaction that is to the immediate detriment of the working class because of the belief that such sacrifices are required in the name of the revolution.

The ethics of responsibility, however, require one to take into account the possible results of one's actions. Weber is very sympathetic to the individual who "is aware of a responsibility for the consequences of his conduct and really feels such responsibility with heart and soul." But for one to have a true "calling for politics," an ethic of ultimate ends and an ethic of responsibility must be balanced, requiring both "passion and perspective."[89] This sensitivity to the dilemmas faced by political leaders is part of a realist tradition dating back to Thucydides, and such thinking influenced twentieth-century writers in the realist tradition such as Hans Morgenthau and Raymond Aron.[90]

International Political Economy

Beyond their domestic political concerns, the eighteenth- and nineteenth-century writers already discussed in this chapter—Montesquieu, Rousseau, Kant, Hegel, and Weber—devoted varying degrees of attention to international politics. In similar fashion, the authors to be discussed subsequently also adopted a world view. However different their theoretical perspectives, explanations, and predictions, they all shared an interest in understanding the relation between economics and politics. An increased attention to political economy was understandable. The eighteenth- and nineteenth-century industrial revolution—the heart of the modernization process—had what could only be described as revolutionary impact on peoples around the globe. For those living in the West, very few areas of life were unaffected, and it was to be expected that some of the best minds turned their attention to analyzing the political, social, and economic implications.[91]

Adam Smith

Though Adam Smith (1723–1790) is often overlooked by contemporary international relations theorists (or portrayed incorrectly by others as a one-sided ideologue), a reading of Smith's *Wealth of Nations* and *Theory of Moral Sentiments* reveals important roots of many subsequent ideas and efforts, particularly in international political economy. The product of the Scottish Enlightenment and a professor at Glasgow University, Smith turned his sights on the workings of markets in a world economy. Read in one way, his approach to finding the ways and means of the wealth of nations was state-centric (and thus in accord with a realist world view). At the same time, however, his notion that states in most instances ought not to place restrictions on the market—thereby allowing investors, producers, workers, and consumers freedom to make economic choices—was consistent with a pluralist world view grounded in liberal principles and opposed to mercantilism.[92]

Smith insisted that freedom in the marketplace should apply to all "social orders," what Marx and others later would identify more specifically as classes.[93] Indeed, Smith expressed anger toward owners of the means of production who were sometimes prone to abridge liberal principles in relation to other social orders—using state power, for example, to restrict the right of workers to bargain for their wages. Smith refers to those working for wages as not always comprehending their interests (what Marx would call a lack of class consciousness) in contrast to landowners receiving rents and owners of capital receiving profits—both of whom were well aware of their interests. Smith stopped short of using such terms as class conflict and exploitation of one class by another, but the threads of such arguments were clearly present. Beyond providing a basis for alternative images of international relations that would be adopted by others, Smith's treatment of the international dimension of political economy was a salient contribution. He did not consider economic matters to be the stuff merely of low politics. Commerce was as much a part of international relations as the security concerns in statecraft dealt with by Machiavelli.

Finally, Smith's brief allusion in book 4 of *The Wealth of Nations* to an "invisible hand" in a free market that allocates factors of production—land, labor, and capital—in ways unintended by those making individual economic decisions is a powerful idea that has found application well beyond Smith's usage. In Smith's words, the individual

> intends only his own gain, and he is in this, as in many other cases, led by an invisible hand to promote an end which was no part of his intention. Nor is it always the worse for society that it was no part of it. By pursuing his own interest he frequently promotes that of the society more effectually

than when he really intends to promote it. I have never known much good done by those who affected to trade for the public good. It is an affectation, indeed, not very common among merchants, and very few words need be employed in dissuading them from it.[94]

From this passage we can draw the idea of a system as a different level of analysis from the individuals, firms, or other groups or units of which it is composed. At the individual level, each actor is expected to act rationally so as to maximize self-interest. In a market of freely competing individuals or firms, the efficiency produced by this competition results in greater aggregate output of goods and services, whatever may be the equity of its distribution across a given society. To Smith, the wealth of nations is enhanced precisely by allowing free market principles to prevail not only domestically, but also internationally.

Smith's view of free markets composed of competitive, interacting units that result in equilibrium prices for quantities produced and supplied to markets would be adapted by neorealists when talking about the equilibrium or balance of power that occurs among competing states. In this sense, the state competing with other states becomes the analog of the firm, much as firms compete in the marketplace. The result in both cases is an equilibrium that may or may not have been intended by any of the actors acting individually.[95] This particular systemic perspective contrasts with alternative realist formulations that emphasize balance of power as a prudent policy that should be followed by statesmen. David Hume, for example, (1711–1776) made such an argument by drawing on the historical analyses of Thucydides and Polybius, while at the same time making one of the earliest arguments for free trade.[96]

Despite Smith's praise of free trade, he expressed reservations about the impact of commerce on society in terms of the ability of a nation to defend itself. He stated that the "bad effect of commerce is that it sinks the courage of mankind, and tends to extinguish the martial spirit." This is the result of the division of labor in advanced economies. Those engaged in commercial activities have no time or interest in performing military service, hence the protection of the country is assigned to military professionals. The result is that "among the bulk of the people military courage diminishes. By having their minds constantly employed on the arts of luxury, they grow effeminate and dastardly." While a commercial country might be formidable abroad due to its navy and standing armies, it tends to be easily overcome when invaded. As an example, he mentions the Carthaginians, who were successful in foreign wars, but not when defending their own territory.[97] Although these observations were presented in the form of lectures and are not critical to Smith's contribution to our understanding of international political economy, they do illustrate a proposition concerning the nature of a society and its ability to defend itself at home and abroad.

Marx

One can find in Smith a basis for arguments later developed by Karl Marx (1818–1883), although Marx and his followers took Smith's ideas far from their liberal moorings. Indeed, an understanding of Marx is incomplete without a reading of Adam Smith. Seeing history in stages with progression from one form of political economy (or mode of production) to another is an idea with its roots in Smith, who also addressed the rise of towns and their relation to the countryside.[98] This connection between Smith and Marx should not be surprising in that Marx, though born and educated in Germany, did much of his work in London at the British Museum library and was intimately familiar with the writings of Smith, David Ricardo, and other classical economists whose work preceded his own efforts. It is to these sources that Marx owed the labor theory of value that figured so centrally in his theoretical work.[99] In this regard, challenges to Marxian use of the labor theory of value have to be understood as critiques of all classical economic theorists, each of whom was wedded to this idea in one form or another.

It is, of course, not our purpose to argue that Marx was dependent intellectually on insights drawn exclusively from Smith. Our only point is that Smith's influences on Marx are usually overlooked, perhaps because their conclusions were so different. Because of his avid and wide reading, Marx was influenced by as diverse a group of writers as Plato, Aristotle, Rousseau, Hegel, and Kant. Thus, as we discussed earlier, class analysis as method and slavery as a form of political economy (or mode of production in Marx's terms) are present in the works of Plato and Aristotle. As noted, the metaphor of the working man in "chains" seems to have been borrowed directly from Rousseau. Friedrich Hegel's view of history as a dialectical clash of ideas was, as is well known, adapted by Marx to emphasize the economic underpinnings of ideas in what is usually referred to as dialectical materialism in history.[100]

Marx was not writing about the political economy of individual states as much as he was about capitalism as a global phenomenon. In describing the world economy, Smith and Marx recognized the different levels of development and the associated wealth of individual countries. Both viewed countries not as isolated entities, but rather as part of a larger whole—a critical element of the globalist perspective on international relations.[101] Indeed, Smith's antimercantilist position rested on his view that the wealth of nations increases in a free trade environment that allows for the accumulation of capital. To see Marx purely in terms of class and class conflict within a given state would also be a misreading. Marx's vision was also internationalist, however much he differed from Smith in his political-economic descriptions or future preferences.

By the nineteenth century the Enlightenment call for liberation and Rousseau's emphasis on national identity resulted in the belief among a number of writers that once nations achieved full independence—a condition in accordance with nature—they would exist in harmony. International relations would then simply consist of the administration of what was basically a homogeneous world community. The underlying assumption, therefore, was that the world was already a natural global community in which peoples' interests could become harmonious. This would be universally perceived if only all of the global community's members could be liberated or educated.[102]

Marx departed from this vision, seeing the world as divided by materially based class conflict. These horizontal, transnational class divisions cut across state boundaries and were a prime source of conflict, an analysis in direct contrast to the realist emphasis on conflict arising from interstate competition. Nevertheless, Marx was hopeful. Growing class consciousness of the proletariat would reach its climax in a proletarian revolution, he believed. Over an unspecified period of time, the state—and, consequently, international relations—would fade away. Marx's work, therefore, is an interesting blend of determinist and voluntarist inclinations, as reflected in the statement that "men make their own history, but they do not make it just as they please; they do not make it under circumstances chosen by themselves, but under circumstances directly found, given, and transmitted from the past."[103] In sum, Marx believed that human beings are able to understand the historical process, and that "reality is not merely objective datum, external to people, but is shaped by them through consciousness" and action that can enhance the possibility of achieving greater individual freedom and dignity.[104] This epistemological—and not merely normative—perspective is quite different from the positivist epistemology that traditionally has informed much of the work in international relations. Such work seeks to discern essentially ahistorical universal laws and very often assumes that empirical and normative concerns can—or at least should—be separated. Nevertheless, Marx's belief that people have the ability to shape their world is reflected in the literature that attempts to develop a critical theory of international relations.[105]

Cobden and Liberalism

The assumption of the potential for harmony among states and peoples in conjunction with the faith that unrestricted economic activity would enhance the possibility of achieving that harmony came together in the works of nineteenth-century liberals and utilitarians.[106] Richard Cobden (1804–1865) was perhaps the foremost exponent of this perspective. Entering the

British House of Commons in 1841, he was the leader of the Anti-Corn Law League and managed to get this act repealed in 1846 against the wishes of the protectionist landed interests. While his arguments for free trade emphasized that such a policy would enhance the nation's prosperity, he also addressed the issues of the relation between free trade and peace, the influence of military establishments on war, and the pernicious effects of balance of power policies.

Cobden made three rather ambitious claims concerning the impact of free trade on peace. First, he asserted that most wars were fought by states to achieve their mercantilist goals. Free trade would show leaders a much more effective—and peaceful—means to achieve national wealth. Second, even in the case of wars not arising from commercial rivalry, domestic interests that would suffer from the interruption of free trade because of war would restrain and oppose hostilities. Finally, Cobden hypothesized that with an expansion of free trade, contact and communication among peoples would expand. This, in turn, would encourage international friendship and understanding. "Free Trade! What is it? Why, breaking down the barriers that separate nations; those barriers, behind which nestle the feelings of pride, revenge, hatred, and jealousy, which every now and then burst their bounds, and deluge whole countries with blood."[107] This posited relation between international trade and international peace has been a recurrent proposition, and indeed is found in some of the present-day works on interdependence and in arguments that international trade can have pacifying effects on the behavior of states.[108]

While the expansion of free trade contributes to the growth of coalitions favoring peace over war, Cobden argues that military organizations would be against such developments as they would in effect virtually render militaries obsolete. But he assumed, as did other liberals, that "the great masses of mankind are disposed for peace between nations," and hence he was optimistic that they would, through the power of public opinion, negate the power of those who had a vested interest in the maintenance of international conflict.[109] As the threat of war receded, a peace dividend would become apparent to all as tax dollars would be diverted to domestic programs.

Finally, Cobden argues that an important obstacle to the reduction in spending on armaments was the policy of balance of power. Cobden's attack on the balance of power is as passionate as it was sweeping. He first notes—as have a number of modern theorists of international relations—that the balance of power suffers from vague and multiple definitions.[110] He then argues that as a policy for Britain, it is little more than a smokescreen for British interests, with the word balance designed "to please the public ear; it implied something of equity; whilst England, holding the balance of Europe in her hand, sounded like filling the office of Justice herself to one-half of the globe."[111] But, in fact, the balance of power has been the cause of wars and a "pretence for maintaining enormous standing armaments." In ringing prose he claims, "The balance of power is a chimera! It is not a fallacy, a mistake, an imposture—it is an undescribed, indescribable, incomprehensible nothing."[112] In sum, Cobden's emphasis on free trade as a means to mitigate the aggressive tendencies of states, his faith in the ability of political leaders to learn alternative means to achieve national interests, and his analysis of the important role played by domestic constituencies in foreign affairs epitomize nineteenth-century liberal thought on international politics. These ideas have also contributed to the development of the pluralist image of international relations.

Hobson

While Cobden's arguments concerning the link between capitalist free trade and international peace influenced a great number of people, a more pessimistic line of thinking developed by Karl Marx also had its advocates. This is most clearly exhibited in the works on imperialism that have contributed to the globalist image of international politics. One of the most influential analyses was by a non-Marxist, the English economist John A. Hobson (1858–1940). In his work *Imperialism: A Study* (1902), Hobson discussed what he termed the "economic taproot of imperialism." He noted that capitalist societies suffered from three interrelated problems: overproduction of goods due to the efficiency of modern machinery; underconsumption of these products by the lower classes, whose meager wages did not give them sufficient purchasing power to buy the excess goods; and oversavings on the part of the capitalists, aided by paying workers low wages.[113] For capitalists, the supposed solution to the problem of excess goods and capital was to find new markets. Western capitalist markets, however, all suffered from the same maladies, so they could not be the outlet for another state's goods and capital. Capitalists therefore urged their governments to lay claim to the underdeveloped territories in parts of Asia and Africa that represented untapped markets. The result according to Hobson is imperialism, defined as "the endeavour of the great controllers of industry to broaden the channel for the flow of their surplus wealth by seeking foreign markets and foreign investments to take off the goods and capital they cannot sell or use at home."[114] For Hobson, such factors as the "spirit of adventure" or a "mission of civilization" were "clearly subordinate to the driving force of the economic factor."[115]

According to some analysts, imperialism is "inevitable" as "everywhere appear excessive powers of production, excessive capital in search of investment."[116] Hobson disagreed. It was the "mal-distribution of consuming power" that prevented the absorption of goods and capital within a particular country. The solution, therefore, was to divert from the capitalists "their excess of income and make it flow, either to the workers in higher wages, or to the community in taxes." Either policy would increase domestic consumption, and as a result "there will be no need to fight for foreign markets or foreign areas of investment."[117] As for the "possessing classes," social reform will not "inflict upon them the real injury they dread." To the contrary, it is actually in their best interest in that the current use of surplus capital and goods forces "on their country a wrecking policy of Imperialism."[118]

Lenin

The impact of Hobson's analysis can be seen in perhaps the most famous work in this genre, Vladimir Ilyich Lenin's *Imperialism: The Highest Stage of Capitalism* (1916). Writing during World War I, Lenin was interested in not only explaining the capitalist exploitation of lesser-developed countries, but also the causes of war among advanced capitalist states. More important, he had the expressly political purpose of trying to convince Marxists that the time was ripe for revolutionary action.[119] The result of Lenin's efforts was a highly influential theory of international political change. From Hobson, Lenin accepted the critical importance of underconsumption and overproduction as stimuli for the search for foreign markets and hence colonialism. From the German Social Democrat, Rudolph Hilferding (1877–1941), Lenin adopted the argument that the critical feature of imperialism is not so much industrial capital, but rather finance capital. As Lenin concludes:

> Imperialism is capitalism at that stage of development at which the dominance of monopolies and finance capital is established; in which the export of capital has acquired pronounced importance; in which the division of the world among the international trusts has begun, in which the division of all territories of the globe among the biggest capitalist powers has been completed.[120]

Marx had argued that the internal contradictions of capitalism and its inherently exploitative nature would eventually lead to working class or proletarian revolutions. When the predicted revolutions failed to occur, disciples of Marx attempted to explain what had happened. For Lenin, imperialism was the answer. Imperialism provided the European working class a taste of the spoils resulting from the exploitation of colonies, thus dampening proletarian discontent.

But such a breathing space was not to last. Once the "whole world had been divided up, there was inevitably ushered in the era of monopoly possession of colonies." There then followed a "particularly intense struggle for the division and the redivision of the world."[121] This struggle among capitalist states was intensified by the continual, yet uneven growth of capitalism, which saw the rise of some states and the relative decline of others:

> The only conceivable basis under capitalism for the division of spheres of influence, interests, colonies, etc., is a calculation of the *strength* of those participating, their general economic, financial, military strength, etc. And the strength of these participants in the division does not change to an equal degree, for the *even* development of different undertakings, trusts, branches of industry, or countries is impossible under capitalism. Half a century ago Germany was a miserable, insignificant country, if her capitalist strength is compared with that of Britain of that time; Japan compared with Russia in the same way. Is it "conceivable" that in ten or twenty years' time the relative strength of the imperialist powers will have remained *un*changed? It is out of the question.[122]

What Lenin posited, therefore, was a version of power transition theory, although one that relied almost exclusively upon economic determinants at the expense of political factors. His emphasis on the exploitative nature of capitalism and its universality has also contributed to the globalist image of international politics.

Conclusion

The writers we have discussed throughout most of this chapter and the previous one were observing the development of a new world order—a state and capitalist world system. The evolution of this system required a fundamental change in mindset from medieval notions of the essential unity of the heavenly and earthly orders. New concepts and ideas were introduced. For those writers in the realist and pluralist traditions, states had come to be understood as sovereign entities with no authority above them. Greater attention was paid to analyzing the nature of the international system itself as opposed to viewing international conflict as stemming only from the nature of humanity or the nature of states and societies. In this new world, statecraft was recognized as a most important enterprise. How much opportunity there is for statesmen to influence events effectively (or how much is determined by the environment external to the state) is an important question still facing theorists and policy makers. But writers such as Kant and the nineteenth-century liberals actually favored constraints such as republicanism and public opinion being placed on decision makers, whose excess "voluntarism" was often viewed as a major cause of war.

For realists, power and power politics were seen as resulting, whether intended or not, in balances of power among states. For pluralists and globalists, markets and commercial relations came to be viewed as transcending national borders, with important political consequences. For pluralists, such economic transnationalism could have an integrating and pacifying effect on relations among states. For globalists, the spread of capitalism was a destructive and exploitative process that would inevitably end in war. These were powerful ideas with a long shelf life. Just as scholars debated these ideas during the years between World Wars I and II, the insights and observations offered by these writers remain with us to the present day, underpinning much of contemporary thinking and theorizing about international relations.

Notes

1. Leo Strauss and Joseph Cropsey, eds., *History of Political Philosophy* (Chicago: Rand McNally, 1963), 379. Descartes was following the lead of Francis Bacon, who was an enthusiast of the belief that through Machiavellian politics one could increase the possibility of mastering fortune or nature.

2. "Enlightenment," *Encyclopedia Britannica*, vol. 8 (Chicago: William Benton, 1973), 601.

3. "Enlightenment," 602.

4. Strauss and Cropsey, *History*, 487, 490.

5. Montesquieu, *The Spirit of the Laws*, ed. David Wallace Carrithers (Berkeley: University of California Press, 1971), XXX.

6. Strauss and Cropsey, *History*, 470.

7. Montesquieu, *The Spirit*, I:3.

8. IX:2.

9. I:3.

10. I:3.

11. IV:1.

12. XXVI:1.

13. I:3.

14. XXVI:23; see also I:3, IX:6.

15. X:2, 3.

16. "Rousseau," *Encyclopedia Britannica*, vol. 19 (Chicago: William Benton, 1973), 659–61.

17. Jean-Jacques Rousseau, "Discourse on the Origin of Inequality," part II, in *Basic Political Writings*, trans. and ed. Donald A. Kress (Indianapolis, Ind.: Hackett, 1987).

18. Rousseau, "Discourse," part II.

19. For an argument that such collaboration is possible because hunters could "make informal rules regulating the separate or cooperative hunting of hares," see Ernst B. Haas, *Beyond the Nation-State* (Stanford, Calif.: Stanford University Press, 1964), 69–71. For a discussion of game theory and games—including stag hunt—see Robert Axelrod and Robert O. Keohane, "Achieving Cooperation Under Anarchy," *World Politics* 38, no. 1 (Oct. 1985): 226–54.

20. Rousseau, "Discourse," part II.

21. part II.
22. part II.
23. part II.
24. Jean-Jacques Rousseau, "On the Social Contract," in *Basic Political Writings*, IV:1.
25. II:2.
26. II:2.
27. I:6.
28. Rousseau, "Discourse," part II.
29. Rousseau, "On the Social Contract," I:4.
30. I:4.
31. I:1.
32. As quoted by Michael Howard, *The Lessons of History* (New Haven, Conn.: Yale University Press, 1991), 145.
33. Stanley Hoffmann, "Rousseau on War and Peace," *The American Political Science Review*, 57, no. 2 (June 1973): 326.
34. Kenneth N. Waltz, *Man, the State and War* (New York: Columbia University Press, 1954, 1959), 188.
35. Hoffmann, "Rousseau," 329.
36. Ibid., 330.
37. See Hannah Arendt, *Lectures on Kant's Political Philosophy*, ed. Ronald Beiner (Chicago: University of Chicago Press, 1982), 16, 28.
38. W.B. Gallie, *Philosophers of Peace and War: Kant, Clausewitz, Marx, Engels and Tolstoy* (London: Cambridge University Press, 1978), 33.
39. Immanuel Kant, *Perpetual Peace*, ed. Lewis White Beck (New York: Macmillan, 1957), 51.
40. Ibid., 16, 18.
41. Ibid., 31.
42. Ibid., 31.
43. Ibid., 27.
44. Ibid., 10.
45. Ibid., 16.
46. Ibid., 17.
47. Ibid., 31.
48. Ibid., 32.
49. Ibid., 41.
50. Ibid., 45.
51. Ibid., 46, 35.
52. See Edward Hallett Carr, *The Twenty Years' Crisis, 1919–1939* (New York: Harper and Row, 1939, 1964), 11–13.
53. Kant, *Perpetual Peace*, 31.
54. Arendt, *Lectures*, 16.
55. Ibid., 52, 54.
56. Ibid., 75.
57. Kant, *Perpetual Peace*, 18–19. For a discussion of Wilson's argument that democracies that have been created through national self-determination facilitate peace and international cooperation, see Arnold Wolfers and Laurence W. Martin eds., *The Anglo-American Tradition in Foreign Affairs* (New Haven, Conn.: Yale

University Press, 1956), 263–79. See also Michael W. Doyle, "Liberalism and World Politics," *American Political Science Review,* 80, no. 4 (Dec. 1986): 1151–69; Michael W. Doyle, "Kant, Liberal Legacies and Foreign Affairs," *Philosophy and Public Affairs,* 12, nos. 3 and 4 (1983) 205–35 and 323–53.

58. Kant, *Perpetual Peace,* 32. See also Arendt, *Lectures, 75,* where she constructs a categorical imperative implicit in Kant's writings on peace through federation. "Always act on the maxim through which this original compact can be actualized into a general law." As she frames it, this would be a corollary of Kant's categorical imperative in ethics that what is right is that which we would will to be a universal law or maxim for conduct. As is well known, to treat human beings as ends worthy in themselves and not merely as means is another categorical imperative or universal obligation identified by Kant.

59. Such themes are to be found in a number of the essays—including by those scholars who accept the realist assumption of power-maximizing states acting in an anarchic environment—in Stephen D. Krasner, ed., "International Regimes," special issue of *International Organization,* 36, no. 2 (Spring 1982).

60. John Jay, *The Federalist Papers,* No. 5 (New York: The New American Library, 1961), 51.

61. Alexander Hamilton, *The Federalist Papers,* No. 6, 54. The comment on "external danger" is from No. 8, 67.

62. Ibid., No. 6, 56–58.

63. James Madison, *The Federalist Papers,* No. 10, 82.

64. Ibid., No. 51, 324.

65. For two conceptions of American politics as group conflict, see Arthur F. Bentley, *The Process of Government* (Chicago: University of Chicago Press, 1908); and David Truman, *The Governmental Process* (New York: Alfred A. Knopf, 1951).

66. Pierre Hasner, "Georg W.F. Hegel," in *History of Political Philosophy,* ed. Leo Strauss and Joseph Cropsey (Chicago: Rand McNally, 1963), 628–29. As Hegel states, "The only Thought which Philosophy brings with it to the contemplation of History, is the simple conception of *Reason*; that Reason is the Sovereign of the World; that the history of the world, therefore, presents us with a rational process. . . . Reason is not so powerless as to be incapable of producing anything but a mere ideal, a mere intention — having its place outside reality. . . . That this 'Idea' or 'Reason' is the *True,* the *Eternal,* the absolutely *powerful* essence; that it reveals itself in the World, and that in that World nothing else is revealed but this and its honor and glory—is the thesis which, as we have said, has been proved in Philosophy, and is here regarded as demonstrated." *Philosophy of History* (New York: P.F. Collier and Son, 1900), 52–53.

67. Andrew Linklater, *Men and Citizens in the Theory of International Relations* (New York: St. Martin's Press, 1982), 122.

68. Leo Strauss, *Natural Right and History* (Chicago: University of Chicago Press, 1953), 15. Strauss, a severe critic of historicism, argued: "Historicism asserts that all human thoughts or beliefs are historical, and hence deservedly destined to perish; but historicism itself is a human thought; hence historicism can be of only temporary validity, or it cannot be simply true." p. 25.

69. Linklater, *Men and Citizens,* 122–24.

70. Heinrich von Treitschke, "The State Idea," in *The Theory of International*

Relations: Selected Texts from Gentili to Treitschke, ed. M.G. Forsyth, H.M.A. Keens-Soper, and P. Savigear (New York: Atherton Press, 1970), 326.

71. Hegel, *Philosophy of History,* 87, 96.

72. Georg W.F. Hegel, *Hegel: The Essential Writings,* ed. Frederick G. Weiss (New York: Harper and Row, 1974), 298. For Hegel's discussion of sovereignty and related issues concerning international relations, see pages 284–306.

73. The historicist emphasis on history and culture, challenges to Enlightenment conceptions of man and society, and an interest in works dealing with the linguistic construction of reality are reflected in much of the "critical theory" work on international relations that question positivist–empiricist approaches to knowledge. R.B.J. Walker, for example, argues that "Sovereignty is not a permanent principle of international order. On the contrary, it has been constituted and reconstituted historically. Nor can it be said that sovereignty is passé. Rather, to focus on the principle of state sovereignty is to engage with deeply entrenched discourses about political life." *State Sovereignty, Global Civilization, and the Rearticulation of Political Space,* World Order Studies Program, Occasional Paper No. 18 (Princeton, N.J.: Princeton University, Center of International Studies, 1988), 3. It should be noted that, far from glorifying the state, critical theorists are concerned with expanding the scope of individual human freedom and defining the human community in a way that transcends state borders. Furthermore, critical theorists emphasize that people are not simply carried along on the tide of historical forces, but can reflect upon their conditions and struggle to shape their circumstances. For an overview of the various elements as well as diversity of critical theory, see Jim George and David Campbell, "Patterns of Dissent and the Celebration of Difference: Critical Social Theory and International Relations," *International Studies Quarterly,* 34, no. 3 (Sept. 1990): 269–93.

74. Max Weber, *From Max Weber: Essays in Sociology,* translated and edited by H.H. Gerth and C. Wright Mills (New York: Oxford University Press, 1946), 82–83.

75. See the introductory essay by Gerth and Mills, "Intellectual Orientations," Weber, *From Max Weber,* 49–55.

76. Weber, *From Max Weber,* 221–22.

77. Ibid., 159.

78. Ibid., 165. See his analysis of imperialism, 162–71.

79. Ibid., 160.

80. Ibid.

81. Ibid., 161.

82. Ibid., 228.

83. Ibid., 215.

84. James G. March and Herbert A. Simon, *Organizations* (New York: Wiley, 1958), 36–37.

85. For example, Graham Allison notes, "While organization theory as such is a newcomer to the intellectual scene, it is a linear descendent of two older disciplines. The classic study of bureaucracy is, of course, [by] Max Weber. . . . The other parent is Taylorism or 'scientific management.'" *Essence of Decision: Explaining the Cuban Missile Crisis* (Boston: Little, Brown, 1971), 298–99, note 2.

86. Note even Weber's choice of words in the following observation: "Every-

where the development of the modern state is initiated through the action of a prince." Weber, *From Max Weber*, 82.

87. According to Strauss, Weber essentially agreed with many present-day social scientists that "Natural right is then rejected today not only because all human thought is held to be historical but likewise because it is thought that there is a variety of unchangeable principles of right or of goodness which conflict with one another, and none of which can be proved to be superior to the others." Strauss, *Natural Right and History*, 36. It has been argued, however, that while Weber was pessimistic about the performance of liberal democracies, the ethical core of his work reflects a "politicized neo-Kantian liberalism: he sees politics as a uniquely human activity, one with the potential both to create and to manifest the responsibility and dignity of individuals in an increasingly secularized world." Mark Warren, "Max Weber's Liberalism for a Nietzschean World," *American Political Science Review*, 82, no. 1 (March 1988): 33.

88. Weber, *From Max Weber*, 117.

89. Ibid., 126–28.

90. Stanley Hoffmann, "Raymond Aron and the Theory of International Relations," *International Studies Quarterly*, 29, no. 1 (March 1985): 22; S. Turner and R.A. Factor, *Max Weber and the Dispute over Reason and Value* (London: Routledge and Kegan Paul, 1984), 168–79; Raymond Aron, "Max Weber and Power-Politics," in *Max Weber and Sociology Today*, ed. Otto Stammer (New York: Harper and Row, 1971), 83–100.

91. See Karl Polanyi, *The Great Transformation* (Boston: Beacon Press, 1944, 1957); and E.J. Hobsbawn, *The Age of Revolution, 1789–1848* (New York: The New American Library, 1962).

92. See Smith's arguments against mercantilist restraints on trade in book 4 of *The Wealth of Nations* (New York: The Modern Library, 1937).

93. Smith mentions these social orders at the end of book 1 of *The Wealth of Nations*. On Marxian class analysis, see (among other of Marx's works) *The German Ideology* (1846), *The Communist Manifesto* (1848), *The 18th Brumaire of Louis Bonaparte* (1852), *The Civil War in France* (1871), and *Critique of the Gotha Program* (1875).

94. *The Wealth of Nations*, IV, Ch. 2, 423.

95. As Kenneth Waltz states, "Balance-of-power theory is a theory about the results produced by the uncoordinated actions of states." *Theory of International Politics* (Reading, Mass.: Addison-Wesley, 1979), 122. Although Waltz argues that only two states are required for a balance of power, many writers have looked to five as an ideal number of great powers. One finds this in Machiavelli's time in the five competing states on the Italian peninsula (not counting interventions by two other states—France and Spain). The Congress of Vienna created a balance of power among five then-key states—England, France, Russia, Prussia, and Austria. Though intended for collective security (and not balance of power as such), the United Nations Security Council has five permanent members—the United States, Russia, the People's Republic of China, Great Britain, and France. More recently (in the early 1970s), Henry Kissinger proposed an order composed of five poles—the United States, the Soviet Union, Europe, Japan, and China.

96. As Hume states, "Thucydides represents the league which was formed against Athens, and which produced the Peloponnesian war, as entirely owing to

this principle [the balance of power]. And after the decline of Athens, when Thebans and Lacedemonians disputed for sovereignty, we find that the Athenians (as well as many other republics) always threw themselves into the lighter scale, and endeavoured to preserve the balance." In the case of the expansion of the Roman Empire, those rulers who were more interested in "gratifying their private passions" failed to pursue a balance of power policy, and as a result "they were forging their own chains." David Hume, "Of the Balance of Power," in *Essays: Moral, Political and Literary* (London: Oxford University Press, 1963), 339, 343.

97. Adam Smith, *Lectures on Jurisprudence,* ed. R.L. Meck, D.D. Raphael, P.G. Stein (Oxford: Clarendon Press, 1978), pp. 540–41.

98. One can find Smith's overview of the history of Europe since Rome in book 3 and his discussion of primitive economy in book 2 of *The Wealth of Nations.*

99. The concept of surplus value is implicit in Smith's discussion in book 1 of *The Wealth of Nations,* in which he observes how the productivity of skilled labor stemming from the division of labor allows for some in civilized society not to be producers themselves. On Marxian economics and political economy, also see Karl Marx's *Capital,* especially volume 1 (1867) and portions of volume 3 (published posthumously); *Economic and Philosophic Manuscripts* (1844), *Wage-Labour and Capital* (1848), and the *Grundrisse.*

100. For Marx's discussion of dialectical materialism in history, see the first part of *The German Ideology* and *The Communist Manifesto.*

101. The emphasis on capitalism as a global phenomenon and the need to view states and other social forces as part of a larger whole is evident in the works of Immanuel Wallerstein. See, for example, *The Capitalist World-Economy* (Cambridge: Cambridge University Press, 1977). On the Smith–Marx connection in the context of the globalist literature, see Robert Brenner, "The Origins of Capitalist Development: A Critique of Neo-Smithian Marxism," *New Left Review,* 104 (July-Aug. 1977): 25–92.

102. Howard, *The Lessons of History,* 143.

103. Karl Marx, "The Eighteenth Brumaire of Louis Bonaparte" in *The Marx–Engels Reader,* ed. Robert C. Tucker (New York: W.W. Norton, 1972), 436.

104. John Maclean, "Marxist Epistemology, Explanations of 'Change' and the Study of International Relations," in *Change and the Study of International Relations: The Evaded Dimension* ed. Barry Buzan and R.J. Barry Jones (New York: St. Martin's Press, 1981), 55. As Maclean goes on to note, "The pragmatic or management view of social reality [associated with such scholars as Karl Popper] starts with the epistemological premise that people adapt to a given, pre-existing and external environment, whereas Marx's fundamental starting point is people's intrinsic capacity to shape their world." (page 55).

105. See, for example, Andrew Linklater, *Beyond Realism and Marxism: Critical Theory and International Relations* (New York: St. Martin's Press, 1990); James Der Derian and Michael J. Shapiro, eds., *International/Intertextual Relations: Postmodern Readings of World Politics* (Lexington, Mass.: Lexington Books, 1989); "Speaking the Language of Exile Dissidence in International Studies," special issue of *International Studies Quarterly,* 34, no. 3 (Sept. 1990). As Richard K. Ashley states, "Nowhere in neorealist categories do we find room for the idea that men and women who are the objects of theory can themselves theorize about their lives; are in fact engaged in a continuing struggle to shape and redefine their understandings

of themselves, their circumstances, their agencies of collective action, and the very categories of social existence; do indeed orient their practices in light of their understandings; and, thanks to all of this, do give form and motion to the open-ended processes by which the material conditions of their practices are made, reproduced, and transformed." "The Poverty of Neorealism," in *Neorealism and Its Critics,* ed. Robert O. Keohane (New York: Columbia University Press, 1986), 291.

106. The argument is developed at length by Kenneth N. Waltz, *Man, the State and War* (New York: Columbia University Press, 1959), 80–123.

107. "Richard Cobden," in Wolfers and Martin, *The Anglo-American Tradition,* 193.

108. As Richard Rosecrance states, "The main thesis of this book is that a new 'trading world' of international relations offers the possibility of escaping such a vicious cycle [episodes of chaos and warfare] and finding new patterns of cooperation among nation-states. Indeed, it suggests that the benefit of trade and cooperation today greatly exceeds that of military competition and territorial aggrandizement." *The Rise of the Trading State: Commerce and Conquest in the Modern World* (New York: Basic Books, 1986), ix.

109. Ibid., 197.

110. See, for example, Ernst B. Haas, "The Balance of Power: Prescription, Concept or Propaganda?" *World Politics,* 5, no. 4 (July 1953): 442–77.

111. Richard Cobden, in M.G. Forsyth, et al., eds., *The Theory of International Relations: Selected Texts from Gentili to Treitschke* (New York: Atherton Press, 1970), 308.

112. Ibid., 309.

113. John A. Hobson, *Imperialism: A Study* (Ann Arbor: University of Michigan Press, 1965).

114. Ibid., 85.

115. Ibid., 74. Nor is imperialism an irrational "objectless disposition on the part of a state to unlimited forcible expansion," as argued by Joseph Schumpeter. See Schumpeter's *Imperialism and Social Classes,* trans. Heinz Norden, ed. Paul M. Sweezy (Oxford: Basil Blackwell, 1951), 6.

116. Hobson, *Imperialism,* 81.

117. Ibid., 85–86.

118. Ibid., 89.

119. "Lenin's concern was not to construct an abstract historiography of the development of capitalism: it was rather to convince all those who called themselves Marxists that the time had now arrived when revolutionary action to overthrow capitalism had become imperative." Neil Harding, *Lenin's Political Thought,* vol. 2 (Atlantic Highlands, N.J.: Humanities Press, 1983), 69.

120. V.I. Lenin, "Imperialism, the Highest Stage of Capitalism," in *The Lenin Anthology* ed. Robert C. Tucker (New York: W.W. Norton, 1975), 244.

121. Ibid., 271.

122. Ibid., 267.

10
Conclusion: The Historical Development of Ideas

In chapter 2 we pose six questions related to the study of international relations. The first question, which concerns the relative importance of the overall nature of the international system, the nature of the international system's political units, and human nature, dominates the discussion in this book and has been answered in different ways by different writers. Explanation at the level of the international system is reflected in Thucydides' focus on the changing distribution of power between Athens and Sparta, Hobbes' characterization of the international system as one with "no common power" and analogous to the state of nature, Rousseau's discussion of the implications of international anarchy, and Lenin's law of uneven development. Anarchy was viewed as what Kenneth Waltz has labeled a "permissive" cause of war; the decentralized nature of the system and state concern for security inevitably generated suspicion, distrust, and tension. While not addressing international relations, Adam Smith's perspective on the rise of economic markets has been used by some contemporary realists as an analog to a systems-level explanation of the behavior of states. Finally, Marx viewed capitalism as a global phenomenon, with states being part of a larger whole. Contemporary globalists adopt a similar perspective.

While realists tended to be pessimistic about the possibility of changing such a system, writers in the pluralist tradition, such as the Stoics, Seneca, and Marcus Aurelius, hoped that humanistic, universal values discovered through the process of right reason could create a sense of fellowship and global community that would go beyond loyalty to one's own political community. Similarly, Aquinas and other religious writers during the Middle Ages argued for the supremacy of religious doctrine, thus advancing church authority as a means to unify the Western world. Conversely, Dante placed his hope in a powerful secular emperor presiding over a world empire.

A recurrent theme at the state-societal level of analysis concerns the nature of a polity, its security, and its foreign policy behavior. Herodotus argued that states governed by laws are best able to inspire citizens to fight for freedom against outside powers. For Aristotle, a mixed form of government enhances stability and security, an argument also made by Polybius and Cicero. Machiavelli, following Livy, argued that republican forms of government not only are the most stable, but also aid in expansionism. Montesquieu and Kant emphasized how the nature of the states making up the international system—not simply human nature—is a critical factor in determining the extent of conflict. Republican state systems were deemed more conducive to peace, an argument Hamilton found unconvincing. Cobden argued that states that allowed private organizations and entrepreneurs to engage in free international trade would be more peaceful. Marx, on the other hand, argued that conflict is endemic and inevitable in capitalist societies and laid the groundwork, along with Hobson, for Lenin's argument that imperialism, the highest stage of capitalism, accounted for international wars.

The essence of human nature, and its effect on war and peace, were also subject to dispute. For Homer and Herodotus, war is simply a fact of life and a recurrent expression of one aspect of human nature. Thucydides added the observation that the worst side of human nature is exposed in times of war, as the thin veneer of civilization is stripped away and uncontrolled passions take hold. For Augustine, the causes of war are to be found at the individual level of analysis, but for him the corruption of the soul is at the heart of the problem. Given their faith in reason, Stoics such as Seneca and Marcus Aurelius essentially were optimists with regard to human nature and the ability of individuals to live in harmony. Rousseau glorified the innocence and fellowship of individuals in the state of nature and argued that war is an artifact of society that principally stems from the privatization of property. Like Montesquieu, however, Rousseau placed great faith in education, by which individuals would be prepared for "civil life." Generally, however, the authors surveyed held a pessimistic view of human nature.

For some, such as Thucydides and Livy, not much could be done to alter the situation. For others, Plato and Aristotle, human nature and potential could be elevated by active participation in a political community or, according to Augustine, by a commitment to God. For Kant, despite the selfish inclinations of human beings, the ability to reason in conjunction with nature's design encourages the search for peace. For Machiavelli and Hobbes, strong leadership in a political commonwealth could mitigate the worst aspects of human nature and keep passions somewhat under control. Compared to Grotius, these two authors did not have much faith in the power of international norms or law as a means to mute the excesses of human nature. For still others, Marx and Lenin, the revolutionary transformation of one type of social and economic system into another ultimately would liberate mankind and lead to dramatic improvements in the human condition.

In order to answer the second question of how the international economy and the international political system are related one must turn initially to the ancient Greeks, although for the most part their work has a domestic focus. Class analysis was an important theme in the works of Plato and Aristotle. In terms of international relations, the Greeks were generally suspicious of the cultural contamination resulting from commercial transactions with other peoples. By contrast, Polybius noted how commerce aided in the development of a "sense of humanity and equality" among city-states of the Peloponnese. But international political economy was not really addressed in a systematic way until the age of mercantilism, when the issue of the relation between "power" and "plenty" came to the fore.[1] Thereafter, classical economists such as David Ricardo and Adam Smith suggested that unfettered markets would improve the lot of the greatest number of people. Kant argued that economic imperatives contribute to peace among nations, with liberals such as Cobden claiming categorically that free trade policies lead to international peace. To the contrary, Marx and then Lenin posited that capitalism is the root cause of revolution, with imperialism accounting for modern war.

The third question, on why it is so difficult to predict the course of international events, was more often commented upon than answered. The difficulty encountered with chance phenomena is particularly troublesome in warfare. As Thucydides was quoted earlier, war is "governed by the total chances in operation and can never be restricted to the conditions that one or the other of the two sides would like to see permanently fixed." Polybius felt similarly: "We are no more than mortal men, and we should at all times make due allowance for the unexpected, and especially in time of war." The implication of these observations for a science of international relations is sobering. Even if one could identify all the relevant variables in a particular case and chart the manner in which they could interact and influence one another, successful prediction would be difficult at best. The response, of course, is that science need not attempt to predict the course of particular events, but rather should deal with general tendencies. Some argue that we may have to be satisfied primarily with post-hoc explanations that may provide general guidance for future action.[2] The result, however, is that the past may seem to be "overdetermined" and the future "underdetermined."[3]

This problem of prediction is compounded by the issues raised in the fourth question: How much control do statesmen have over international events? This issue is cast in terms of determinism and voluntarism or free will, with Homer's *The Iliad* first setting out these parameters. Scholars writing about international relations have tended to pose this question in the narrow manner suggested, focusing, as did Plutarch, on statesmen. Constraints resulting from the structure of the international system, the type of society or government, or human nature are emphasized to different degrees by the authors we have discussed.

Without exception, however, all of the authors under study here also argued that choice still exists. Polybius warns against assuming that all outcomes are merely acts of God, and Marcus Aurelius asserts that "the robber of your free will does not exist." Similarly, Machiavelli, following Livy, states that effective choice in terms of influencing outcomes is also possible: "So as not to rule out free will, I believe that it is probably true that fortune is the arbiter of half the things we do, leaving the other half or so controlled by ourselves." If leaders are completely dependent upon the whims of fate, then there would be no purpose in Machiavelli's and More's insistence that political leaders need to solicit sound advice, or little reason for Plutarch to record the efforts of statesmen to affect the course of history.

It has been argued by some theorists, however, that constraints on statesmen are not necessarily all bad. For nineteenth-century liberals, public opinion is a positive restriction on the actions of political leaders, just as the eighteenth-century authors of *The Federalist Papers* had believed competing factions within a state would limit the power of any one group. Kant's republicanism plays a similar role, as does his faith in nature: "The guarantee of perpetual peace is nothing less than that great artist, nature. In her mechanical course we see that her aim is to produce a harmony among men, against their will and indeed through their discord." So it was with Adam Smith, who noted how the competitive economic interactions of individuals lead to unanticipated yet positive outcomes—a theoretical insight that has been applied to relations among states.[4]

For the Stoics, the starting point in their philosophy was the individual, and their primary concern was to provide a philosophical basis so that people in general—not just political elites—could deal with the vicissitudes of life. Social contract theorists placed their faith in the power of human reason—that individuals would see that it is in their best interest to cooperate and would do so. For Adam Smith, by contrast, the interest of all would be served by individuals free to act in their own self-interests, however unintentional their service to collective or common interests might be. Cicero, Hobbes, Rousseau, Montesquieu, and international law theorists such as Grotius all attempted to explain why it is rational for otherwise competitive individuals to cooperate. Furthermore, as Kant later emphasized, learning to cooperate is possible over time. Even for Hegel and Marx, the ability of individuals to comprehend the nature of the historical process and to reflect upon their circumstances gives them some power to change their life circumstances.

The fifth question on the relation between morality and power in international affairs was a topic of concern to a number of writers. The issue of just war was addressed, among others, by Cicero, Augustine, Aquinas, Grotius, and Rousseau. The larger issue of morality and politics, however, pervades the vast majority of the works, including those of such supposedly hardcore realists as Thucydides and even Machiavelli. The traditional practice of dichotomizing thinking about international relations into realist and idealist camps would seem to be an example of attempting to achieve clarity at the cost of accuracy. We found E.H. Carr's observations on the limitations of such an approach to be quite apt, particularly as he addresses at the same time the issue of voluntarism. Carr, while applauded by realists for demolishing "the hollowness of the utopian edifice," also argued that realism alone is inadequate as it "does not provide us with the springs of action which are necessary even to the pursuit of thought." Carr would agree with Aristotle that human beings are political animals who by nature pursue particular, valued goals. As a result, the notion "that human affairs can be directed and modified by human action and human thought is a postulate so fundamental that its rejection seems scarcely compatible with existence as human beings." The bottom line, therefore, is that "any sound political thought must be based on elements of both utopia and reality"—a blend of values and power.[5] To accept this perspective, however, is to reinforce further the argument that outcomes in international relations may well be indeterminate and that, as a result, one should hold suitably low expectations concerning the successful prediction of specific international events.

As for the sixth question of how one should approach the study of international relations, a number of important points were made. Thucydides' distinction between the underlying and immediate causes of war is still used today, and very likely influenced Polybius' discussion of causes, beginnings, and pretexts. Plato's dialectical approach to knowledge, which emphasizes the consideration of alternative hypotheses and arguments, encouraged systematic thinking about politics. Similarly, Aristotle's devotion to empirical research and an interest in categorizing political phenomena has left a legacy for students of international relations. Polybius placed great store in relating observation to theory, thus making one of the earliest and strongest arguments that the search for causation should be the fundamental goal of researchers. Seneca agreed. A similar interest in causation and patterns of behavior characterizes the work of every writer surveyed, beginning with Machiavelli, with faith in scientific methods particularly pronounced in Weber.

The Three Images

The realist, pluralist, and globalist images that influence present-day theorists have ancient roots. From our review of the literature, we can observe that the realist understanding of world politics is the oldest tradition. It was already well established in Homer and Herodotus, and their writings directly influenced Thucydides, who made realism a centerpiece of ancient international relations thought. Thucydides, however, did not take an extreme realist position that excluded values from his analysis. The competition between power and values in international relations was as apparent to Thucydides as it would be to E.H. Carr more than two millenia later.

While realism was present in the writings of Plato, Aristotle, and Polybius, one also finds in their work the origins of other ideas that would inform present-day pluralism. But it was the outward-looking intellectual orientation of the Greco-Roman Stoics that was responsible for an extension of emerging liberal concepts to encompass relations that stretched beyond the borders of a particular political community. Present-day pluralism with its emphasis on transnational phenomena and the importance ascribed beyond states to individuals, groups, and other nonstate actors can be understood not just as a product of eighteenth- and nineteenth-century liberal thought, but also as a perspective with intellectual roots in Greco-Roman Stoic writings.

Although globalism as an image owes its development primarily to the nineteenth-century work of Marx and others in his intellectual debt, concepts associated with globalism such as class, class conflict, the labor theory of value, and political economy as mode of production can be found in Plato, Aristotle, and Livy. This is not to say that these ancient writers were globalists, much less that they were Marxists or even pre-Marxists. To make such an assertion would be to construct no more than a caricature of intellectual history. Globalism, as we have defined the image, is a nineteenth- and twentieth-century development, but one that incorporates concepts with ancient roots in Western thought.

Current realist, pluralist, and globalist perspectives on international relations reflect different emphases and foci within each image. Realists, for example, agree on the centrality and relative autonomy of states (buttressed by such concepts as sovereignty and reason of state), the preoccupation of leaders with the security of the state, and the importance of international anarchy to the generation of conflict. Not all realists, however, emphasize a drive or struggle for power as being rooted in human nature. Indeed, "neo" or "structural" realists do not focus so much on human nature; they place greater emphasis on the rational actor assumption for state behavior and argue that anarchy and various distributions of power among states lead them to be preoccupied with security and hence the enhancement of power or capabilities. One critic of neorealism, however, has suggested that this version of realism, in attempting to be more scientific, has in fact betrayed earlier realist works that were more sensitive to history and context.[6] Not all would agree, of course, that neorealism's emphasis on structural or systemic factors is necessarily any less sensitive to history and context than classic realists with their emphasis on human nature.

Similar differences within the pluralist literature can also be found. Historical conceptions of world order, for example, are not necessarily benign. While writers during the Middle Ages recognized social and political diversity, their ideal order was that of a hierarchy dominated by secular and religious elites. Similarly, Dante's solution to the international anarchy of his time was a universal empire. The Stoic heritage, by contrast, is not one of drawing unity from diversity by centralizing authority or by force of arms. Rather, Stoic universalism is achieved through the power of reason. Furthermore, particularly in the work of Seneca, it is also a philosophy that celebrates the individual. While Stoicism aimed to provide a philosophical basis for linking the individual to a wider humanity beyond the confines of one's particular political community, it also respected the autonomy of the individual.

The emphasis of the liberal heritage on the individual has also contributed directly to the development of the pluralist image. What has been termed "republican liberalism" is exemplified by the works of Kant, while "commercial liberalism" is represented by the peace-through-trade arguments of Cobden.[7] "Liberal institutionalism" more recently has gone through a number of incarnations—functionalist integration theory (1940s and early 1950s), neofunctionalist integration theory (1950s and 1960s), and interdependence theory (1970s).[8] Present-day literature associated with "neoliberal institutionalism," while recognizing the existence of international anarchy, reflects the Grotian tradition by emphasizing how the interaction of states and the development of international norms interact with domestic politics and international organizations in such a way that states may redefine their interests and learn how to cooperate.[9] Finally, the literature on organizational and bureaucratic politics, small group dynamics, crisis decision making, and individual psychology shares liberalism's skepticism about the unified, rational actor states.[10] In sum, the pluralist image of international politics—as befits its name—subsumes a number of approaches and cannot simply be equated with idealism.

As for the globalist image, there are at least three schools of thought: orthodox Marxists, dependency theorists, and world-systems theorists. Orthodox Marxists are highly critical of both the dependency and world-system literature. Dependency theorists argue that the underdevelopment of the Third World is the result of external exploitation. Such states produce only those commodities required by the more advanced capitalist states, at the same time providing an outlet for capital. Hence, an exploitative international division of labor exists.[11] Orthodox Marxists contend that exploitation is less a result of external demands than it is an outcome of the type of class structure within a dependent state. Hence, one should pay greater attention to relations between the owners of the means of production and the laboring classes, and less to external exploitation as such.[12] Furthermore, some Marxists with voluntarist inclinations claim that by ignoring class relations in favor of external relations of unequal exchange (particularly trade), the possibilities for revolution in exploited countries are underestimated.[13] As world-system theorists have tended to draw on the dependency literature, they also have come under attack from orthodox Marxists. Immanuel Wallerstein's ambitious attempt to trace the historical development of capitalism (utilizing such well-known concepts as core, periphery, and semiperiphery) has been subject to criticism from a wide variety of both hostile and sympathetic scholars.[14]

While we have noted differences among various authors associated with the realist, pluralist, and globalist images, what unites these images is more important than what divides them. Realists, for example, tend to emphasize the underlying continuity of international politics. This focus is well expressed in one realist's belief that international politics is "the realm of recurrence and repetition; it is the field in which political action is most regularly necessitous," and least "susceptible of a progressivist interpretation."[15] Conversely, a writer in the pluralist tradition states, "My perspective is more permissive of the workings of volition, of a kind of free will, than is allowed by many popular theories of international politics."[16] Similarly, while realists emphasize the overriding importance of military-political factors in their analyses, globalists give precedence to economic considerations, and pluralists argue the relative weight of these factors will vary depending on the issue area.[17]

The Historical Development of Ideas

A pervasive theme throughout this work is the familiarity of authors with the works of their predecessors. Rousseau, for example, did not begin with an empty slate. He was intimately familiar with the work of Montesquieu who, in turn, drew inspiration from Polybius and other writers who preceded him. Inspiration came not just from points of agreement, but also from opposition; both Montesquieu and Rousseau took issue with Hobbes. Similarly, the work of Immanuel Kant and Adam Smith had roots in Aristotle and the Greco-Roman Stoics, even as they were themselves part of an emerging eighteenth- and nineteenth-century liberal tradition. One cannot claim to have any more than a partial understanding of Machiavelli without an appreciation of his reliance on the works of Livy, Polybius, Thucydides, and other Greco-Roman writers.

Thus a deeper understanding of the thought of any theorist does not come from viewing that person's work in isolation. Identifying links to earlier writers reveals the degree to which arguments are a response not only to contemporary events and the unfolding of history as a given scholar or scholars understand it, but also to the intellectual currents that preceded their own theoretical efforts. In a very real sense, international relations theory has been evolutionary in relation both to observed events and to ideas. Put another way, the evolution of international relations theory has been based on sensitivity to (and an understanding of) both changing political circumstances and the intellectual heritage of previous work. Such an appreciation for one's intellectual precursors as well as for the continuity and change of international politics is something any scholar should hope to achieve.

Notes

Multiple citations within notes are listed in the order in which the quotations appear in the text.

1. Jacob Viner, "Power vs. Plenty as Objectives of Foreign Policy in the Seventeenth and Eighteenth Centuries," *World Politics*, 1, no. 1 (Oct. 1948): 1–29.

2. As E.H. Carr argues, "The clue to the question of prediction in history lies in this distinction between the general and the specific, between the universal and the unique. The historian . . . is bound to generalize; and, in so doing, he provides general guides for future action which, though not specific predictions, are both valid and useful. But he cannot predict specific events, because the specific is unique and because the element of accident enters into it." *What Is History?* (Harmondsworth, Eng.: Penguin Books, 1973), 68–69.

3. James Kurth, as cited by Robert O. Keohane, *International Institutions and State Power: Essays in International Relations Theory* (Boulder, Col.: Westview Press, 1989), 21.

4. By way of example, Kenneth Waltz notes, "According to the common American definition of power, a failure to get one's way is proof of weakness. In politics, however, powerful agents fail to impress their wills on others in just the ways they intend to. The intention of an act and its result will seldom be identical because the result will be affected by the person or object acted on and conditioned by the environment within which it occurs." *Theory of International Politics* (Reading, Mass.: Addison-Wesley, 1979), 192.

5. E.H. Carr, *The Twenty Years' Crisis: 1919–1939* (New York: Harper Torchbooks, 1964), 89, 92, 93.

6. Richard K. Ashley, "The Poverty of Neorealism," in *Neorealism and Its Critics*, ed. Robert O. Keohane (New York: Columbia University Press, 1986), 255–300. Michael Doyle distinguishes between what he calls "minimalist," "fundamentalist," and "structuralist" forms of realism. "Thucydides: A Realist?" in *Hegemonic Rivalry: From Thucydides to the Nuclear Age*, ed. Richard Ned Lebow and Barry S. Strauss (Boulder, Col.: Westview Press, 1991), 170–72. For a discussion of realism in terms of its various definitions in political theory and everyday discourse, see R.N. Berki, *On Political Realism* (London: J.M. Dent and Sons, 1981).

7. The terms are those of Robert O. Keohane, "International Liberalism Reconsidered," in *Economic Limits to Modern Politics*, ed. John Dunn (Cambridge: Cambridge University Press, 1989), 165–94.

8. Joseph M. Grieco, "Anarchy and the Limits of Cooperation: A Realist Critique of the Newest Liberal Institutionalism," *International Organization*, 42, no. 3 (Summer 1988): 486. On functionalism, see David Mitrany, *A Working Peace System* (Chicago: Quadrangle Press, 1966). On neofunctionalism, see Ernst B. Haas, *The Uniting of Europe: Political, Economic, and Social Forces, 1950–1957* (Stan-

ford, Calif.: Stanford University Press, 1958). On interdependence, see Edward S. Morse, "The Transformation of Foreign Policies: Modernization, Interdependence, and Externalization," World Politics, 22 (April 1970): 371–92.

9. Joseph S. Nye, "Neorealism and Neoliberalism," World Politics, 40, no. 2 (Jan. 1988): 238; and Robert O. Keohane, "Neoliberal Institutionalism: A Perspective on World Politics," in International Institutions and State Power, 1–20.

10. Grieco, "Anarchy and Cooperation," 489, note 13, citing Graham T. Allison, Essence of Decision: Explaining the Cuban Missile Crisis (Boston: Little, Brown, 1971); Irving L. Janis, Victims of Groupthink (Boston: Houghton Mifflin, 1972); Ole R.. Holsti, Crisis, Escalation, War (Montreal: McGill-Queen's University Press, 1972); Robert Jervis, Perception and Misperception in International Politics (Princeton, N.J.: Princeton University Press, 1976).

11. See, for example, Andre Gunder Frank, Latin America: Underdevelopment or Revolution? (New York: Monthly Review Press, 1969); Andre Gunder Frank, World Accumulation, 1492–1789 (New York: Monthly Review Press, 1978); F.H. Cardoso and Enzo Faletto, Dependency and Development in Latin America (Berkeley: University of California Press, 1979); Samir Amin, Imperialism and Unequal Development (New York: Monthly Review Press, 1977).

12. See, for example, Robert Brenner, "The Origins of Capitalist Development: A Critique of Neo-Smithian Marxism," New Left Review, 104 (July-Aug. 1977): 25–92.

13. Augustin Cueva, "A Summary of Problems and Perspectives of Dependency Theory," Latin American Perspectives, 3, no. 4 (Fall 1976): 12–16; and Raul A. Fernandez and Jose F. Ocampo, "The Latin American Revolution: A Theory of Imperialism, Not Dependency," Latin American Perspectives, 1 (Spring 1974): 30–61.

14. Brenner, "The Origins of Capitalist Development"; and, for a more sympathetic critique, Theda Skocpol, "Wallerstein's World Capitalist System: A Theoretical and Historical Critique," American Journal of Sociology, 82, no. 5 (March 1977): 1075–91. See also Robert A. Denemark and Kenneth P. Thomas, "The Brenner-Wallerstein Debate," International Studies Quarterly, 32, no. 1 (March 1988): 47–65. Wallerstein has written many books and articles on world-systems theory. See, for example, The Modern World-System I: Capitalist Agriculture and the Origins of the European World-Economy in the Sixteenth Century (New York: Academic Press, 1974); The Capitalist World-Economy (Cambridge: Cambridge University Press, 1979).

15. Martin Wight, "Why Is There No International Theory?" in Diplomatic Investigations: Essays in the Theory of International Politics, ed. Herbert Butterfield and Martin Wight (Cambridge, Mass.: Harvard University Press, 1966), 26.

16. Ernst B. Haas, When Knowledge Is Power: Three Models of Change in International Organizations (Berkeley: University of California Press, 1990), 7. See also James N. Rosenau, Turbulence in World Politics (Princeton, N.J.: Princeton University Press, 1990). Rosenau, like Haas, puts emphasis on volition and learning. And as Robert O. Keohane states, "My own interest in international cooperation and discord—in particular, the conditions under which governments develop patterns of collaboration—reflects my personal aversion to conflict and violence, and my belief in the ability of human beings, through a combination of reason and empathy with others, to improve the world. I am a child of the Enlightenment—a chas-

tened child, to be sure, but nevertheless a believer in the *possibility* of progress, though by no means in its inevitability." *International Institutions and State Power,* 21.

17. Another example: Despite the fact that neorealists and world-systems theorists adopt "structuralist" approaches, for neorealists system structure is defined in terms of the observable attributes of states, which are a given. World-systems theorists, however, define structure in terms of the organizing principles of the capitalist world economy that underlies and actually generates the state actors themselves. Alexander E. Wendt, "The Agent-Structure Problem in International Relations Theory," *International Organization,* 41, no. 3 (Summer 1987): 335.

Acknowledgments

We wish to thank Karl Pieragostini, Dina Zinnes, Michael Fry, and Joseph Lepgold for their comments on the initial draft of this book.

Index

Alexander the Great, 70, 75, 80, 115
Alfarabi, 6*n*
Alliances, 12, 23*n*, 29, 31–32, 37–38,
    113–14, 157–58, 167. *See also*
    Balance of power
    bandwagoning, 57–61
    balancing, 57–61
Allison, Graham T., 66*n*
Anarchy, 11, 16, 42, 53, 128, 140,
    151, 153, 164–65, 167, 170–71,
    174–75, 189, 191, 195, 200,
    227*n*
Aquinas, Thomas, 3, 9, 75, 105, 124–
    25*t*, 133–39, 140–42, 144–46*n*,
    156, 171–73, 186, 219, 222
Aristophanes, 33
Aristotle, 3–5, 18, 21, 23, 25, 29, 36,
    69–71, 73, 75–80, 87, 89, 90*n*,
    95–97, 102–3, 107, 109–10,
    120, 134–35, 140–42*n*, 153–54,
    162, 185, 206, 219–21, 223–24,
    226
Aron, Raymond, 66*n*, 203
Augustine, St., 3, 105, 124–125*t*,
    133–39, 140–42, 144–46*n*, 155–
    56, 173, 220, 222
Aurelius, Marcus: *see* Marcus
    Aurelius

Bacon, Francis, 163
Balance of power, 22, 29, 39, 42, 44–
    45, 61, 63, 87, 95, 147, 173,

183, 199, 201, 205, 208–9,
    216*n*–17*n*. *See also* Alliances
Bodin, 3, 75, 101, 147–48*t*, 169–70,
    174, 181
Botero, Giovanni, 148*t*, 162–63, 174
Bueno de Mesquita, Bruce, 66*n*
Bull, Hedley, 174
Burke, Edmund, 101

Caesar, Julius, 101
Calvin, John, 148*t*–49
Capabilities: *See* Power
Capitalism, 15–16, 103, 124, 131–
    32, 150, 183, 201, 204–12, 219–
    20, 225, 228*n*
Carr, E. H., xiii, 61, 63, 196, 223,
    227*n*
Causation, 19*n*, 24, 27, 82–86, 106,
    110–11, 113. *See also* War
Christendom (Christianity), 121, 126,
    131–33, 135–36, 139–41, 143*n*–
    144*n*, 147, 149, 155–56, 159,
    168, 170, 174, 195
Church: *See* Christendom
Cicero, 81, 93–95, 100–105, 111,
    115, 118, 133, 137–38, 153–54,
    173, 220, 222
Class analysis (class), 36, 72, 74, 78–
    79, 107, 116–17, 204, 206–7,
    220, 225
Clausewitz, 26, 48
Cobden, Richard, 182*t*, 182, 207–9,
    218*n*, 220–21

231

About the Authors

MARK V. KAUPPI received his Ph.D. from the University of Colorado and his M.A. from the University of California at Berkeley.

PAUL R. VIOTTI earned his Ph.D. from the University of California at Berkeley and masters degrees from Georgetown University and the George Washington University.

They are also authors of *International Relations Theory: Realism, Pluralism, and Globalism* (Macmillan, 1987, 1992).

STAR TREK®

CAPTAIN'S LOG

STAR TREK created by Gene Roddenberry
Special Thanks to Risa Kessler and John Van Citters at CBS Consumer Products.

www.**IDWPUBLISHING**.com   ISBN: 978-1-60010-887-7   14 13 12 11   1 2 3 4

STAR TREK: CAPTAIN'S LOG. MARCH 2011. FIRST PRINTING. Star Trek is ™, ® and © 2011 CBS Studio, Inc. STAR TREK and related marks are trademarks of CBS Studios Inc. IDW authorized user. All Rights Reserved. © 2011 Idea and Design Works, LLC. IDW Publishing, a division of Idea and Design Works, LLC. Editorial offices: 5080 Santa Fe St., San Diego, CA 92109. Any similarities to persons living or dead are purely coincidental. With the exception of artwork used for review purposes, none of the contents of this publication may be reprinted without the permission of Idea and Design Works, LLC. Printed in Korea.
IDW Publishing does not read or accept unsolicited submissions of ideas, stories, or artwork.

Ted Adams, CEO & Publisher
Greg Goldstein, Chief Operating Officer
Robbie Robbins, EVP/Sr. Graphic Artist
Chris Ryall, Chief Creative Officer
Matthew Ruzicka, CPA, Chief Financial Officer
Alan Payne, VP of Sales

PIKE
Written by Stuart Moore
Art and colors by J.K. Woodwar
Lettering by Robbie Robbins
Edits by Scott Dunbier

SULU
Written by Scott and David Tipt
Art by Federica Manfredi
Colors by Andrea Priorini
Color assist by Chiara Cinabro
Lettering by Neil Uyetake
Edits by Scott Dunbier

Harriman
Written by Marc Guggenheim
Art by Andrew Currie
Colors by Moose Bauman
Lettering by Neil Uyetake
Edits by Scott Dunbier

Jellico
Written by Keith R.A. DeCandido
Art by J.K. Woodward
Lettering by Chris Mowry
Edits by Scott Dunbier

Collection edits by
Mariah Huehner and
Justin Eisinger

Book design by Robbie Robbins

PiKE

"IT'LL BE GOOD TO COME DOWN TO EARTH FOR A WHILE.

"REGROUP... RETHINK..."

...AND REPLENISH OUR DEPLETED CREW.

STARFLEET WANTS A FULL DEBRIEF AFTER THE TALOS INCIDENT. THEY SAID A STARBASE WOULDN'T DO—THEY WANT US HOME.

BUT GIVEN THE LOSSES WE'VE SUSTAINED, I'D SAY IT'S FORTUITOUS TIMING.

IDLE CONVERSATION ISN'T MY STRONG SUIT, CAPTAIN. AND YOU'RE NOT HOLDING UP YOUR END.

WHAT'S WRONG?

IT'S JUST... THE MASSACRE ON RIGEL. ALL THOSE CREW MEMBERS LOST... AND THEN, THE THINGS WE SAW ON TALOS IV...

THIS IS MY LIFE, NUMBER ONE. MY CAREER. I'VE SACRIFICED EVERYTHING TO BECOME MASTER OF A STARSHIP... AND YET I CAN'T STOP WONDERING...

...IS IT ALL WORTH IT?

I THOUGHT I'D GOTTEN RID OF THESE DOUBTS. BUT I KEEP THINKING... THINKING ABOUT...

NUMBER ONE... WHEN WE WERE DOWN IN THE KEEPER'S CAVERN. YOU, ME, YEOMAN COLT... AND VINA...

CAPTAIN.

I CAN'T HELP YOU.

I DON'T HAVE YOUR ANSWERS.

KRUNKKKK

RED ALERT. SENIOR OFFICERS TO THE BRIDGE.

CAPTAIN PIKE TO THE BRIDGE!

KRUNKHHH

THANK YOU, YEOMAN.

I AM ALL RIGHT!

MINIMAL DAMAGE TO SHIP'S SYSTEMS. BUT OUR SHIELD STRENGTH IS DROPPING WITH EACH HIT.

SIR, THAT SHIP IS CHARGING WEAPONS AGAIN.

I'M PLOTTING AN ELLIPTICAL COURSE AWAY FROM JUPITER'S GRAVITY WELL—

NO.

I'M TIRED OF BEING AMBUSHED.

NUMBER ONE, PREPARE A COUNTERATTACK. SAFEGUARD *ENTERPRISE*, BUT SEE IF YOU CAN DO THAT THING SOME DAMAGE.

YEOMAN COLT—

—YOU'RE WITH ME.

...THINK I CAN GET YOU THROUGH THEIR SHIELDS, CAP'N.

JUST NEED A MINUTE TO COMPENSATE FOR THAT STRANGE RADIATION...

SPOCK SAYS THEIR WARP ENGINES ARE CONTAINED IN THE AFT QUARTER OF THE SHIP, CHIEF. GET US AS CLOSE TO THAT SECTION AS YOU CAN.

AND KEEP A LOCK ON OUR FREQUENCIES.

EVERYBODY STAY SHARP. THIS'LL BE A QUICK RAID—CRIPPLE THEIR ENGINES, THEN BEAM RIGHT OUT.

ZZZRRAPP

...BEST SUBLIGHT SPEED TO EARTH, NUMBER ONE.

YES, SIR.

MISTER SPOCK... ANY I.D. ON THAT SHIP?

STARFLEET IDENTIFIES IT AS *HALOGIAN*, CAPTAIN—A PLANET ON THE OUTER RIM. BUT I HAVE NO FURTHER INFORMATION THAN THAT.

WONDERFUL.

TWO MORE DEATHS... FOR NO REASON WHATSOEVER.

MAYBE SOMEDAY...

CAPTAIN... I...

YOU DID GOOD WORK OVER THERE, YEOMAN. I INTEND TO RECOMMEND YOU FOR IMMEDIATE PROMOTION.

MEANWHILE...

...I SUGGEST YOU CONTINUE YOUR STUDIES.

...

...YES SIR.

TWELVE YEARS LATER.

"GOOD TO SEE YOU AGAIN..."

U.S.S. EXETER
NCC - 1788

...CAPTAIN COLT.

CONGRATULATIONS ON YOUR PROMOTION.

AND YOURS, SIR. BUT I MUST ASK...

WHAT EXACTLY IS A "FLEET CAPTAIN," ANYWAY?

IT'S SORT OF LIKE AN OLD-STYLE FLAG ADMIRAL. IN THE EVENT OF A LARGE-SCALE MILITARY MISSION, I'LL BE DIRECTING THE MOVEMENTS OF AN ENTIRE SQUADRON.

IT'S NOT A COMMON RANK. BUT STARFLEET IS GEARING UP FOR THE POSSIBILITY OF OPEN CONFLICT WITH THE KLINGONS.

I HAVEN'T BEEN ON ONE OF THESE OLD CLASS J'S FOR A WHILE.

NOT TOO MANY AMENITIES, AS I RECALL...

THEY'RE ONLY USED FOR TRAINING MISSIONS, THESE DAYS.

I'VE GOT A COMPLEMENT OF *VERY* GREEN CADETS. I THINK THEY'RE GRADUATING THEM YOUNGER THAN EVER.

THEY ARE.

THE KLINGONS.

THE KLINGONS...

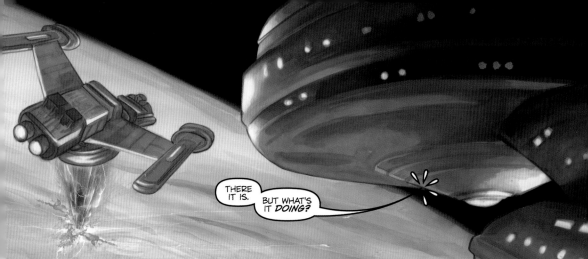

THERE IT IS. BUT WHAT'S IT *DOING*?

THAT RADIATION BEAM IS GENERATING INTENSE HEAT.

AND IT'S AIMED STRAIGHT AT JUPITER'S CORE...

MY GOD.

JUPITER IS BASICALLY A GIANT BALL OF GAS. THERE'S A THEORY THAT IT'S A FAILED STAR—A TWIN TO THE SUN.

I THINK THAT SHIP IS TRYING TO *IGNITE* IT.

IS THAT POSSIBLE?

I DON'T KNOW.

BUT IF THEY SUCCEED... IT'LL WIPE OUT ALL LIFE IN THE SOLAR SYSTEM.

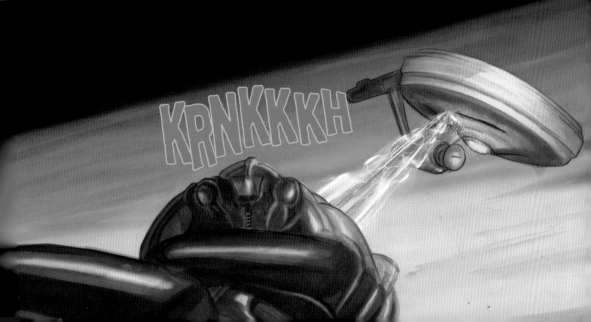

KRNKKKH

...TREMENDOUS NERVE DAMAGE TO HIS ENTIRE SYSTEM. THERE WAS VERY LITTLE WE COULD DO.

HE SHOULD BE ABLE TO MANEUVER THIS CHAIR AROUND, AND OPERATE THE BLINKING LIGHT... BUT THAT'S ABOUT IT.

WHAT ABOUT HIS MIND?

IT'S FINE.

JUST TRAPPED INSIDE THAT SHELL.

I'LL LEAVE YOU WITH HIM. BUT DON'T EXPECT MUCH.

ONE BLINK MEANS YES, TWO MEANS NO.

CAPTAIN?

I—I THOUGHT YOU'D WANT TO KNOW. THE HALOGIANS HAVE BEEN TURNED DOWN FOR FEDERATION MEMBERSHIP FOUR TIMES IN THE PAST THIRTEEN YEARS.

YOU SAVED MY CREW, CAPTAIN. WE HAD ZERO CASUALTIES FROM THE BATTLE.

BUT WHAT A PRICE TO PAY...

APPARENTLY A SMALL GROUP OF THEM HAVE BEEN SEEKING REVENGE ON EARTH, FOR THE INSULT.

OH, CHRIS...

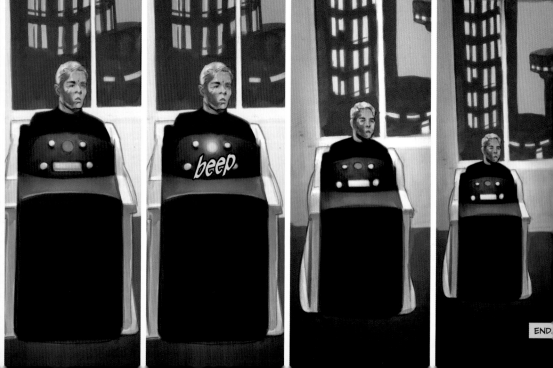

END

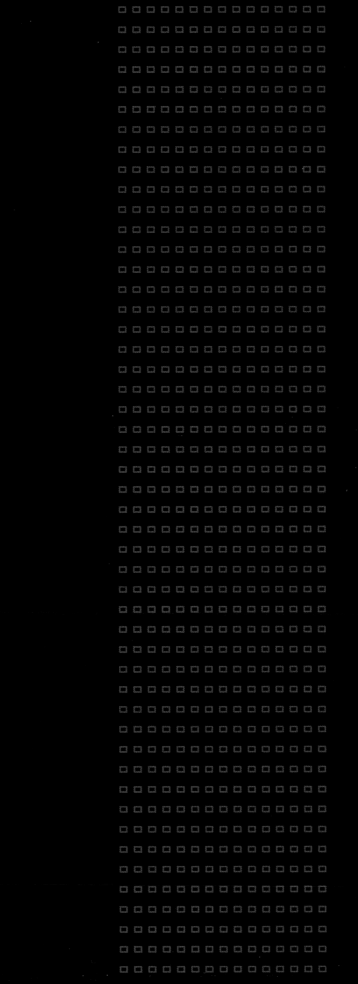

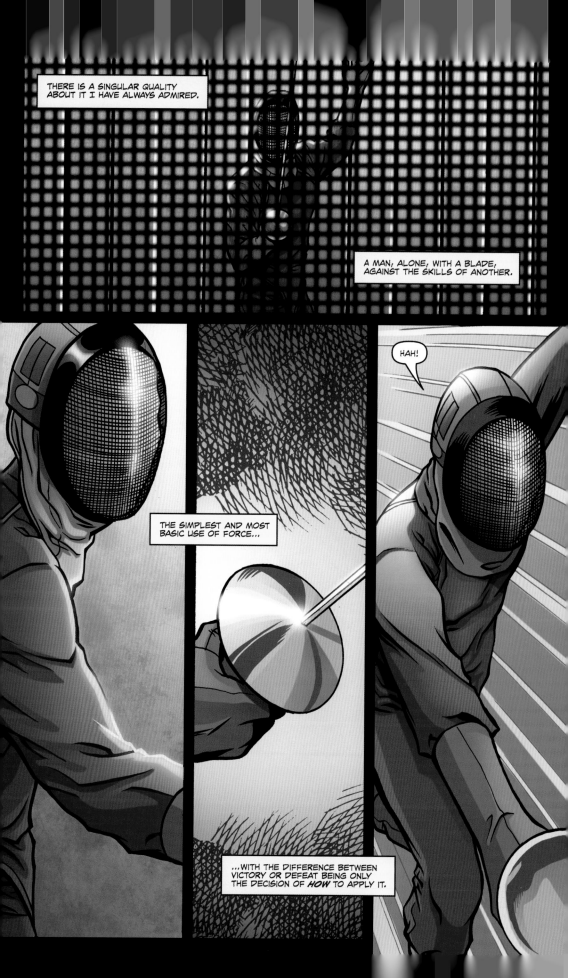

THE NEWS ISN'T ALL BAD. STARFLEET INTELLIGENCE TELLS US THAT ALL THIS POSTURING IS PROBABLY MORE ABOUT INTERNAL THOLIAN POLITICS THAN ANY SORT OF REAL INTEREST IN CONFLICT.

WE THINK THIS CAN ALL BE SMOOTHED OVER WITH SOME DIPLOMATIC SAVVY AND CHARM. WE'VE TOLD THE THOLIANS THAT WE WANT TO TAKE THIS OPPORTUNITY TO RENEW OUR NON-AGGRESSION PACT WITH THEM.

THE THOLIAN DIPLOMATS WILL MEET WITH YOU IN ORBIT AROUND THE VYELL 4 BORDER STATION. I'M SENDING A SECURE DIPLOMATIC BRIEFING PACKET TO YOUR COMMUNICATIONS OFFICER RIGHT NOW.

UNDERSTOOD, ADMIRAL.

HIKARU, I DON'T THINK THIS WILL BE DIFFICULT. I'D LIKE TO THINK THAT THE THOLIANS ARE AS EAGER TO PATCH THIS UP AS WE ARE. HOWEVER...

...I RECOMMEND THAT YOU NOT SHOW UP LATE. RENSHAW OUT.

THE THOLIANS. SPLENDID.

SO WHAT WAS THAT "LATE" BUSINESS ABOUT?

THE THOLIANS PLACE AN EXTREMELY HIGH VALUE ON PUNCTUALITY. SOME MIGHT SAY IRRATIONALLY SO.

I TAKE IT WE'LL TALK TO THEM OVER SHIP-TO-SHIP COMMUNICATIONS? AND THEY CAN'T LEAVE THEIR SHIPS BECAUSE OF THE TEMPERATURE DIFFERENTIAL, RIGHT?

INDEED. IN AN ENVIRONMENT LIKE OURS, A THOLIAN WOULD FREEZE AND SHATTER.

YOU'VE ENCOUNTERED THEM BEFORE, HAVEN'T YOU?

BEEN READING UP ON ME, HAVE YOU?

BROWSING THROUGH THE ENTERPRISE RECORDS SEEMED LIKE A DECENT IDEA, CAPTAIN.

FAIR ENOUGH. AND YES, WE HAD A SKIRMISH WITH THE THOLIANS. ONE WE BARELY ESCAPED, AS IT HAPPENED...

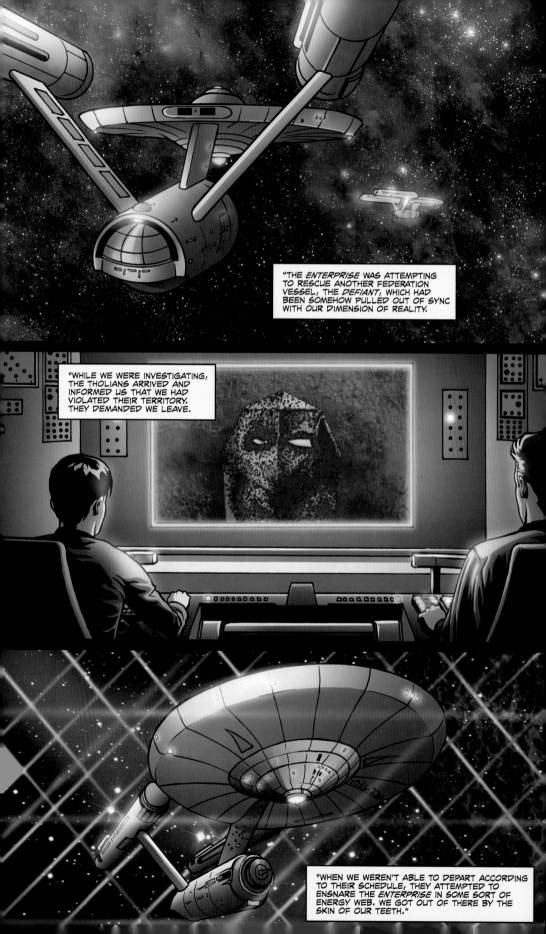

"THE *ENTERPRISE* WAS ATTEMPTING TO RESCUE ANOTHER FEDERATION VESSEL, THE *DEFIANT*, WHICH HAD BEEN SOMEHOW PULLED OUT OF SYNC WITH OUR DIMENSION OF REALITY."

"WHILE WE WERE INVESTIGATING, THE THOLIANS ARRIVED AND INFORMED US THAT WE HAD VIOLATED THEIR TERRITORY. THEY DEMANDED WE LEAVE."

"WHEN WE WEREN'T ABLE TO DEPART ACCORDING TO THEIR SCHEDULE, THEY ATTEMPTED TO ENSNARE THE *ENTERPRISE* IN SOME SORT OF ENERGY WEB. WE GOT OUT OF THERE BY THE SKIN OF OUR TEETH."

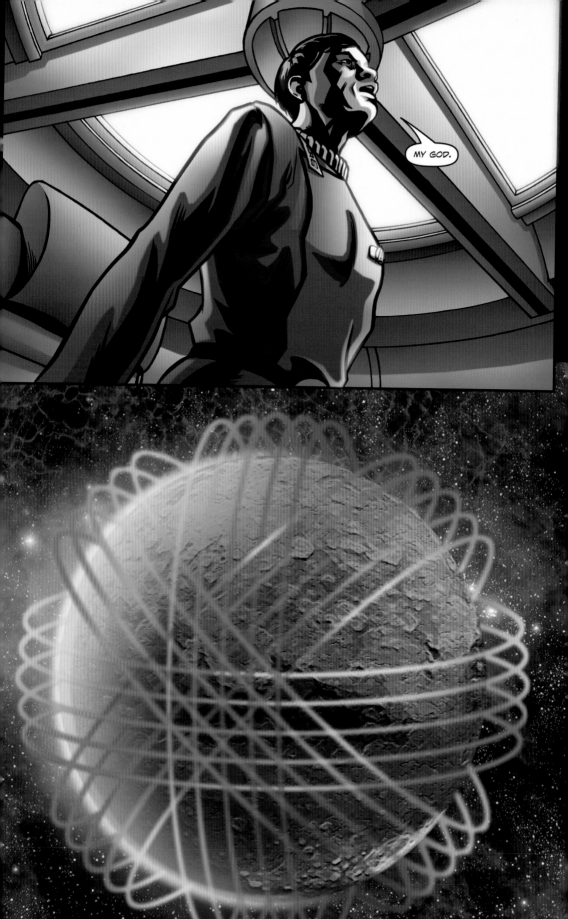

"RECEIVING A HAIL FROM THE THOLIAN COMMANDER, CAPTAIN."

YOU WILL WITHDRAW!

NOBODY WILL BE WITHDRAWING, COMMANDER.

NOW, YOU HAVE OUR APOLOGIES FOR BEING 37 MINUTES LATE TO THE NEGOTIATIONS. THE DELAY WAS UNAVOIDABLE, AS WE WERE FORCED TO STOP FOR RESCUE OPERATIONS.

BUT IS THAT AFFRONT REALLY WORTH THE LIVES OF THE COLONISTS BELOW, NOT TO MENTION PLUNGING BOTH OUR PEOPLES INTO A NEEDLESS WAR?

ALL FOR 37 MINUTES.

OR, YOU COULD DEMONSTRATE THAT THOLIAN RESPECT FOR MERCY IS GREATER THAN OUR RESPECT FOR PUNCTUALITY.

OR YOU CAN CONTINUE ON YOUR CURRENT PATH; IN WHICH CASE WE'LL BE FLYING THE EXCELSIOR DIRECTLY DOWN YOUR THROAT. THE CHOICE IS YOURS.

HELMSMAN, TAKE US DIRECTLY TOWARD THE LEAD THOLIAN VESSEL. MATCH THEM MOVE FOR MOVE. FULL IMPULSE POWER.

AYE, SIR.

20,000 METERS AND CLOSING, CAPTAIN.

15,000 METERS AND CLOSING.

STEADY, MR. DAILEY.

10,000...

WE'RE BEING HAILED BY THE THOLIAN COMMANDER, CAPTAIN!

ON SCREEN! FULL STOP, MR. DAILEY!

WE HAVE CONCLUDED THAT MERCY IS AN ACCEPTABLE EXCUSE FOR YOUR TARDINESS. DESTRUCTION OF THE COLONY REMAINS AS OF YET UNNECESSARY. WE SHALL RETURN TO VYELL AND COMMENCE DISCUSSIONS. ARE WE IN AGREEMENT?

WE ARE IN AGREEMENT. EXCELSIOR OUT.

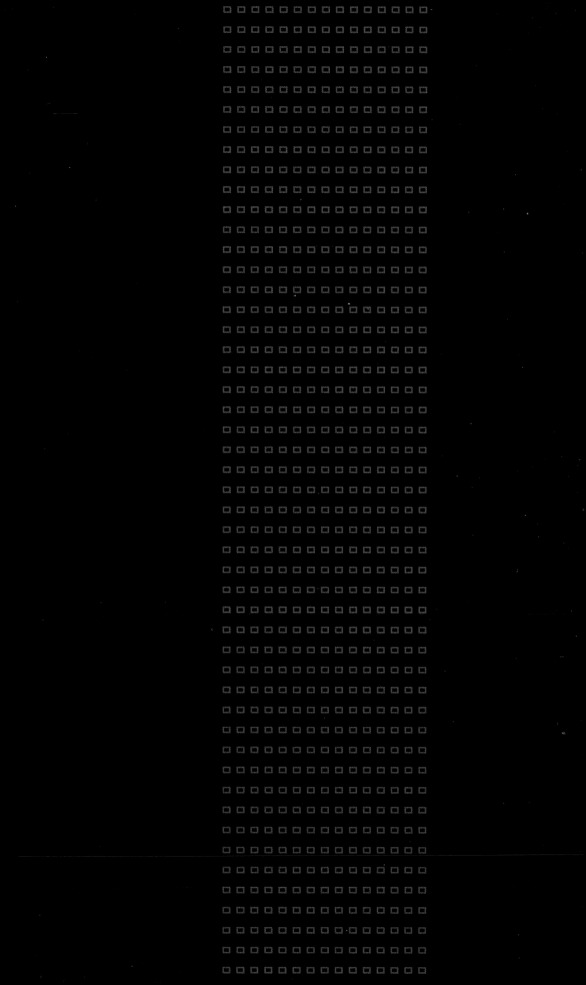

Harriman

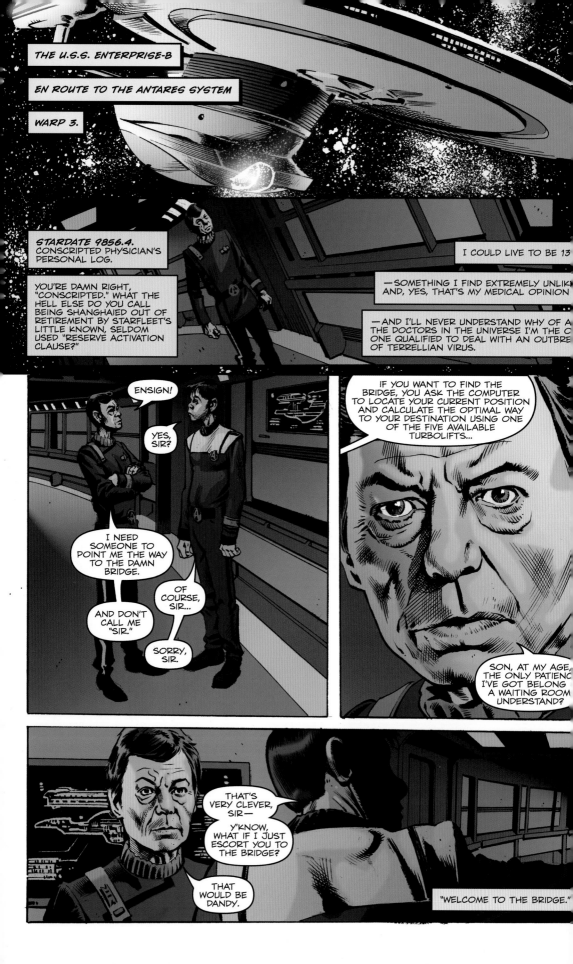

KLINGON BATTLECRUISER
VENGEANCE

IN ORBIT AROU[N]
ANTARES

"THERE SHALL BE NO PEACE AS LONG AS KIRK LIVES."

GENERAL CHOROTH, COMMANDING

SIR?

JUST... MUSING, KURR.

THE EMPIRE, AS EVER, WAS AS GOOD AS ITS WORD. KIRK IS DEAD AND NOW PEACE IS UPON US.

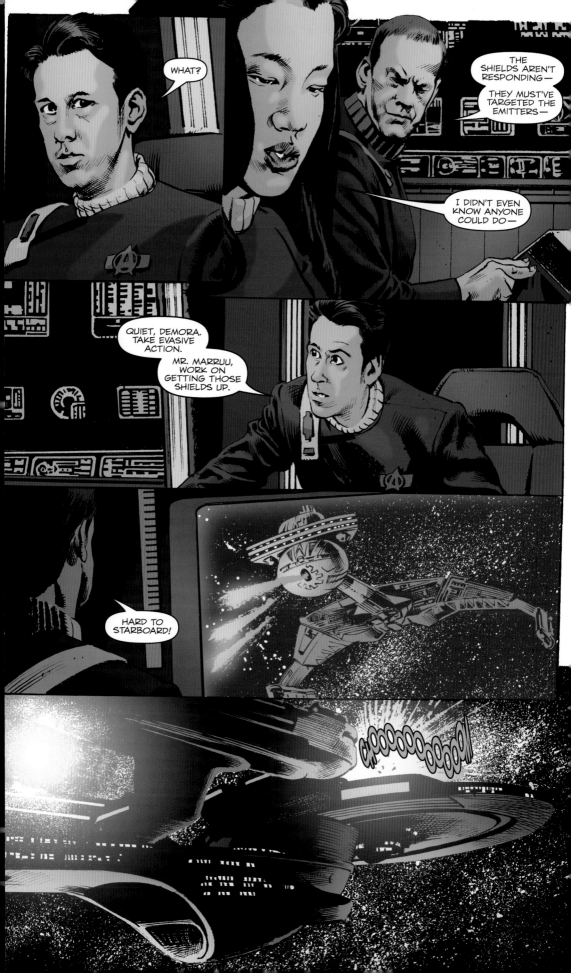

TIME IS UP, ENTERPRISE.

VERY WELL. ENGAGING TRANSPORTERS...

AKACHOOOOO

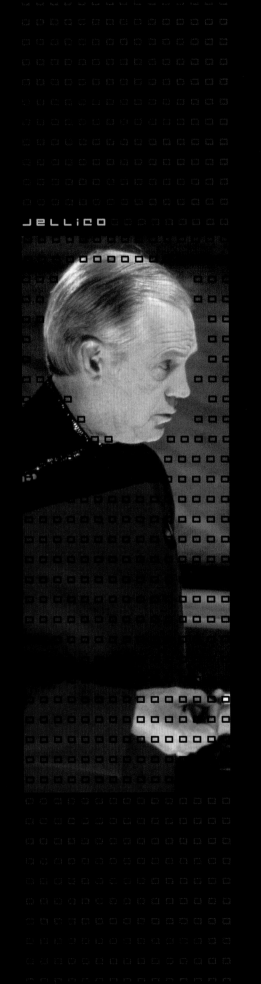

JELLICO

PERSONAL LOG, COMMANDER LESLIE WONG, STARDATE 45921.3.

AFTER MY TENURE AS AN INSTRUCTOR AT STARFLEET ACADEMY ENDED, I HAD REQUESTED AN ASSIGNMENT TO STARBASE 375.

INSTEAD, I HAVE BEEN POSTED TO THE *U.S.S. CAIRO*, AN *EXCELSIOR*-CLASS SHIP, AS HER NEW FIRST OFFICER.

I HAVE RENDEZVOUSED WITH THE VESSEL AT CAMPAGNA STATION, A CIVILIAN SCIENCE OUTPOST IN THE SOLARION SYSTEM.

I'LL BE SERVING UNDER CAPTAIN EDWARD JELLICO.

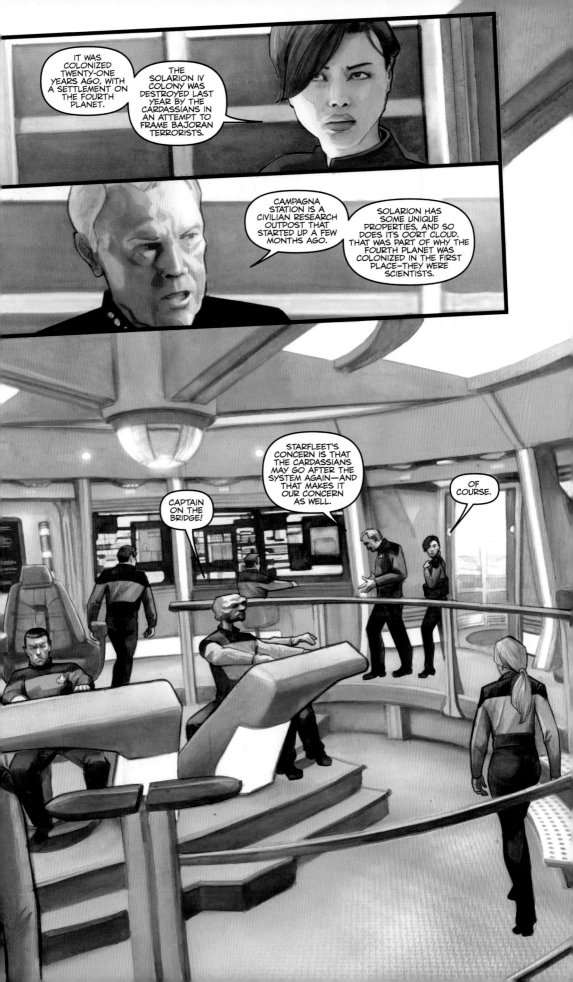

PERSONAL LOG, SUPPLEMENTAL.

IT HAS BEEN AN INTERESTING FIRST DAY ON THE CAIRO.

I WAS RATHER SURPRISED TO SEE A SHIFT CHANGE AT 1200 HOURS. TRADITIONALLY, THE THREE EIGHT-HOUR SHIFTS END AT 0800, 1600, AND 2400.

CAPTAIN, THE LAST SHIFT CHANGE WAS ONLY SIX HOURS AGO.

THAT'S CORRECT.

BUT THEN THERE WAS ANOTHER SHIFT CHANGE AT 1800.

THE CAIRO HAS BEEN ON A FOUR-SHIFT ROTATION SINCE I FIRST TOOK HER OUT.

OH.

OKAY.

I FIND MYSELF WONDERING HOW A CREW OF FOUR HUNDRED CAN CONTORT ITSELF INTO FOUR SIX-HOUR SHIFTS INSTEAD OF THE USUAL THREE EIGHT-HOUR ONES.

HOWEVER, THINGS SEEM TO RUN EFFICIENTLY.

THE *EXCELSIOR* CLASS IS CLOSE TO A CENTURY OLD. ONCE IT WAS THE VANGUARD OF A NEW BREED OF SHIPS.

NOW IT'S ONE OF THE OLD WORKHORSES OF THE FLEET.

YELLOW ALERT!

WHAT?

FIGURES, THE BAJORAN OVERREACTS.

WHAT DO YOU EXPECT?

WHAT WAS THAT, LIEUTENANT, ENSIGN? THE REST OF THE BRIDGE DIDN'T CATCH IT.

NOTHING, COMMANDER.

WE WERE JUST—

YOU WERE JUST INSULTING A FELLOW CREWMEMBER BY ASSUMING THAT SHE LETS HER HOMEWORLD'S HISTORY WITH THE CARDASSIAN UNION COLOR HER JUDGMENT.

THANK YOU, COMMANDER.

DON'T—IT JUST MEANS THAT I'M ASSUMING YOU JUMPED THE GUN ON YELLOW ALERT BECAUSE YOU'RE YOUNG AND STUPID, NOT BECAUSE YOU'RE BAJORAN.

GIVE ME A FULL SCAN OF THE CARDASSIAN SHIP. I'LL BE IN THE READY ROOM WITH THE CAPTAIN.

THE *HARKON* IS A MODIFIED *YRCAN*-CLASS SCIENCE VESSEL.

WHAT KIND OF MODIFICATIONS?

NOT SURE, CAPTAIN—BUT THEY DO HAVE SOME ODD E.M. EMISSIONS.

HOWEVER, THEY ONLY HAVE ONE LOW-GRADE DISRUPTOR CANNON AND FIVE PHOTON TORPEDOES, WITH ONE LAUNCHER.

GOOD WORK, ENSIGN.

ALL RIGHT, MAINTAIN COURSE FOR NOW, BUT GO TO YELLOW ALERT.

AND MAINTAIN REGULAR SCANS ON THE *HARKON.*

PERSONAL LOG, SUPPLEMENTAL.

THAT'S TWICE THAT CAPTAIN JELLICO HAS CHEWED ME OUT IN FRONT OF THE ENTIRE BRIDGE CREW.

CAN'T SAY I'M PARTICULARLY THRILLED WITH THAT—

—ESPECIALLY WHEN HE THEN TURNS AROUND AND COMPLIMENTS ENSIGN SIM.

I WILL GIVE SIM CREDIT, THOUGH—SHE'S WORKING EXTRA SHIFTS. MAYBE SHE WANTS MORE ATTENTION FROM THE CAPTAIN.

I, ON THE OTHER HAND, MAY WANT LESS. ONCE THIS BORD[E]R PATROL IS OVER, I THINK I'M PUTTING IN FOR A TRANSFER TO A POST WHERE THE CAPTA[IN] DOESN'T FEEL THE NEED TO EMBARRASS ME IN PUBLIC.

THE *HARKON* DOESN'T NEED TO BE THIS CLOSE TO THE BORDER IN ORDER TO CONDUCT SCANS OF THE OORT CLOUD.

LET ME GUESS—JELLICO SAID WE ONLY HAD AN HOUR AND TO GET IT DONE?

GOOD GUESS.

BEEN SERVING ON THIS SHIP A WHILE NOW. YOU GET USED TO WORKING EXTRA SHIFTS FOR NO GOOD REASON.

LIEUTENANT HONIGSBERG'S WORDS WERE BORDERLINE INSUBORDINATE, BUT I GOT WHERE HE WAS COMING FROM.

AND HE AND HIS PEOPLE KNOW THEIR STUFF. HE PULLED PEOPLE FROM OFF-SHIFT AND GOT THEM WORKING ON THE PROBLEM.

IN EXACTLY FIFTY-SEVEN MINUTES, THE *CAIRO* WAS ONE BIG, SUPER-EFFICIENT LONG-RANGE SENSOR.

THE SCAN'S COMPLETE, CAPTAIN.

THE *HARKON* IS ACTUALLY INSIDE THE ORBIT OF THE SEVENTH PLANET, EVEN THOUGH THEY'RE OUTSIDE THE ORBIT OF THE EIGHTH.

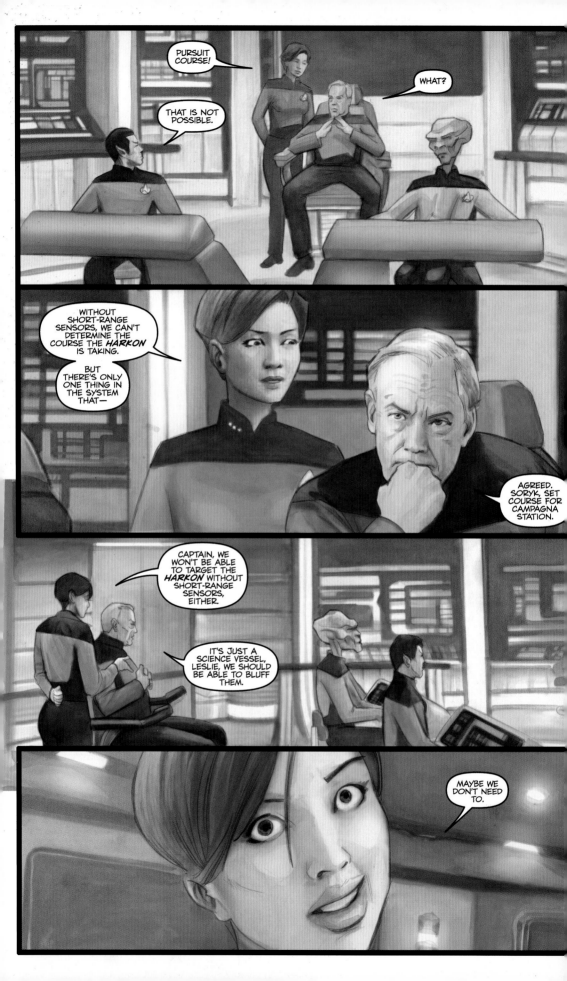

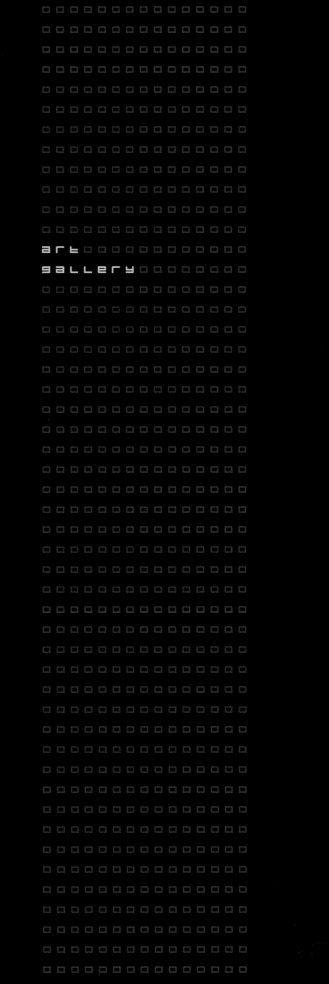

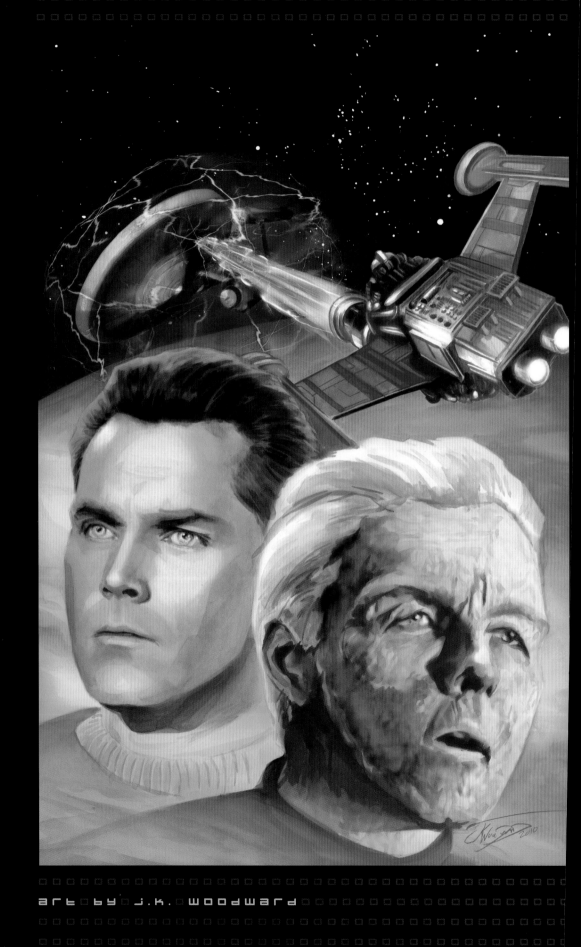

art by j.k. woodward

STAR TREK ®

CAPTAIN'S LOG